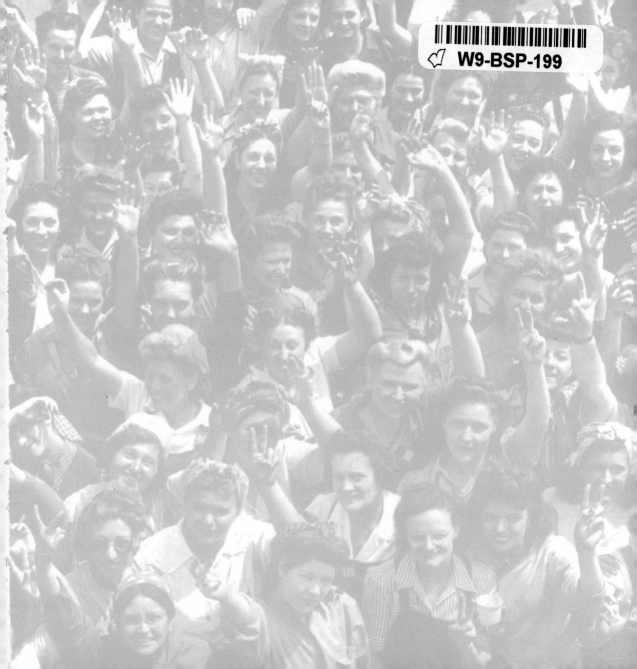
W9-BSP-199

SHEROES

SHEROES

Bold, Brash, and Absolutely
Unabashed Superwomen

From Susan B. Anthony to Xena

Varla Ventura

Foreword by Vicki Leon

CONARI PRESS
Berkeley, CA

NEW HANOVER COUNTY
PUBLIC LIBRARY
201 CHESTNUT STREET
WILMINGTON, NC 28401

© 1998 CONARI PRESS

All Rights Reserved. No part of this book may be used or reproduced in
any manner whatsoever without written permission, except in the case of brief
quotations in critical articles or reviews. For information, contact
Conari Press, 2550 Ninth St., Suite 101, Berkeley, CA 94710.

Conari Press books are distributed by Publishers Group West.

We gratefully acknowledge permission to reprint the following: From *Sappho and the
Greek Lyric Poets* by Willis Barnstone, translator. Copyright © 1962, 1967, 1988 by Willis Barnstone.
Reprinted by permission of Schocken Books, distributed by Pantheon Books,
a division of Random House, Inc.

The photos herein are reprinted by permission of Archive Photo, with the exception of the
following, which are used courtesy of Corbis-Bettmann: Cover photos,
(Lucy Lawless and Gillian Anderson), pp. 1, 19, 45, 75, 101, 123, 183, 213, 265, 325.

Cover design: Kathy Warrinner, Aufuldish and Warrinner
Art direction: Ame Beanland
Interior design: Suzanne Albertson

ISBN: 1-57324-128-8

Library of Congress Cataloging-in-Publication Data
Ventura, Varla, 1958–
Sheroes : bold, brash, and absolutely unabashed superwomen from
Susan B. Anthony to Xena / Varla Ventura : foreword by Vicki Leon.
p.   cm.
Includes bibliographical references and index.
ISBN 1-57324-128-8 (trade paper)
1. Women heroes—Biography.   I. Title.
CT3203.V46   1998   98-12936
920.72—dc21   CIP

Printed in the United States of America on recycled paper
1   3   5   7   9   10   8   6   4   2

I dedicate this book to the sheroes of my family:

my mother Helen who supports my quest to be a writer,
my sister Lola Kay for her fire burning bright,
and sister Martha who always watched out for me and still does

Much love and many thanks to all of you.

"For every hero in this world, there's at least one shero."

—Johnetta B. Cole, president of
Spelman College

I see the wise woman.

She carried a blanket of compassion. She wears a
robe of wisdom. Around her throat flutters a veil of shifting
shapes. From her shoulders, a mantle of power flows. A story
band encircles her forehead. She stitches a quilt; she spins
fibers into yarn; she knits; she sews; she weaves. She ties
the threads of our lives together. She forms a
web of spiraling threads.

—Susan Weed from *Healing Wise*

Contents

Foreword

Sheroes *provokes a question I've asked myself dozens of times:* Where was this treasure-house of a book when I went to school? From the first grade on, I sat at my desk, listlessly listening to the cliched tales of heroes from history, all of them—or so it seemed—male. Meanwhile, as I grew up in the Pacific Northwest of the fifties, many of the women profiled in this book were busy making history, making changes, making intellectual contributions, and making waves. Did I hear about any of them in school? In the media? On that shiny new world of communications called television? Rarely, if ever.

Would my life have been different if I'd had these daring examples to aspire to, to take courage from, to lean on as my own personal support group from history? Most definitely.

For instance, when my mother and father pushed me toward a particular college, I asked what they saw me doing with my education, and they said, "A nurse perhaps. Or a teacher." I turned angrily from their narrow vision and their well-meant path of higher education. It was decades before I saw that learning (as valid when enrolled in the university of life as well as in more traditional institutions) would set me free, free to become whatever I set my mind to be.

Over the years, as I made my way as a writer and researcher, many of the sheroes in this book became my personal sheroes, too. The lives and deeds of women like Mary Leakey, Karen Silkwood, Margaret Mead, Rachel Carson, and Eleanor Roosevelt moved me deeply and helped me grow. As a thirtysomething college reporter, for instance, I got to write my first news story about Billie Jean King's rout of Bobby Riggs—and in so doing, the sheer audacity of Billie Jean's actions struck home. *Sheroes* brings all of my favorites, and hundreds more women, to luminous life—a brilliant and an encyclopedic achievement for one book.

Of late, I've been thinking a lot about just how and why the jigsaw of our whole human history came to have so many female pieces missing. Since 1995, the publication date of *Uppity Women of Ancient Times,* my first book about real-life female achievers of long ago, I've given hundreds of lectures, workshops, and talks to audiences about the frisky, risk-it-all women from our ancient, medieval, and Renaissance past. I point out that many of these trailblazers were famous—or infamous—in their own day. Invariably, someone in the audience asks: "If these women were household words, how and why did they become invisible?"

At this point, I mention a trio of female names and say: "What do these names mean to you?" After having given this pop quiz to several thousand people now (many of them well-read women whose educations far exceed my own), I regret to say that no one has known the answers. No one. Not one person has identified three key women who I selected at random from our own, very recent American history.

This response—or lack of one—leads me to my most telling point. "You see? Even in the late twentieth century, the historical invisibility process often begins immediately—in a woman's own lifetime."

Sheroes, Varla Ventura's book, is a perfect antidote to that process, a bold and colorful portrait of women who dared to pursue their dreams. In that pursuit, they themselves become raw material, the ideal matrix for other women's dreams. They become, in a word, sheroes—a word, and a notion, whose constituency is going to grow ever more clamorous in the brave new second millennium.

—Vicki León, author of the Uppity
Women in history series, published by
Conari Press

P.S. Take my "invisible women" quiz yourself, and see how well you do. Identify the following twentieth century women: Junko Tabei, Sally Louisa Tompkins, and Gerti Cori.

Junko Tabei—first woman to climb Mount Everest, on May 16, 1975. This housewife led an all-woman Japanese team to the top.

Sally Louisa Tompkins—only woman to be named an officer in the Confederate Army, where she ran the hospital she'd already established (at her own expense) with the lowest mortality rate of any soldier's hospital in the South.

Gerti Cori—first female doctor to win a Nobel prize; awarded in physiology and medicine in 1947 and shared with her husband.

Answers

The Shero with Ten Thousand Faces

Women have always been powerful. So much so, in fact, that several millennia of oppression have only made us stronger. And no amount of witch burnings, stiletto heels, and lack of basic human rights have stopped the blossoming forth of the boldest, bravest wave of women and girlpower ever, here at the dawn of the new millennium.

Women have always been heroes. But, it is no longer enough to say so. As we shake off the last traces of a major patriarchal hangover, women need a new language, a new dialect, and a freshly forged paradigm to express an untrammeled femininity that has nothing to do with bondage—unless, of course, that's your bag. Women of courage, in addition to taking back their power, must have a name of their own. Any wise woman can tell you that words have power. As Rumpelstiltskin knew, the naming of a person or thing, is to have ownership and power over the named. He was quaking in his leathery dwarf boots for fear that the princess he had imprisoned (so she could spin straw into gold for his moldering coffers) would figure out his name. Sure enough, our girl psyched it out with good, old-fashioned women's intuition and his game was up. As sheroes, all women can fully embrace and embody all their fiery fempower and celebrate the unique potency of our gender-tribe. By taking, telling, and proudly touting the title and banner of sheroes, women can identify with the traits of strength, courage, and no-holds-barred individuality, thus sharing and spreading the power around. Taking back power doesn't necessarily mean that power has to be taken away from someone else; there is enough for all. No need to repeat the mistakes of the past.

Power. Share it; it grows!

What Is a Shero?

Packing estrogen and, not infrequently, a pen and a sword, sheroes come in every imaginable shape, size, and color, and manifest their sheroism in infinite ways. Our sheroic foremothers of the past centuries paved the way for the cybersheroes and screen goddesses of today at a time when women were relegated to the status of second-class citizens, if they were fortunate enough to be citizens at all. Their accomplishments are stunning in light of the fact that there was, for all practical purposes, a tacit caste system with one gender on top. Battling exclusion and seclusion, these incredible women risked it all to create the freedom we enjoy and uphold today. Women warriors, the sheroes of herstory didn't take no for an answer and went to the head of the class without passing go, oftentimes through a gauntlet of disapproval, bad press, and every other odd against them.

The Shero's Journey

Heroes and their trips have gotten plenty of air time thanks to the erudite scholarship of the late mythographer Joseph Campbell who popularized the genre. His delineation of the hero's journey begins with restlessness and hearing the call to action; it moves to the middle road of dragon slaying and an underground passage through hell and back where the hero faces death, to the culmination of the visionary quest in self-awareness and the return home.

The heroic archetype was brought to the world's attention when George Lucas extrapolated Campbell's explication of the hero's journey in the *Star Wars* trilogy. It is important to bear in mind that not every would-be hero who sets upon the path to greatness succeeds. In fact, the most promising candidates may fall—look at Lancelot, the flower of France and the finest knight in King Arthur's court who betrayed his liege lord and lost his honor. Heroism is no guarantee! The question for us to consider here is how a shero's journey differs, if at all, from the hero's journey. Having obsessed with this very question for the better part of a year, I have concluded that it is, indeed, different.

Interestingly, Campbell himself never tackled the subject, but commented that the question always came up after his lectures. (Can't you just see the Sarah Lawrence women giving him the business?) His position was that "if a woman engages in the man's task of achievement, then her mythology will be essentially the same as that of the male hero." Aside from the fact that achievement in and of itself is not the true hallmark of a human's psychospiritual evolution, women have been achieving great things since women took primitive society from hunting and gathering to agricultural-based communities. For that matter, we might as well go back to the beginning to Eve, who would've burned her bra if she'd had one, and her predecessors among the first femmes, including the first feminist Lilith, whom Yahweh attempted to hook up with the utterly human Adam. Lilith, being semidivine, would have none of this mundane human-beingness and bailed immediately. But, according to the early Christian Gnostic Gospels, before there was Adam and before there was God even, there was Sophia, the primordial and very female entity embodying ultimate wisdom associated with the unknowable heart of darkness.

Marion Woodman, doubtless one of the preeminent Jungian analysts of our time, does examine the "heroine's journey," as she calls it, deeply and brilliantly. In her excellent book on the subject, *Leaving My Father's House,* Woodman cuts to the heart of the repression of women's adventurous and powerful energies and advocates a transcendence of the old patri-archal model for women through dumping obsolete control systems and dangerous daddy complexes to illuminate the world with our true spirit and our excellence. "So long as a woman accepts a man's archetypal projection, she is trapped in a male understanding of reality," she notes. The shero's journey, she explains, is an awakening to consciousness and "staying with the process is what matters." The shero needn't necessarily go underground; she can turn inside to the intuitive, and occasionally superconscious wisdom at the core of their being—Sophia, divine feminine wisdom. Woodman urges women to share these sto-ries of transformation and growth to "open the path to freedom" for other women.

Sheroes is a collection of the life stories of the harbingers of female transformation. Each of the sheroes in this book, and the legions who are not, have done this work. They have released their full energy and, in so doing, changed the world for us by blazing trails, breaking down barriers, and empowering other women to do the same.

Sister-sheroes, suffragists, amazons, and priestess-healers laid the foundations for the post-modern sheroes of today who are making new strikes in arts and letters, the business world, and in the power and sports arenas. From Madeleine Albright who declared politics "is not a fraternity anymore!" to the courageous televised outing of lesbian Ellen DeGeneres, women are making enormous strides today that should see us to a fabulously feminized twenty-first century. A delightful irony I've noticed is that the aforementioned Star Wars trilogy contains the perfect parallel journey of hero and shero, although that hasn't seemed to get nearly the air time among all the hype of the incredible international success of this mythical sci-fi series. You will recall that Luke Skywalker has a twin sister, none other than princess Leia Morgana. While Luke was playing with droids and scooting around his planet in jerry-rigged spacecrafts, Princess Leia was masterminding the rebellion against the fascist Darth Vader. Talk about leaving your father's house!

Tripping the Light Femtastic

This book of sheroes is intended to be a call to action as well, and a challenging exhortation to honor bold and brave women by telling their stories. This book is only the tip of the sheroic iceberg, however. If I had my way, it would never end because I wanted to include every shero who ever lived. My greatest hope is that it will spark something in you, the reader—who are your personal sheroes? Let me know (see the personal note in the back of the book).

Ethnographer Marina Warner, in her compelling examination of women in fairy and folktales, From the Beast to the Blonde, concludes that words and the wielding of words is the realm of women: "The story itself becomes the weapon of the weaponless. The struggles of women, for example, are not resolved by combat on the whole (one or two Amazons heroines excepted), as the contests of men may bring heroic epic . . . women's arts within fairy tales are very marked, and most of them are verbal: riddling, casting spells, conjuring, understanding the tongues of animals, turning words into deeds." Storytelling is a way of weaving the fabric of consciousness, introducing new strands, new awareness. In this way, the shero stories can, on an archetypal level, shift, transform, and create new reality for ourselves, and, most importantly, for young women and girls. Imagine a neo-Amazonian utopia where every adolescent girl has sky high self-esteem— no Ophelias to revive! Estrogen empowered, full-esteem ahead, and absolutely, unabashedly glorious.

This brings me back to the original point of this storytelling adventure for me. In the beginning was the word. Logos. Sophia. In the new beginning was the word—sheroes! The term *women heroes* is no longer sufficient for a post-patriarchal populace and the auditory twinning of heroine to the supremely addictive opiate is certainly a turn-off, and reason enough to embrace the mantle of sheroism. For this, I must thank poet shero Maya Angelou, who used the word in a speech and sparked the muse for me. Let's get shero into Webster's Dictionary, Scrabble, the collective consciousness, and, most importantly, the common parlance! (For your convenience, we've provided a form in the back of the book addressed to the publishers of Webster's, which you can cut out and send in.) The word *sheroes* has potential to be a "meme," defined by Constance Hale in her handy reference guide for pomo word slingers, *Wired Style,* as a "virus of the mind . . . a unit of cultural inheritance" that changes consciousness, changes society, and creates new ways of thinking and perception as it tunnels its way through the global body of communication.

In closing, I want to thank all the sheroes who set the standards and knocked down the walls of oppression, brick by brick. Often, as I researched the lives of these women, I was moved to tears with the realization of what they went through for their magnificent accomplishments—by, among others, Elizabeth Blackwell who got into medical school on a joke and had the last laugh, by supermodel superwoman Waris Dirie battling against the scourge of female circumcision, and by every working-class shero who demands her due. I dedicate this book to every shero whose story remains untold and whose unquenchable spirit lives on!

WarriorSheroes:
Amazons Among Us

1

S ince the fall of Troy, Amazons have never gone out of style. Now, at the fall of the millennium, they have never been hotter! The global phenomenon of Xena, Warrior Princess and her Amazon sidekick, Gabrielle, is proof positive that Amazons are, once again, ruling the world. Archetypically, Amazons represent aggressiveness on the part of women. (Say, if you can call upon the muse, why can't you invoke Amazonian courage? And tell me why, for that matter, has there yet to be a self-help book for empowering women by "embracing your inner Amazon"?)

The myth of the Amazon nation tells of an all-woman country by the river Thermodon with a very advanced gynocentric government and the finest army on earth. Occasionally, they socialized with the men of other nations for the purpose of begetting children. The fate of male babies in Amazonia was woeful; they were neutered and enslaved. The ancient historian Diodorus Siculus recorded stories of Amazon military campaigns on swift and well-trained horses, sporting bows, arrows, double-headed axes, and a single breast (they would cut off one breast in order to wear their special shields), with which they conquered a wide swath from Asia Minor to Egypt.

Greece and Africa weren't the only cultures to celebrate womanly valor. Norse mythology has a sort of afterlife Amazon, the Valkyries, "choosers of the slain" from Old Norse. Handmaidens of Odin, the Valkyries pick the most valiant warrior from among the slain on battlefields to be in the celestial army of the gods. In the Edda, the Valkyries include Gondul, "she-wolf"; Skuld; death-bringer Skorn; Brunnhilde, "she who calls out"; Hrist, "storm"; and Thrud, "force" who ride through the heavens on charging horses getting ready for Ragnarok, the battle marking the end of the world.

These and all other avenging angels and hell-spawned hags break all stereotypes about women as the gentler gender. Epitomizing the "take no prisoners" attitude, these women warriors punched, kicked, stabbed, shot, and charioteered their way to the top. Gorgons, furies, pirate queens, warrior princesses, martial nuns, maenads, gladiatrices, and guerrillas from antiquity to the twenty-first century represent sheroism at its most visceral and thrilling.

Penthesilea:
The Real Thing

The daughter of Orithia, Penthesilea was the ruler, along with her sister Hippolyte, of Amazonia, the Bronze Age Amazon nation in an area of the Black Sea. A fierce warrior, Penthesilea's name means "compelling men to mourn." During Orithia's reign, repeated attacks from Greek war parties eroded the borders of their once widespread empire. The nation of Amazonia itself, however, lived in peace; its women warriors were regarded as the most highly skilled soldiers among all the armies of the world. Even the piratical adventurers of myth, the Argonauts, dropped their plans to invade Amazonia when they saw how peaceful and self-sufficient the country was.

Penthesilea was the greatest Amazon of all times. At first, her excellence with weaponry was primarily for the purpose of hunting. When her sister died falling on Penthesilea's spear during a hunt, Penthesilea chose to channel her grief and rage into battle. At the request of Queen Hecuba, she liberated the city of Troy, under siege by the Greeks for years. The link between Troy and Amazonia predates Homer and Euripides by centuries and many scholars believe that Homer adapted his famous story from the Egyptian poetess Phantasia and reoriented it toward the patriarchal tastes of his Greek audience.

Essentially, Penthesilea's Achilles heel was her desire to lead the attack on Troy, the last Goddess worshiping city-state in Mediterranean Asia Minor. The legends vary, but consensus among herstorians is that Achilles took one look at the powerful and pulchritudinous Penthesilea and fell deeply in love. They battled ruthlessly one-on-one, and the Amazon queen proved to be the only soldier Achilles had ever encountered who was his equal. One version depicts the great Penthesilea taking Achilles and dozens of Greeks' lives in the battlefield surrounding Troy, only to be confounded when the God Zeus brings Achilles back to life. In this version, she died but Achilles' grief was so severe that he killed several of his allies who had mutilated her corpse (in one version he rapes her corpse in a wanton necrophilic lust). Other tellings of the tale have Penthesilea brutally killing the Greek and falling in love with him as his dying eyes locked with hers, then setting upon his corpse and devouring him, in a final act of savage love.

Only sections of the ancient poem *Aethiopis* that describe Penthesilea and the liberation of Troy managed to survive from antiquity. They include a suffragistic speech made by the amazing amazon herself: "Not in strength are we inferior to men; the same our eyes, our limbs the same; one common light we see, one air we breathe; no different is the food we eat. What then denied to us hath heaven on man bestowed? O let us hasten to the glorious war!"

Other Fighting Femmes of the Ancient World

Marpesia, "The Snatcher," was the ruler of the Scythian Amazons along with Lampedo. In frenzies, Maenads were fierce creatures, not to be toyed with, especially after a few nips of ritual new grape wine. Agave wrestled and tore off the head of her own son, Pentheus, in one of her ecstasies, mistaking him for a lion. She then paraded around proudly holding his decapitated head up for all to see. Her husband met a similar end in another rite. Agave was a Moon-Goddess and was in charge of some of the revelries that were the precedent for Dionysus' cult. Euripes celebrated the ferocity of Agave and her fellow Maenads, **Ino** and **Autonoë** in his *Bacchae* as soldiers report how "we by flight hardly escaped tearing to pieces at their hands" and further describing the shock of witnessing the semi-divine females tearing young bulls limb from limb with their terrible "knifeless fingers." In his version, Pentheus dies while trying to spy on the private ritual of the Maenads in transvestite disguise.

Aba was a warrior who ruled the city of Olbe in the nation of Tencer around 550 B.C. She got support from some very high places such as the likes of Cleopatra VII and Marc Antony! Tencer remained a matriarchy after her rule, passing to her female descendants.

Abra was the Queen of Babylon, according to medieval Spanish accounts. Along with Queen Florelle and a flotilla of 50,000 expert women archers, Abra defended her kingdom against the Greeks.

Ada was Artemesia's (Queen of Caria and military advisor to Xeres) sister and a warrior-queen (circa 334 B.C.) in her own right. The brilliant military strategist Alexander helped her regain her throne from her invasive brother. She led and triumphed in the siege of the capital's acropolis, after which she was able to take the city. Her ferocity was aided by the intense emotions of a cross-gender civil war within her family, "the siege having become a matter of anger and personal enmity," according to Strabo.

Hercules was the fiercest, that is, until he ran up against **Admete,** aka "The Untamed," who bested him and made him serve the Goddess Hera, the wife of Zeus who detested Hercules. Hera rewarded Admete for her loyalty and excellence by appointing her head priestess of the island refuge Samos; Admete, in turn honored her Goddess with her evangelical fervor, expanding the territory of Hera's woman cult to the far reaches of the ancient world.

Aëllopus was a Harpy who fought the Argonauts; her name means "Storm-Foot."

Cratesipolis was Queen of Sicyon around 300 B.C. She stood in battle beside her husband, the famous Alexander the Great, and fought on even after he died. She ruled several important Greek cities very successfully and managed a vast army of soldier-mercenaries. She went on to take Corinth for Ptolemy and nearly married him, but the plans fizzled.

Larina was an Italian Amazon who accompanied Camilla in the *Aeneid* along with fellow comrades-in-arms, Tulia, Acca, and Tarpeia. According to Silver Latinist poet Virgil, "they were like Thracian Amazons when they make the waters of the Thermodon tremble and make war with their ornate arms, either around Hippolyte, or when warlike Penthesilea returns in her chariot and the female armies exult, with a great ringing cry and the clashing of crescent-shaped shield."

Rhodogune, queen of ancient Parthia in 200 B.C., got word of a revolt when she was taking a bath. Vowing to end the uprising before her hair was dressed, she hopped on her horse and rushed to lead her army to defense. True to her word, she directed the entire, lengthy war without ever bathing, or combing her hair. Portraits of Rhodogune always faithfully depict her dishevelment. (Another queen of the ancient world, **Semiramis,** also pulled herself from the bath to the battlefield act when her country needed a brave leader.)

Of the royal lineage of Cleopatra, **Zenobia Septimus** preferred the hunt to the bath and boudoir. She was queen of Syria for a quarter-century beginning in 250 A.D. and was quite a scholar, recording the history of her nation. She was famed for her excellence on safari, specializing in the rarified skill of hunting panthers and lions.

When the Romans came after Syria, Zenobia disgraced the empire's army in battle, causing them to turn tail and run. This inspired Arabia, Armencia, and Periso to ally with her and she was named Mistress of Nations. The Romans licked their wounds and enlisted the help of the barbarians they conquered for a Roman army including Goths, Gauls, Vandals, and Franks who threatened to march Zenobia's league of nations. When Caesar Aurelius sent messengers requesting her surrender, she replied, "It is only by arms that the submission you require can be achieved. You forget that Cleopatra preferred death to servitude. When you see me in war, you will repent your insolent proposition." And battle they did. Zenobia fought bravely, holding her city Palmyria against the mass of invaders for longer than anyone thought possible. Upon her capture, Zenobia was taken to Rome in chains, jewels, and her own chariot, and she was given her own villa in Rome where her daughters intermarried into prominent families who ruled Rome.

Boudicca's name means "victorious" in the language of the Celts. She is the legendary warrior-queen of the Iceni of Norfolk who led a rebellion against the invading Romans in the year 61 A.D., and sacked the Roman's settlements, including Verulamium and Londinium, which she put to the torch. She took the lives of 70,000 Romans in her battles and was reputed to be "tall of person, of a comely appearance, and appareled in a loose gown of many colors. About her neck she wore a chain of gold and in her hand she bore a spear. She stood a while surveying her army and, being regarded with a reverential silence, she addressed them an eloquent and impassioned speech." She died in battle, at her own hand, taking poison rather than be killed by an enemy of the Celts. Many women fought to defend their land and culture; the Celtic army consisted of more women than men!

European Battle Axes and Freedom Fighters

The Germanic princess **Modthryth** referenced in *Beowulf* was an actual female ruler in 520 A.D., "a good folk queen" with soldierly aspirations. According to folktales handed down in Sweden, any man who looked upon her with desire was challenged to fight her and be felled by her sword!

Lathgertha was also a ruler immortalized in *Halfdanar Saga*, which tells her story under the name Hladgerd. She rallied to hero Halfdanar's cause, leading twenty ships in battle to save the day. She is also commemorated in a Saxo Grammaticus tale where he supplied more background about what inspired Lathgertha to take up the battle girdle—she and a group of noblewomen were taken for slaves by invading Norwegians who locked them into a prison brothel. The noblewomen refused to suffer this indignation and turned the tables on their captors, taking their weapons and going into battle. Grammaticus describes her as endowed with "a man's temper in a woman's body. With locks flowing loose under her helm, she fought in the forefront of the battle, the most valiant of warriors. Everyone marveled at her matchless feats."

Aethelburg was an ancient British battle-queen of Ine. According to the writings of Damico, she erected a fortress in Taunton in 722 A.D.

One hundred-fifty years after Aethelburg's rule, **Aethelflaed** took up the sword and swore herself to chastity-belted celibacy after her intensely unpleasant experience of childbirth. She and her husband became friends and fellow warriors. When her husband died in 912 A.D., she kept on fighting to defend her father, Alfred the Great, and his kingdom against invading Danes. She had a brilliant tactical mind, uniting the pre-England kingdoms of Wales and Mercia. She died in battle at Tammoth in the borough of Stratsfordshire and her one child, daughter **Aelfwyn**, ascended the throne until her jealous, power-hungry uncle managed a coup.

Good King Wenceslas was actually quite mad. His wife, **Queen Sophia** of Bohemia had to hold by herself the royal stronghold against German's invading emperor Sigismund and a barbarous cyclopean Bohemian named Ziska who fancied he would overtake and rule Bohemia himself. **Ziska's Army of Women**, was a ragtag bunch of Bohemian reformers and patriots, largely women and children, who took down Sophia's professional soldiers with such original tactics as removing their clothes and tossing them on the battlefield to entangle the legs of the warhorses the Bohemian Royal Army rode.

The Knights Templar are quite well known, but their counterparts, the numerous crusading battle nuns known as the **Martial Nuns** are not, having been effectively "whited-out" of history—probably by jealous scribe monks! But there were armed nuns who accompanied fighting monks in the Crusades in the 1400s. But even nuns who stayed home were often armed—they had to defend their convents by themselves in the aggressively territorial Dark Ages. For example, when the anti-Christian Espartero invaded Spain in his famous siege, the nuns of Seville fought back and won. One nun who took up the pen and the sword wrote of her crusade to Jerusalem at the time of Saladin's attack on the holy city, "I wore a helmet or at any rate walked on the ramparts wearing on my head a metal dish which did as well as a helmet. Woman though I was I had the appearance of a warrior. I slung stones at the enemy. I concealed my fears. It was hot and there was never a moment's rest. Once a catapulted stone fell near me and I was injured by the fragments."

Careful study of European military history shows a number of women armies, including many women of the cloth. Ultimately, success was too threatening to the men they fought beside and several popes declared such women to be heretics. **Joan of Arc**, or course, was the most famous. She was burned at the stake in 1431 on the letter of a law that was hundreds of years old that forbade women from wearing armor. At the time, Joan was the national shero of France, having led the battle to free the French from the foreign power of England, at the advice of the voices of saints. Several women were inspired by Joan's example and moved to courage by her murder. The most successful was **Joan, the Maid of Sarmaize,** who attracted a religious following that supported her in Anjou. She claimed to be the Joan of Arc returned and, like her predecessor, dressed in men's clothing and armor. Several of

Joan of Arc's friends and family took her in and accepted her. Her actual identity was never known.

Onorata Rodiani was an ahead-of-her time portrait and mural painter who was busy immortalizing the Tyrant of Cremona in oils when an "importunate nobleman" barged into the sitting. Onorata whipped out her dagger and ended the rude noble's life on the spot, but was forced to go underground as a fugitive. She put down the brush and took up the sword as the captain of a band of mercenaries and died in 1472 in an attempt to defend her birthplace of Castelleone.

In 1745, a Scottish woman named **Mary Ralphson** fought at Fontenoy right beside her husband. Known as "Trooper Mary," she wasn't deterred by having only five fingers and one thumb, living through war to the grand age of 110.

The Amazon of the Vendeans, **Mademoiselle de la Rochefoucalt** fought the Republicans when Louis XVI was murdered. She was only a teenager, but was famed for her speeches on the battlefield, "Follow me! Before the end of the day we either sign our victory on earth, or hymns with the saints in heaven."

Alexandra Dourova was a Russian shero who fought against Napoleon as a colonel in the Fourth Hussars. In World War I, the very same regiment enlisted another fighting woman—**Olga Serguievna Schidlowskaia.**

Major **Tamara Aleksandrovna** was in charge of an all-female air force for Russia in World War II. Their phenomenal success is evidenced by their record of flying 125 combats, 4,000 sorties, and shooting down 38 Nazi aircraft. Other amazonian aviatrixes were **Captain Budanova, Nancy Wak** of New Zealand who flew for the allies in France and **Ludmilla Pavlichenko** who killed 309 Nazis by herself!

Nina Teitelboim, called "Little Wanda with the Braids," was an anti-Nazi fighter who commanded a special force of Poland's People's Guard which blew up the elite Cafe Club, a hang-out for the top-ranking Gestapo. Thus empowered, she was part of a raid on the Nazis, stealing back the enormous stockpiles of cash the Nazis themselves had stolen from the people of Warsaw. After this success, the price on her head was higher than ever, and she was captured and executed.

Florence Matomelo was a soldier in the anti-apartheid resistance movement. In 1965, she was arrested for her role in the African National Congress (Pro Azanian or black South African rebel government) and confined to solitary where she was starved, beaten, interrogated, and deprived of the insulin she needed for her diabetes. She died after five years of this abuse, leaving behind several children. She had led a life of constant courage, defying and protesting the unfair practices of apartheid laws, and she died for her cause, having made invaluable contributions to the changes that finally freed black South Africans from the racist rule set up by colonial whites.

Fierce Asiatic Females

In the year 39 A.D., the Vietnamese Trung sisters led a revolt against China. **Phung Thi Chinh** was in the last stages of pregnancy, but fought beside the other women, gave birth in the middle of the rebellion, and kept on fighting with her babe bound to her back with cloth.

Hangaku was a medieval noble's daughter with topnotch archery skills. Born to the Taira shogunate, she fought beside the men to defend the family's castle. She was fully acknowledged for having superior bow and arrow skills in comparison with her father, brothers, and husband, "shooting a hundred arrows and hitting a hundred times." In 1201, a fateful attack on the familial fortress occurred, during which Hangaku dressed like a boy and stood, unhidden, raining arrows down upon the attackers. Even her flawless archery couldn't save the Tairas that round, and she was felled by an arrow and captured as a prisoner-of-war.

Afra'Bint Ghifar al-Humayriah was a veil-less Arab woman who fought in the legendary tent-pole battles with Khawlah in the seventh century. These resourceful women rebelled against the Greeks who had captured them with the only available weapon—the poles of the tents they were imprisoned in!

Hindustan's warrior queen of Gurrah, **Durgautti** led a bold and colorful army of 1,500 elephants and 6,000 horseback soldiers. "Like a bold heroine, mounted within her elephant's howdar, armed with lance and bow and arrow," writes herstorian Eleanor Starling, she bested the invasive Mongol Asaph Khan and his army of 6,000 horses and 12,000 foot soldiers. When he later turned the tables on her, she killed herself with her elephant handler's dagger rather than endure defeat.

Lakshmi Bar, the Rani of Jhansi is one of India's national heroines. Raised in a household of boys, she was fearless and brilliant as a military strategist. When her husband died, she came out of purdah to fight the British, becoming the key figure in the Indian Mutiny of 1857. She was a wrestler, athlete, boxer, and equestrienne extraordinaire who trained women for her army with special care. These women came to be known as the "amazons of Jhansi." Lakshmi herself was famous for calmly taunting enemy generals, "Do your worst, I will make you a woman." Her fame spread like wildfire throughout India, making her their national shero when she broke through an encircling ambush of British soldiers during battle and escaped on horseback to a hundred miles away in just twenty-four hours with a ten-year-old boy clinging to her back. She and the boy were the only two survivors of the slaughtered Indian troops. It should also be noted that Lakshmi was in full armor in a sweltering heat of 120 degrees. She died on the battlefield of Gwalior when she was barely thirty; a British general called her the "greatest hero" he'd ever seen.

Qui Jin was called a "Heroine Among Women" by Sun Yat-Sen. She was simply amazing! Born in 1874, her hobbies included cross-dressing and riding through the streets of Chinese cities and villages. She founded the first newspaper for women in China, founded a school for girls, and escaped from her arranged marriage to pursue her revolutionary goals of overthrowing the Qing Monarchy. Quite the intellectual, she wrote poetry and took a vow of silence during her imprisonment upon being arrested for plotting the assassination of the Qing governor. Her daughter followed in her mother's pioneering footsteps by becoming China's first aviatrix.

Women Warriors of the Americas

Coyolxauhqui was an Aztec divinity who fought her own mother, Coatlicue, for defending the warrior-god she had birthed (her brother, I suppose, but enemy nevertheless!) Coyolxauhqui's daunting name means "the one whose face was tattooed with rattlesnakes."

According to herstorian Carolyn Niethammer, **Pohaha** was a brave battle axe with a sense of humor for whom the heat of battle was quite rousing. Of North American Tewa Indian tribal origin, Pohaha's name tells the tale: "po" referred to the wetness between her legs caused by her excitement in battle and "ha ha" was a name given her because of her shrieks of laughter as she warred. Pohaha wanted to make sure her enemies knew they were up against a woman warrior and would lift her skirt to prove her gender.

Weetamoo, the Squaw Sachem of Pocasset, lived in the area of what is now Tiverton, Rhode Island, from 1650 for a quarter-century of legendary sheroism. She commanded an army of 300 women warriors and stunned all who encountered her with her incredible beauty and charisma. She was a good tactician and courageous in battle. When her husband, Wamsutta, was poisoned by the English, Weetamoo went native in a big way and decided to try to eradicate the white invaders from her land. She joined her brother-in-law Metacom and their armies fought side-by-side against the English in King Phillip's War. During the Great Swamp fight of 1675, she drowned in the Tetcut River while being chased by Brits. The Redcoats fished her body out of the flood-swollen river, cut off her head, and put it on display.

Bowdash was an Indian woman who acted as a guide for white men explorers. Born to the Kutenai tribe in Montana, she was a folk shero in her part of the west, celebrated for being a peacemaker, prophet, messenger, and warrior in song and story, passed down orally through generations. Her story is both gory and glorious. According to Kutenai legend, when she was being killed by her enemies by their knives, her wounds magically sealed up.

Elizabeth Custer was the very independent wife of the famous Major General George A. Custer who traveled west after the Civil War. "Libbie" rode with the Seventh Cavalry beside her husband and other notables such as Wild Bill Hickok and Medicine Bill Comstock. She was an extraordinary horsewoman, able to ride forty miles a day easily. Her overprotective (to say the least!) husband instructed his regiment to kill her themselves rather then let her fall to enemy Indians. This never happened, because she and her sister missed out on the Battle of Little Big Horn when they left the fort for some horseback adventure of their own. Libbie also traveled to India and rode a horse through the Khyber Pass to Afghanistan. She lived to the ripe old age of ninety-two and was buried in West Point's military cemetery beside George.

Pauline Cushman was a gypsy woman of great beauty who fought in the Civil War and gained the rank of major for her courage in fighting behind enemy lines in Tennessee. Her life was incredibly colorful—after the war, she went out west and gave speeches in full Union uniform. She also acted, amazing audiences, favoring the role and costume of an Amazon. For a time, she settled in Arizona where she ran a hotel and kept the peace with her trusty Colt 45. Upon moving to the Wild West outpost of San Francisco, she took the law into her own hand again and bullwhipped a man in public for libeling her. No doubt, people thought twice before speaking ill of gypsy soldier gal Pauline Cushman after that!

▲ *This colorful San Franciscan was Pauline Cushman: Civil War Shero.*

Poker Alice Ivers was one of the special breed of "Wild West Amazons" who ran a casino, smoked cigars, and sported a six-shooter she used with skill. In the 1880s, she ran across a card dealer in Pecos who cheated; she waited and watched until the pot got worth taking, held her gun to his head and then made off with the $5,000 prize, shouting, "I don't mind a cheat, it's a clumsy cheat I can't stand."

▶ *Poker Alice Ivers exemplified the "Wild West Amazons."*

▲ *Belle Starr: A yankee spy and legendary outlaw.*

Belle Starr fought for the Yankees as an underground guerilla on the other side of the Mason Dixon Line. Unfortunately for her and a few hundred others, these guerilla groups were outlawed and Belle was on the lam unable to go home. Forced to a life of crime as an accidental fugitive, Belle showed a flair for stickups and cattle rustlings, and generally supported her bad self as a gun-for-hire. Belle has gotten a bum rap as a colorful criminal; she and the others from the underground were patriots who served their country well in extreme danger only to have the rug (or flag, as it were) pulled out from under them.

Calamity Jane was born in 1852 and remains a household name for her skill as a sharpshooter, muleskinner, midwife, gambler, and horseback scout. Her real name was Martha Jane Canary, and she died a pauper in 1903 even though she herself would give the shirt off her back to the needy or sick. She also wouldn't think twice about shooting the hat off any man who disrespected her!

Woman Chief, the "Absaroka Amazon," was a Gros Ventre girl raised by the Crow tribe who captured her in a hunt shortly after her birth, estimated to have been in 1806. Like Shoshoni **Sacajawea**, without whom Lewis and Clark would have made the Donner Party look like a walk in the park, Woman Chief was a highly skilled hunter, guide, negotiator, and translator, who specialized in buffalo hunting, horse thieving, and close-range battle. Her reputation swelled to mythic proportion when she killed and wounded several men in her first skirmish. Her fellow warriors sang songs in her honor, and she made for hot fireside chat. As a hunter, she was reputed as "capable of killing five buffalo during a hunt and then butchering them and loading them on to packhorses singlehandedly." Her sleight-of-hand style of horse trading won her a place on the Council of Chiefs and the title of Woman Chief. She was murdered by a Gros Ventre warrior in the middle of negotiations for peace she was undertaking between the Crows and her native tribe.

Her courage and glory is celebrated in Zapata's revolutionary song, "Adelita." However, **Adelita** was very much a real person, not just a romantic notion in a popular song. She was a gaucha at the turn of the twentieth century in Zapata's and, later, Pancho Villa's army. There were many women soldiers in the peasant armies of the revolution called "soldederas" who started following the army as cooks, water-bearers, and camp followers helping the cause by helping the men. They eventually evolved into their own organization, divided up into ranks of their own design, and they carried pistols, rifles, and knives, becoming "warriors as fierce as the men."

EcoSheroes:
Saving Mother Earth

Whether it is fighting to save gorillas in the mists of Africa or chaining themselves to trees to stop the logging of old growth forests, women have been at the forefront of the green revolution around the world. Indeed the person said to be responsible for the birth of the modern environmental movement was a woman born at the beginning of the twentieth century, Rachel Carson.

Ecosheroism often means putting your very life in danger. Judi Bari of Earth First nearly died when someone planted a bomb in her car when she got too successful in her campaign to save the redwoods of northern California, and hundreds of peasant women in India have looked down the barrel of a gun in their attempts to preserve the trees that maintain their climate and provide the essentials of life in rural villages.

Perhaps it is only natural that the nurturing power of women be directed back toward the source of all life—Mother Gaia. At the cusp of a new millennium we face the continual extinction of species, the razing of precious rainforests—the "lungs" of the planet—and the scare of toxic oceans, thinning ozone, and global warming. Although governmental and corporate spin doctors deny the threat of an overheated planet, environmentalists work assiduously to ensure a healthy world for future generations. The dream of a better, healthy world is an issue that certainly effects every human being. The stories of these courageous women should inspire everyone to do what we can—recycle, reuse, reduce, get out of our cars, plant trees, garden, compost, and work together to protect the environment. This is one area in which we all have infinite opportunities to be sheroes and heroes every day, one small act at a time. This movement has grown to become the critical issue of our day. These ecoheroes and preservationist pioneers are, literally, saving the world!

Rachel Carson:
"The Natural World ... Supports All Life"

World famous ecologist and science writer Rachel Carson turned nature writing on its head. Before she came along, notes *Women Public Speakers in the United States,* "the masculine orientation [to the subject] emphasized either the dominant, aggressive encounter of humanity with wild nature or the distancing of nature through scientific observation." By creating a different, more feminine, relationship to nature, one saw humans as part of the great web of life, separate only in our ability to destroy it; Rachel Carson not only produced the first widely read books on ecology, but laid the foundation for the entire modern environmental movement.

Rachel inherited her love of nature from her mother, Maria, a naturalist at heart, who took Rachel for long walks in woods and meadows. Born in 1907, Rachel was raised on a farm in Pennsylvania where the evidence of industry was never too far away. By the beginning of the twentieth century, Pennsylvania had changed a great deal from the sylvan woodlands named for colonial William Penn. Coal mines and strip mines had devastated some of the finest farmland. Chemical plants, steel mills, and hundreds of factories were belching pure evil into the air.

As she grew, Rachel's love of nature took an unexpected turn toward oceanography, a budding science limited by technological issues for divers. The young girl was utterly fascinated by this particular biological science and, though she majored in English and loved to write, she heard the ocean's siren song increasingly. While in college at Pennsylvania College for Women in the middle 1920s, she changed her major to biology, despite the overwhelming advice of her teachers and professors to stay the course in English, a much more acceptable major for a young woman. Her advisors were quite correct in their assertions that women were blocked from science; there were very few teaching positions except at the handful of women's colleges and even fewer job prospects existed for women.

However, Rachel listened to her heart and graduated with high honors, a fellowship to study at Woods Hole Marine Biological Laboratory for the summer, and a full scholarship to Johns Hopkins in Maryland to study marine zoology. Rachel's first semester in graduate school coincided with the beginning of The Great Depression. Her family lost the farm; her parents and brother came to live with her in her tiny campus apartment. She helped make ends meet with part-time teaching at Johns Hopkins and the University of Maryland, while continuing her studies. In 1935, Rachel's father suffered a heart attack and died quite suddenly. Rachel looked desperately for work to support her mother and brother only to hear the same old discouragements—no one would hire her as a full-time university science professor. Brilliant and hardworking, Rachel was encouraged to teach grade school or, better yet, be a housewife because it was "inappropriate" for women to work in science.

Finally, her unstinting efforts to work in her field were ultimately rewarded by a job writing radio scripts for Elmer Higgins at the United States Bureau of Fisheries, a perfect job for her because it combined her strength in writing with her scientific knowledge. Then a position opened up at the Bureau for a junior aquatic biologist. The job was to be awarded to the person with the highest score: Rachel aced the test and got the position. Elmer Higgins saw that her writing was excellent, making science accessible to the general public. At his direction, she submitted an essay about the ocean to the *Atlantic Monthly,* which not only published Rachel's piece, but asked her to freelance for them on a continuing basis, resulting in a book deal from a big New York publishing house.

By now, Rachel was the sole support of her mother, brother, and two nieces. She raised the girls, supported her mother, and worked a demanding, full-time job, leaving her research and writing to weekends and late nights. But she prevailed nonetheless.

Her first book, *Under the Sea Wind*, debuted in 1941 to a bemused and war-preoccupied public. It was a completely original book, enacting a narrative of the seacoast with the flora and fauna as characters, the first indication of Rachel's unique perspective on nature.

Rachel's second book, *The Sea Around Us*, was a nonfiction presentation of the relationship of the ocean to earth and its inhabitants. This time, the public was ready and she received the National Book Award and made the *New York Times* bestseller list for nearly two years! *The Edge of the Sea* was also very well received, both critically and publicly. Rachel Carson's message of respect and kinship with all life combined with a solid foundation of scientific knowledge found a real audience in postwar America. However, shy and solitary, Rachel avoided the spotlight by accepting a grant that allowed her to return to her beloved seacoast, where she could be found up to her ankles in mud or sand, researching.

As her popularity rose and her income from book royalties flooded in, Rachel was able to quit her job and build a coastal cottage for herself and her mother. She also returned the grant money, asking it be redistributed to needy scientists. In 1957, a letter from one of Rachel's readers changed everything for her. The letter came from Olga Owens Huckins who was reporting the death of birds after airplanes sprayed dichloro-diphenyl-trichloroethane, DDT, a chemical then in heavy use. Rachel Carson was keenly interested in discovering the effects to the natural habitat of DDT. Her findings were shocking: if birds and animals weren't killed outright by DDT, its effects were even more insidious—thin eggshells that broke before the hatchlings were fully developed. It was also suspected of being carcinogenic to humans.

Rachel vowed to write a book about the devastating impact of DDT upon nature "or there would be no peace for me," she proclaimed. Shortly after, she was diagnosed with cancer. Despite chemotherapy, surgery, and constant pain, Rachel worked slowly and unstintingly on her new book. In 1962, *Silent Spring* was published. It was like a cannon shot. Chemical companies fought back, denied, and ran for cover against the public outcry. Vicious charges against Rachel were aimed at what many of the captains of the chemical industry viewed as her Achilles heel—her womanhood. "Not a real scientist," they claimed. She was also called unstable, foolish, and sentimental for her love of nature. With calm logic and cool reason, Rachel Carson responded in exacting scientific terms, explaining the connections among DDT, the water supply, and the food chain.

Ultimately, President John F. Kennedy assigned his Science Advisory Committee the task of examining the pesticide, and Rachel Carson was proven to be absolutely correct. She died two years later, and although her reputation continued to be maligned by the chemical industry, her work was the beginning of a revolution in the responsible use of chemicals and serves as a reminder of the reverence for all life.

> *"Perhaps if Dr. Rachel Carson had been Dr. Richard Carson the controversy would have been minor. . . . The American technocrat could not stand the pain of having his achievements deflated by the pen of this slight woman."*
>
> —Joseph B.C. White, author

Marjory Stoneman Douglas:
Patron Saint of the Everglades

Although not native to the southernmost state, Marjorie Stoneman Douglas took to the Florida Everglades like a "duck to water," becoming, since 1927, the great champion of this rare habitat. She was born to lake country, in Minnesota in 1890, during one of her father's many failed business ventures, which kept the family moving around the country. On a family vacation to Florida at the age of four, Marjorie fell in love with the Floridian light and vowed to return.

Marjory escaped her unstable home life in the world of books. An extremely bright girl, she was admitted to Wellesley College when higher education for women was still quite uncommon. Her mother died shortly after her graduation in 1911.

Feeling unmoored, she took an unrewarding job at a department store and shortly thereafter married a much older man, Kenneth Douglas, who had a habit of writing bad checks.

Leaving for Florida with her father for his latest business pursuit seemed like the perfect way to get away from her petty criminal husband and sad memories. Frank Stoneman's latest ideas, however, seemed to have more merit: founding a newspaper in the scruffy boom town of Miami (the paper went on to become the *Miami Herald*). Marjory eagerly took a job as a cub reporter. Opinionated, forward-thinking, and unafraid

▼ *Marjory Stoneman Douglas: she saved the Everglades from becoming a parking lot!*

to share unpopular views, both Stonemans found their niche in the newspaper trade. One of the causes they were in unswerving agreement on was Governor Napoleon Bonaparte Broward's plan to drain the Everglades to put up more houses. Father and daughter used the paper as their soapbox to cry out against this ghastly idea with all their might.

Roused to action, Marjory educated herself about the facts surrounding the Everglades issue and discovered many of the denizens of Florida's swampy grassland to be in danger of extinction. The more she learned, the more fascinated she became. When decades later, she decided to leave the newspaper to write fiction, she often wove the Everglades into her plots. Marjory learned that the Everglades were actually not a swamp, but rather wetlands. In order to be a swamp, the water must be still whereas the Everglades water flows in constant movement. Marjory coined the term "river of grass" and in 1947 wrote a book about this precious ecosystem entitled *The Everglades: River of Grass.*

More than anything else, Marjory's book helped people to see the Everglades not as a fetid swamp, but as a national treasure without which Florida might become desert. After the publication of her book, Harry Truman declared a portion of the Florida wetlands as Everglades National Park. The triumph was short-lived, however. The Army Corp of Engineers began tunneling canals all over the Everglades, installing dams and floodgates. As if that weren't enough, they straightened the course of the Kissimmee River, throwing the delicate ecosystem into complete shock.

At the age of seventy-eight, Marjory Stoneman Douglas joined in the fight, stopping bulldozers ready to raze a piece of the Everglades for an immense jetport. Almost blind and armed with little more than a big floppy sun hat and a will of iron, Marjory founded Friends of the Everglades, going on the stump to talk to every Floridian about the devastation to this rare resource and building the organization member by member to thousands of people in thirty-eight states. "One can do so much by reading, learning, and talking to people," she noted. "Students need to learn all they can about animals and the environment. Most of all, they need to share what they have learned."

EcoShero Marjory Stoneman Douglas and "Marjory's Army" as her group came to be known, stopped the jetport in its tracks, garnered restrictions on farmers' use of land and chemicals, saw to the removal of the Army's "improvements," and enjoyed the addition of thousands of acres to the Everglades National Park where they could be protected from land grabbing developers. In 1975 and 1976, Marjory was rewarded for her hard work by being named Conservationist of the Year two years in a row. In 1989, she became the Sierra Club's honorary vice president. Protecting the Everglades became Marjory's life work, a job she loved. She has never considered retiring and in her 107th year, is still living in the same house she's been in since 1926 and working every day for Friends of the Everglades.

"Find out what needs to be done and do it!"
—Marjory Stoneman Douglas

Join Marjory's Army!

You can contact Friends of the Everglades through the Internet: www.everglades.org, by phone: 305-669-0858; fax: 305-669-4108; or by writing to 7800 Red Rd., Suite 215K, Miami, FL 33143

Marjorie Kinnan Rawlings:
Bard of the Backwood

Marjorie Kinnan Rawlings used to play "Story Lady" in Washington, D.C., as a girl, making up stories to tell the boys from her neighborhood. As an adult, she and her husband moved to Cross Creek, Florida, where she fell in love with the unique people of south Florida and their heart in the face of hardship, poverty, and starvation, which she immortalized in her memoir *Cross Creek*. Like Marjorie Stoneman Douglas, Rawlings helped focus the nation's attention on an area previously disregarded as a "wasteland" through her O'Henry award-winning short stories like "Gal Young Un" and "The Black Secret" and her novels—*South Moon Under, The Sojourner,* and the children's classic, *The Yearling. The Yearling* shows Rawlings at the top of her craft, with her beautifully rendered story and sense of place winning a Pulitzer prize award in 1939. *The Yearling* was made into a film that received both critical and popular acclaim; both the novel and the film are regarded as classics for their sensitive portrayal of life in the Florida Everglades.

Gertrude Blom:
Bearing Witness

Born in 1901, pioneer rainforest activist Gertrude Elizabeth Loertsher's fascination with native peoples began as a child in Switzerland when she read about American Indians and acted out the stories with her friends after school. She didn't feel the same pull toward academia, however, and pursued horticulture and social work rather than a more traditional educational career. She spent a year in England with a Quaker family whose way of life and pacifist philosophy she found imminently appealing. After a failed marriage to a neighbor's son back home in Bern, Trudi, as she liked to be called, traveled to Germany in the 1930s where she was shocked by the rise of fascism. The daughter of a Jewish mother and a Protestant minister father, Trudi's own sensibility toward peace and justice was poles apart from the Nazi party. Upon Hitler's election as chancellor in 1933, the Nazi's power was dominant; any actions or talk against it were treated as treason.

Trudi's sympathies were entirely anti-Nazi and she risked her life many times to get information about Nazi horror stories to the newspapers in her native Switzerland, outsmarting the ruling party of martinets and murderers again and again. Times got harder and getting out of Germany became increasingly difficult; Gertrude finally inveigled passage to France where she worked for the Resistance, traveling to the United States to aid other European refugees. Upon return to France, she was put in prison after the Nazi takeover.

Ultimately the Swiss government got her out of France, and she made her way to Mexico to rest and get some distance from political strife. She developed a new interest in photography, making women factory workers her subject. Her photographs were compelling, filled with both a beauty and depth in the faces weathered by difficult lives. Mexico itself filled Trudi with awe; it was both a new home and a muse catapulting her toward discovery. She traveled the vast country in search of the meaning she knew lay in the land. Her first sight of the Mexican jungle was an epiphany: "This jungle filled me with a sense of wonder that has never left me," she noted many years later. The mysterious forest and Lacandon Indians who lived there showed her a way to live in the world that was vastly different from her European background. Trudi learned from these people, studying their traditional ways only to discover their life in the jungle was in jeopardy; the rainforest was being cut down to make way for farms and factories, and thousands of Mexican peasants were being relocated to the rainforest state of Chiapos bordering Guatemala and left to scratch a living from the dirt.

Trudi's life was in flux, as well. She met and married Danish archaeologist, cartographer, and traveler, Franz Blom, who shared Trudi's fascination with the Mayan culture and Indian peoples. Together, they pursued their love of the rainforest and thirst for knowledge constantly, mapping the land and recording their findings in journals and Trudi's photography, which they published. The husband and wife team came to a deep understanding of the Lacondan rainforest and its people. They perceived the fragility of this environment and sought to preserve it, founding Na Bolom, a research institution and center for visiting scholars and travelers, anyone caring to learn about the Mayan civilization and its modern descendants.

Trudi also figured a practical way to undo some of the damage Lacandones had suffered. She invited tree experts to assist her in establishing a nursery to replant the rainforest, making the trees free to anyone who would plant them. Trudi worked diligently on the lecture circuit to pay for the seedlings, building the annual crop to 30,000 trees a year before her death in 1993 (her ninety-second year). Na Bolom carries on her work educating and reforesting the Mayan rainforest.

"The time has come for us to wake up to what we are doing and take steps to stop this destruction." —Gertrude Blom

Jane Goodall:
Not Just Monkeying Around

Born in 1934, English zoologist Jane Goodall owes her career to the fact that her divorced mother couldn't afford to send her to college. Instead, the amateur naturalist worked in offices and waitressed in order to pay for travel to feed her great curiosity. In 1960, she received an invitation to visit a friend whose family had moved to Kenya. While there, the young woman worked up the nerve to contact Louis and Mary Leakey who were working there to find evidence of early man in the Oldevai Gorge in the Great Rift. The Leakeys found her to be an able companion, well suited to work in the field looking for fossil fragments or at Kenya's National Museum of Natural History, reconstructing what they found. Despite the fact that she had no formal scientific training, Dr. Louis Leakey asked Jane to go to Tanzania to conduct a lengthy study of chimpanzees in the wild. He believed that by studying chimpanzees, we stand to learn much about the life of early humans.

▼ Jane Goodall: ethnologist, environmentalist, and champion of all chimpanzees.

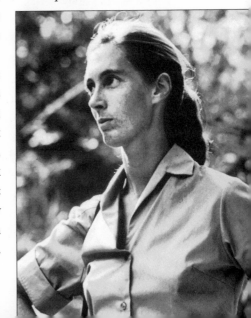

Jane, who was much more interested in animals than in Stone Age ancestors, jumped at the chance—this would be the first such long-term study of this animal in the natural habitat. When the African government refused to allow her to work alone in the animal refuge, Jane's mother offered to accompany her. Despite her lack of training, Jane was well suited to the task of scientific observation; she kept meticulous notes and went to any length to find chimps, hiking miles into the forest each day. Goodall's work was the stuff of scientific revolution.

She disproved many erroneous beliefs about chimpanzees. For example, she learned that they are omnivorous, not vegetarian; make and use tools; have elaborate social structures and a variety of humanlike emotions; and give their young unconditional affection. She has been decried by stuffy male zoologists for giving the chimps names, like Graybeard, instead of numbers in her papers. Jane did it "her way" and outdid all the uptight academics with her commitment, endurance, and plain smarts. In many ways, she received better treatment from her subjects than her peers, especially in the heartwarming moment when a male chimpanzee accepted a nut from Jane's hand, clasping her hand soulfully, before discarding the nut. Jane was touched at his attempt to spare her feelings about the unwanted nut.

In 1964, Jane met and married a young photographer who came to her camp to take photos of the chimps, and they had a son. She went on to earn a Ph.D. in ethnology from Cambridge (one of the only people ever to receive one without a B.A.!), and she has been published widely about her findings. Returning to Africa, she founded the Gombe Stream Research Centre, which is this year celebrating thirty-six years of continuous research in Gombe National Park. In recent years, her work has taken a slightly different turn, however, in protecting the chimpanzees she studied and befriended in Africa through the Chimpanzee Guardian Project. She lectures around the world to raise money to try and stop the continued shrinking of their habitat and their shrinking numbers from more than 10,000 during the time of her study to less than 3,000 today.

The author of six books, and the winner of many awards, Jane Goodall pursues her interests with singular purpose and passion. In a realm where money and education are usually the deciding factors, she started with nothing but her natural intelligence and an open, curious mind. She went on to achieve the top recognition in her field and to become one of the most beloved figures in science today.

*"Every individual matters and has a role to play in this life on earth.
The chimpanzees teach us that it is not only human but also non-human
beings who matter in the scheme of things."* —Jane Goodall

Mary Leakey:
Digging for Truth

Mary and Louis Leakey worked together in the search for the origins of man. Mary's fabled perspicacity for digging and sifting was matched by her acerbic manner and love of good strong cigars. Of the famous duo, Mary was the one with the lucky spade. In 1948, Mary uncovered the skull and facial bones of the much ballyhooed hominid that came to be know as "the missing link." In her trademark no-nonsense manner, Mary mused, "For some reason that skull caught the imagination." In 1959 in the Olduvai Gorge of northern Tanzania, she discovered some teeth and the palate bone of the oldest ancestor of man up to that point. Upon

▲ *Mary Leakey: struck gold in Tanzania
when she dug up "the Missing link."*

finding other bones, they were able to determine that the five-foot, barrel-chested, small-brained, and browless hominid Zinjanthropus had walked upright a million years ago. Three years after Louis Leakey's death in 1972, working widow Mary surpassed her own historical findings when she found the tracks of bipedal creatures which were 3.6 million years old, preserved in volcanic ash, and she later unearthed the jawbones of eleven other humanoids carbon-dated to 3.75 million years old! Mary passed the torch, or rather spade, to her son when she died in December of 1996 at the age of eight-three. We owe a great deal of our new understanding of human evolution to Mary's nose for old bones! "Her commitment to detail and perfection made my father's career," said son Richard E. Leakey. "He would not have been famous without her. She was much more organized and structured and much more of a technician."

Dian Fossey: Gorillas and the Myth

Occupational therapist Dian Fossey felt a primal call to go to Africa where she could study mountain gorillas. Taking out a personal loan, in 1963 she headed to the southern hemisphere, stopping by to say hello to Jane Goodall and the Leakeys, who encouraged her to do a gorilla field study. Traveling to Zaire (otherwise known as the "heart of darkness" to you Conrad fans), she found her research subjects—or rather sniffed out the odoriferous primates. "I was struck by the physical magnificence of the huge jet-black bodies blended against the green palette of the thick forest foliage." Taking the "when in Rome" tack, she won the apes over by mimicking their moves, eventually living among fifty-one gorillas. Indeed, her observations proved that the mountain gorillas were actually peaceful vegetarians in great danger of extinction from poaching and habitat shrinkage.

Dian Fossey defended her gorillas and their turf bravely, earning the enmity of Rwandan tribespeople. She was devastated when her beloved gorilla Digit and two others were slaughtered in what seems to have been a threat to her in 1978. Fossey made a plea to the world to help her save the gorillas, greatly furthered by her book *Gorillas in the Mist* and the eponymous movie featuring Sigourney Weaver in the starring role. After teaching at Cambridge and raising cash for the "Digit fund" to help the mountain gorillas, Dian Fossey (called Nyiramachabelli by the Rwandans—"the old lady who lives in the forest without a man") returned to stay with her gorilla families again, but her reunion was short-lived. She was found murdered on Christmas Eve of 1985 in the gorilla park habitat. Dian Fossey was buried beside Digit. Her murder has never been solved.

Petra Kelly:
Green Knight

Environmental activist Petra Karin Kelly was interested in social issues from a very early age. Born in West Germany in 1947, she moved to Columbus, Georgia, with her mother and stepfather, U.S. Army Lieutenant Colonel John E. Kelly in 1960 where immediately became involved in the civil rights movement. Learning English quickly, during high school she had a weekly radio program on current affairs. For college, she attended the school of International Service at American University where she studied world politics and graduated with honors in 1970. In addition to her studies, she was also very active in campus political movements—antiwar, antinuclear, and feminist—as a volunteer for Robert Kennedy's presidential campaign, and later for Senator Hubert H. Humphrey with whom she maintained a friendship and correspondence.

▲ *Green Party leader, Petra Kelly, was no-nukes and no nonsense.*

Her focus shifted when her sister Grace died from cancer in 1970. Petra created an citizen action group centered in Europe to study the connection between cancer and environmental pollution, eventually campaigning full-time for the Green Party she cofounded in 1979 and spearheading the Campaign for a Nuclear-Free Europe. In one year, she estimated she held more than 450 meetings in order to get the Greens elected to the German parliament, becoming the first German woman at the head of a political party.

Petra had an innate understanding of the inner-workings of politics and, together with her fellow Green Party members, including her lover, Gert Bastian, was surprisingly successful in getting candidates into the governments not only of Germany, but throughout Europe, despite the Green Party's radically pro-environment stances. As time went on, Petra's actions became increasing radical and drew more criticism from conservatives than ever before—she put together a "war crimes tribunal" at Nuremberg on the issue of nuclear weapons and, in 1983, staged a no-nukes demonstration that ended in her arrest, followed by another protest in Moscow. Petra led the Greens into more frays—blockading military bases all over Germany and leading protests in the U.S., Australia, and Great Britain.

Petra was an immensely charismatic leader, capturing the attention of thousands of people, especially young people, around the world. Her pure idealism and willingness to take personal risks captivated the youth of Europe. She received hundreds of letters each week offering support and was in high demand for lectures, articles, and books. Issues pertaining to children were especially close to her heart. She adopted a young Tibetan girl, Nima, and worked to educate the world about Tibetan genocide.

In 1991, Petra and her soulmate Gert, were discovered dead in a suburb of Bonn by police, summoned by Kelly's worried grandmother. They had both been shot and were in an advanced state of decomposition. Police have never been able to solve the double death, although the police believed it to be a double suicide. Others have claimed it was a murder plot from anti-Green neo-Nazis who Gert had decried in newspaper articles.

Police are basing the double-suicide theory on a powder burn on Gert's hand and the lack of other fingerprints or footprints in the apartment, and they have produced background information on Gert Bastian as a former SS agent who had worked for the Nazis in his youth. Thirty years older than Petra, he had once been a virulent right-winger before doing a 180-degree turnaround to join the Green Party. Close friends recall Gert depressedly saying that the "new" Germany reminded him of the old Germany of his fascist youth.

Although we may never know what really happened to Petra Kelly, we do know that while she lived, she made important inroads to drawing the world's attention to nuclear armaments, environmental destruction, children's rights, and world peace. She lived entirely for the betterment of humankind.

Karen Silkwood: Chain Reaction

The story of Karen Silkwood is a mystery wrapped in an enigma. On November 13, 1974, she died in a car crash under suspicious circumstances after she very vocally criticized the safety of the plutonium fuels production plant she worked for in Crescent, Oklahoma. She had been on her way to meet with a New York Times reporter to give him evidence that Kerr-McGee was knowingly passing off defective fuel rods as good.

Prior to her death, she was inexplicably exposed to extremely high levels of plutonium. Karen had learned to routinely test herself for exposure, but nothing prepared her for the discoveries made by the Health Physics Office upon her request. Although no plutonium was found on any surfaces in the lab she was working in, her apartment was found to have been contaminated. Starting with a measure of 1 disintegrations per minute or dpm's as the lowest possible positive result, these measurements were found in her house, according to PBS' online information site: 400,000 dpm on a package of bologna and cheese in the fridge, 25,000 on the stove sides, 6,000 on a package of chicken, and 100,000 on the toilet seat. After her death, an autopsy determined that Karen Silkwood's exposure to plutonium had been very recent and the plant could never come up with an explanation for her exposure. A year after her death, the plant closed.

The speculation surrounding her death has never stopped, but proof of company malfeasance has remained inconclusive. It is known, however, that it was Kerr-McGee who sold rods to the nuclear power plant at Three Mile Island, where defective fuel rods broke down and released radioactivity into the atmosphere.

Wangari Maathai:
Green Goddess

W angari Maathai is a remarkable woman. She set her sights on saving the farm-lands, forests, and grasslands of the most politically unstable continent she calls home—Africa. To that end, she has started the Green Belt Movement. "We wanted to emphasize that by cutting trees, removing vegetation, having this soil erosion, we were literally stripping the Earth of its color," she remarks.

Wangari comes from a sacred spot for all of mankind; the rural village she was born in is beside the Great Rift Valley, the birthplace of the first humans who walked upright. Many call Wangari's home the cradle of life. Early on, she was instructed by her mother about the importance and sanctity of land and that which grows upon it, especially trees. In 1960, she left her village and took a scholarship offered to Kenyans by the United States. She found higher education to be very much her bailiwick, receiving a master of science from the University of Pittsburgh and a doctorate from the University of Nairobi, the first woman ever to do so. She then went on to rack up a number of other firsts in her home-land, including becoming the University of Nairobi's first female professor, first depart-ment chair, and first woman in the anatomy department.

Even though she enjoyed a happy marriage to a member of Kenya's Parliament, had a thriving career, and was raising three children, she still found time to become involved with women's rights. Her Kikuyu background was different from the district in Nairobi her husband was assigned to. As a Kikuyu woman, Wangari had been free to express her opinions and be actively involved in village affairs. In Nairobi, she was regarded as much too uppity for her own good. Proving them right, Wangari decided to run for Parliament and quit her job at the university to work full-time toward for her campaign. When she was told she was ineligible to run for Parliament because she was a woman, the university refused to hire her back.

Wangari then turned her prodigious energy to the environment. On World Environment Day in 1977, she and her supporters planted seven trees in a public park and laid the foundation for the Green Belt movement. Put down by many, and even beaten with clubs, she was accused of throwing her education and talent away. This time, she proved everybody wrong. Wangari discovered that only 3 percent of the Kenyan forest was still standing. As a result, Kenyan villagers were suffering malnutrition, erosion of their farmland, and the subsequent loss of water as springs and creeks dried up. She quite accurately foresaw famine and environmental disaster unless trees were again planted to restore the environment to its natural state. Wangari traveled throughout Kenya, teaching village women how to plant trees and how to start them from seeds they collected. Soon children got involved in the Green Belt planting projects, and by 1988, more than 10,000 trees were planted.

Wangari's brilliant strategy is simple. She doesn't try to convert villagers to the program. She waits for word of the good work and practical results to spread and, soon enough, the Green Belter's are asked to come to another area. In addition to helping to stem the tide of complete destruction of Kenya's ecosystem, Wangari's Green Belt movement has provided many economic opportunities for Kenya's women.

Over the years, Wangari Maathai has received greater recognition for founding the Green Belt movement than any parliamentary seat would have provided. She has received many awards, including a "Woman of the World" award from Diana, Princess of Wales, and the encouragement to continue her invaluable work in the regreening of Africa's precious heartland.

"One person can make the difference." —Wangari Maathai

Tree-Huggers Unite!

The Chipko movement in India began in 1973 when a group of Indian women protested a government action to log near their village. When the loggers decided on a different spot, the women went there to stop the tree-cutting. In a country where widows are still burned with their dead husbands in some places, this concerted action is truly courageous. A year later, the tree action moved to yet another location. Gaura Devi, a respected elder and widow from the village of Reni, was tipped off by a little girl herding cows that loggers were on the way. Gaura flew into action and got a troop of women. When a logger threatened Devi with a gun, she replied with a fierce calm, "Shoot us. Only then will you be able to cut down the forest." From this point on, the strength of the Chipko movement increased tremendously and even got requests from men to join. Chipko means "to hug"; these grassroots environmentalists encircle their trees, holding hands to protecting their fellow beings from destruction.

Judi Bari:
Shero of the Forest Movement

The day after Judi Bari died, someone wearing an Earth First! t-shirt lowered the Willits Post Office Flag to half-mast. The flag stayed grieving until the postmaster put it back up some time later. The postmaster had to do a lot of raising the flag that week because every day the flag was lowered until the day of her wake, when the city hall flag stayed at half-mast for the day.

Judy was loved because she was an inspiration; she was admired and vilified because she was a great organizer. She knew how to organize all kinds of people—hippie kids to homesteaders—into an alliance that, by 1991, was beginning to include loggers and other timber workers. And for this she was bombed. She had the astute sense when to invade the neighborhood and when not to. And for this she was bombed. She had the principled courage to stand in the face of macho Earth First!-ers and renounce tree-spiking; and she continued to do this in spite of being crippled and in chronic, unrepairable pain for the last six years of her life.

Here was the shero's journey: to achieve the respect and honor due her work from loggers and other timber workers. Loggers who were tired of slogging right and left to cut baby trees to make a living; millworkers who saw that the company didn't care for them any more than it cared for the forest. She brought them to understand that the company was cutting them out of a job; she was good at pointing out that putting the quarterly report before the health of the forest would destroy it for our children. And workers were beginning to understand her message; and "Big Timber" couldn't stand that kind of message, so she was bombed. By somebody who is still out there.

A veritable army of people, whose desire to vilify Judi seemed endless, was led by the FBI, who labeled her a terrorist, charged her with bombing herself, and accused her one month before her death of faking cancer to gain sympathy from the public. Why on earth, why? I believe it was because she espoused and lived by a philosophy she called "biocentrism," which holds that humankind as a species is only one of a continuum, an organism, and therefore had little right to exploit the resources of the planet to the resources' destruction. She believed that giant corporations were betraying the public trust by the extraction of resources for obscene profit; naturally, this was appalling to those guardians of corporate America. So, if bombers could not destroy her body, then the FBI would destroy her reputation. If she could not be stopped from forming an alliance with workers, then she could be slowed down by intimidation, threats, isolation, and misinformation. It didn't work; she came back, and came back, and never stopped until cancer struck her down six years after the bombing.

That was her sheroism. She challenged all kinds of macho forces on their own ground. When Louisiana-Pacific Security shoved her to the ground and conned the cops into arresting her falsely, she replied a few days later by leading a circle of women through their gate at Albion, surrounded the security officer while chanting the many names of the Great Goddess. "My God, they've cast a spell on me!" he cried, eyes rolling back in his head. When in the process of discovery she obtained Oakland Police Department photos of her bombing, she looked at them over and over until she could harden herself to reliving the trauma, and actively conduct her case against the FBI for harassment, slander, and other equally slimy machinations conducted by their COINTELPRO.

Judi inspired many of us to embrace Earth First! principles, because she lived and worked by those principles and the principles of nonviolent direct action. She inspired us to learn the principles of forest management from all sides. She saw clearly and led us to see that the trust of honest men, who believed the forest would still be there for their children the way it was for them, had been betrayed and broken by the giant corporations. She inspired us to work to save the trees of our backyards, stretching through northern California to the Oregon border and beyond: the Cascades, the Siskiyous, the Talmiopsis Wilderness, Clayoquot Sound, clearcut after clearcut all the way to the Brooks Range.

Six years—the last of her life—of relentless organizing true to her shero's mission, cleaning up the corporate Augean Stables as if the corporate steeds were eating and eliminating the world. She never gave up, and she never lost her laugh. Great, deep, holding all the world laughter, even through the pain of her last months. She was cut off too soon—way too soon. What the bombing didn't do, breast cancer—the woman's neutron bomb—did. Judi made the sheroic decision to die with dignity, surrounded by her children, her family, and her friends. In the months left to her after Headwaters Rally, the greatest mass civil disobedience in the history of the U.S. forest movement (1,033 arrests that day; over 200 actions in the months following) she organized, explained, and delegated the mountains of material she had amassed: from the stuff for making banners (her last hangs on the Skunk Train Line proclaiming L-P OUT! and it's coming true) to extensive files on her case against the FBI.

In that time, she also had the opportunity to see how much the hometown folks loved her. There was a benefit tribute a month before she died. Judi was there and took the time to express her joy and thanks by singing, "I am a warrior of the earth; I came alive in the Ancient Redwoods," clutching all the while a bottle of Headwaters water, and, lastly, toking a bit of medical marijuana and blowing it into the Willits High School Auditorium air. "I've liberated Willits High!" she cried, and as we cheered and cried and howled to see that ephemeral smoke ascend the shaft of the spotlight, we knew we would never be the same for knowing her, having seen the Spirit pass among us once more with her great belly laugh. Viva, Judi! Presente Siempre.

"The woman brave enough to sit in the crotch of a tree had hers blown up today." —Robin Rule, on the bombing of Judi Bari

SportSheroes:
Leveling the Playing Field

Greek mythology tells us of the first female Olympian, Atalanta of Boetia. Born to Schoeneus, she cared not for weaving, the kitchen, or for wasting her precious time with any man who couldn't hold his own against her athletic prowess. Her father, proud of his fleet-footed Boetian babe, disregarded the norms of ancient Greek society and didn't insist on marrying his daughter off for political or financial gain, and supported her decision to marry the man who could out-run her. Her suitors were, however, given a head start, and Atalanta "armed with weapons pursues her naked suitor. If she catches him, he dies." She was outfoxed by Hippomenes who scattered golden apples as he ran, slow-ing down the amazonian runner as she stopped to pick them up. Well matched in every way, they were happy together, even going so far as to desecrate a shrine to Aphrodite by making love on the altar! For this, the Goddess turned Atalanta into a lioness where she ruled yet again with her wild and regal spirit.

In real life, women athletes have been crashing down barriers and high jumping their way to fame since the nineteenth century. In 1972, they got a bit of help from the federal government in the form of Title IX. Although

President Richard Nixon signed the law stating, "No person in the United States shall, on the basis of sex, be excluded from participation in, be denied the benefits of, or be subjected to discrimination under any education program or activity receiving federal financial assistance." The legislation is still hotly debated as to whether this is enough to give women parity. Since the passage of Title IX, statistics have shown a 7 percent increase in the ratio of women athletes in high school. Although this is a definite improvement, there's still a long way to go to reach the 50 percent mark.

Even without full equality in funding, sports is an arena where women can compete with men openly again now, thanks to such sheroic trailblazers as tennis star Billie Jean King who went up against Bobby Riggs in the heavily hyped match of 1973. Riggs, with preening braggadocio and banty-rooster crowing declared that he would exhaust King because men were "stronger" and "better tennis players." Telecast from Houston's Astrodome, the world watched while Billie Jean King beat the shorts off the chauvinist Riggs and leveled the playing fields (and courts!) for every woman and girl on that herstoric day. Like King, and today's rising star, Venus Williams, the sheroes portrayed here have bucked the odds with passion, pure guts, and sheer ability to make it to the top of their games.

Babe Didrikson Zaharias:
The Greatest

B abe (real name Mildred) Didrikson always strived to be the best at any activity she undertook. Insecure, she figured sports was a great way to build herself and her self-esteem up. She got that right! She excelled at every sport she tried: running, jumping, javelin throwing, swimming, basketball, and baseball to name just a few. In her prime, she was so famous that she was known around the world by her first name.

Babe had a supportive home environment for the sporting life; her mother, Hannah Marie Olson, was a figure skater. Babe's family was loving, but they had a tough time making a living in the hardscrabble Texas town from whence they hailed. As a youngster in the twenties, Babe worked after school packing figs and sewing potato sacks at nearby factories, but somehow she still found time to play. No matter what the game, Babe was always better than the boys.

In high school, Babe tried out for basketball, baseball, golf, tennis, and volleyball; her superior athletic skills created a lot of jealousy among her peers. A Dallas insurance company offered her a place on their basketball team; Babe worked at the firm, finished high school, and played on the team. In her very first game, she smoked the court and outscored the other team all by herself. Fortunately for her, Employers Casualty also had track, diving, and swim teams. Track held a particular lure for Babe; she set records almost immediately in the shot put, high jump, long

▼ *Babe Didrikson: the greatest all-sport athlete of all time.*

jump, and javelin throw. In 1932, Babe represented the Lone Star State as a one-woman team, and out of eight competitions she took awards for six. In 1932, Los Angeles was the site of the Summer Olympics; Babe drew the eyes of the world when she set records for the 80-meter hurdles and the javelin throw. She would have won the high jump too, but the judges declared her technique of throwing herself headfirst over the bar as unacceptable. There is no doubt she would have taken home even more gold except for the newly instated rule setting a limit of three events per athlete.

For Babe, making a living was more important than the accolades of the world. Unfortunately the options for women in professional sports were extremely limited in the 1930s. She made the decision to become a professional golfer; although she had little experience, she took the Texas Women's Amateur Championship three years later. In typical Babe Didrikson style, she went on to win seventeen tournaments in a row and also took part in matches against men, including a memorable match against the "crying Greek from Cripple Creek," George Zaharias, whom she married in 1938. Babe quickly saw the need for equality in women's golf and helped found the Ladies Professional Golf Association. Babe died at forty-three, after making a stunning comeback: winning the U.S. Open by twelve strokes less than a year after major surgery for intestinal cancer. She is thought by many to have been the greatest female athlete of all time.

"It's not enough to swing at the ball. You've got to loosen your girdle and really let the ball have it." —Babe Didrikson Zaharias

Alice Coachman: Running for Her Life

Boy could Alice Coachman run and jump! Because of World War II, however, national competitions were as far as an athlete could aspire in the forties, and the young African American athlete held the national titles for the high jump for twelve consecutive years. Her chance to achieve international recognition finally came in the 1948 Olympics; Alice was thought to be past her prime, but she decided to go for it anyway. Her teammates lost every race; finally it was Alice's turn for the high jump. She took the gold, defeating an opponent who towered above her in height, to become at age twenty-four, the first black woman to win Olympic gold and the first American woman to go for the gold in track and field.

Alice was warmly welcomed back to America with an invitation to the White House, a victory motorcade through her home state of Georgia, and a contract to endorse Coca Cola. Not surprisingly, the racist and sexist America of the forties didn't fully embrace Alice as it should have. She was, however, lionized in the black community as a favorite daughter and truly was the trailblazer for every black woman athlete to come after her.

Althea Gibson:
Never Give Up

From the ghetto to the tennis court, Althea Gibson's story is pure sheroism. At a time when tennis was not dominated by whites but by upper-class whites at that, she managed to serve and volley her way to the top.

Born in 1927 to a Southern sharecropper family, Althea struggled as a girl with a restless energy that took years for her to channel into positive accomplishments. The family's move to Harlem didn't help. She was bored by school and skipped a lot; teachers and truant officers predicted the worst for Althea, believing that she was a walking attitude problem whose future lay as far as the nearest reform school.

Although things looked dire for Althea, she had a thing or two to show the naysayers. Like many sheroes, Althea had to bottom out before she could get to the top. She dropped out of school and drifted from job to job until, at a mere fourteen, she found herself a ward of New York City's Welfare Department. This turned out to be the best thing that could have happened to Althea—a wise welfare worker not only helped her find steady work, but also enrolled her into New York's police sports program. Althea fell in love with paddle ball and, upon graduating to real tennis, amazed everyone with her natural ability. The New York Cosmopolitan Club, an interracial sports and social organization, sponsored the teen and arranged for her to have a tennis coach, Fred Johnson. Althea's transformation from "bad girl" to tennis sensation was immediate; she won the New York State Open Championship one year later. She captured the attention of two wealthy patrons who agreed to sponsor her if she finished high school. She did in 1949—and went on to accept a tennis scholarship to Florida Agricultural and Mechanical University.

Althea's battles weren't over yet, though. She aced nine straight Negro national championships and chafed at the exclusion from tournaments closed to nonwhite players. Fighting hard to compete with white players, Althea handled herself well, despite being exposed to racism at its most heinous. Her dignified struggle to overcome segregation in tennis won her many supporters of all colors. Finally, one of her biggest fans and admirers, the editor of *American Lawn Tennis* magazine, wrote an article decrying the "color barrier" in tennis. The walls came down. By 1958, Althea Gibson won the singles and doubles at Wimbledon and twice took the U.S. national championships at the U.S. Open as well.

Then, citing money woes, she retired; she just couldn't make a living at women's tennis. Like Babe Zaharias, she took up golf, becoming the first black woman to qualify for the LPGA. But she never excelled in golf as she had in tennis, and in the seventies and eighties she returned to the game she truly loved, serving as a mentor and coach to an up and coming generation of African American women tennis players.

▲ *Althea Gibson: this champion broke through the "color barriers" in tennis.*

Through sheer excellence and a willingness to work on behalf of her race, Althea Gibson made a huge difference in the sports world for which we are all indebted.

Martina Navratilova:
Always Herself

▲ *Martina Navratilova: uncloseted and almost unbeatable tennis star.*

One of the all-time tennis greats, Martina Navratilova was a Czechoslovakian native who defected to the United States so she could manage her own career, rather than having the Czech government tell her what to do and where to go. During the eighties, she was the top-ranked women's tennis player in the world with a career record of seventy-five straight wins. She approached her career and training as serious business, a pure athlete in the truest sense. One of the first openly gay celebrities, Martina has been linked amorously with writer Rita Mae Brown, who penned a novel about their affair, and was sued in a "galimony" suit by another lover, Judy Nelson, who went on to share a bed with Rita. Opines Martina, "I never thought there was anything strange about being gay."

The All-American Girls Baseball League:
Backward and in High Heels

For the briefest time in the 1940s, women had a "league of their own." And while it was not intended to be serious sports so much as a marketing package, the All-Girls Baseball League stormed the field and made it their own. The league was the brainchild of chewing gum magnate Phillip K. Wrigley, whose empire had afforded him the purchase of the Chicago Cubs. He came up with the concept of putting a bunch of sexy girls out on the field in short skirts and full makeup to entertain a baseball-starved population whose national pastime was put on hold as baseball players turned fighting men.

He was right—the gals did draw crowds, enough to field teams in several mid-sized Midwestern cities. (At the height of its popularity, the league was drawing a million paying customers per 120 game season.) A savvy businessman catering to what he believed were the tastes of baseball fans, Wrigley had strict guidelines for his "girls"— impeccable appearance and maintenance, no short hair, no pants on or off the playing field. Pulchritude and "charm" were absolute requirements for players. Arthur Meyerhoff, chairman of the league, aptly characterized it as: "Baseball, traditionally a men's game, played by feminine type girls with masculine skill." For Meyerhoff, "feminine type" was serious business and he kept a hawkeye on his teams for the slightest sign of lesbianism. He also sent his sandlot and cornfield trained players to charm school to keep them on their girlish toes.

Although the rules seemed stringent, the players were eager to join these new teams called the Daisies, the Lassies, the Peaches, and the Belles because it was their only chance to play baseball professionally. Pepper Pair put it best in the book she and the other AAGBL players are profiled in, "You have to understand that we'd rather play ball than eat, and where else could we go and get paid $100 a week to play ball?" After the war, men returned home and major league baseball was revived. However the All-Girls league hung on, even spawning the rival National Girl's Baseball League. With more opportunity for everyone, teams suddenly had to pay more money to their best players in order to hang on to them and both leagues attracted players from all around the U.S. and Canada.

Penny Marshall's wonderful film, *A League of Their Own* did a credible job portraying the hardship and hilarity of professional women athletes trying to abide by the rules and display feminine "charm" while playing topnotch baseball. Ironically, the television boom of the fifties eroded the audience for the AAGBL as well as many other semi-pro sports. The death blow to the women's baseball leagues came, however, with the creation of the boys-only Little League. Girls no longer had a way to develop their skills in their youth and were back to sandlots and cornfields, and the AAGBL died in 1954.

"The fans thought we were the best thing that ever came down the pike."

—player Mary Pratt

Joan Joyce: Perfect Pitch

Joan Joyce should be a household name. In the words of a tournament umpire who watched her pitch a game, she was "one of the three best softball pitchers in the country, and two of them are men." Joan ended up in softball when she was blocked from playing baseball in the fifties. She recalled in an interview in *Sports Illustrated*, "I started playing softball at eight because my father played it and because it was the only sport open to me at the time." By her teens, she was astounding players, coaches, and parents alike with a fast ball clocked at 116 miles per hour. At eighteen, she joined the Stratford, Connecticut, all-girl team, the Raybestos Brakettes, and pitched the team to three consecutive national championships. Soon, the Brakettes were the force to be reckoned with in amateur softball, winning a dozen championships in eighteen seasons. Joyce's record was an unbelievable 105 no-hitters and thirty-three perfect games.

Joyce's reputation as an "unhittable" pitcher led to a challenge in 1962 between Joyce and Ted Williams, then a batting champion with a .400 average per season. A roaringly appreciative crowd watched her fan thirty pitches past the bemused Williams. He managed only a few late fouls and one limp hit to the infield. On that day, Joan Joyce showed she was not only just as good, but better than any man!

Wilma Rudolph:
La Gazelle

Runner Wilma Rudolph's life is the story of a great spirit and heart overcoming obstacles that would have stopped anyone else in their tracks, literally! Born in Bethlehem, Tennessee, in 1955, Wilma contracted polio at the age of four and was left with a useless leg.

Wilma's family was in dire straits with a total of eighteen children from her father's two marriages. Both parents worked constantly to feed the burgeoning brood, her father as a porter and her mother as a house cleaner, and it was more important to feed Wilma and her siblings than it was to get the medical attention Wilma needed to recover the use of her leg. Two years later circumstances eased a bit and, at the age of six, Wilma started riding the back of the bus with her mother to Nashville twice a week for physical therapy. Although doctors predicted she would never walk without braces, Wilma kept up her rehabilitation program for five years and not only did the braces come off, but "by the time I was twelve," she told the *Chicago Tribune*, "I was challenging every boy in the neighborhood at running, jumping, everything."

Her exceptional ability didn't go unnoticed. A coach with Tennessee State University saw how she was winning every race she entered in high school and offered to train her for the Olympics, which Wilma hadn't even heard of. Nevertheless, she qualified for the Olympics at sixteen and took home a bronze medal in the 1956 Summer Games for the 100-meter relay. Still in high school, she decided to work toward a gold medal for the 1960 games.

Well, she did that and more. The three gold medals she won in the 1960 Olympics in Rome—in the 100-meter dash, the 200-meter dash, and the 4 X 100 relay—turned her into a superstar overnight. Wilma was the first American woman ever to win triple gold in a single Olympics. People were stumbling over the top of each other to find the superlatives to describe her. The French named Wilma "La Gazelle," and in America she was known as "The Fastest Woman on Earth." Wilma was everybody's darling after that with invitations to the JFK White House and numerous guest appearances on television. The flip side of all the glory was, however, that Wilma received hardly any financial reward for her public appearances and had to work odd jobs to get through college.

One year later, Wilma again set the world on fire by breaking the record for the 100-meter dash: 11.2 seconds. Unpredictably, Wilma sat out the '64 Olympic Games and stayed in school, graduating with a degree in education and returning to the very school she attended as a youngster to teach second grade. In 1967, she worked for the

Job Corps and Operation Champion, a program that endeavored to bring star athletes into American ghettos as positive role models for young kids. Wilma herself loved to talk to kids about sports and supplied a powerful symbol with her inspiring story.

That Wilma touched the lives of children is best evidenced in a letter writing campaign taken up by a class of fourth graders in Jessup, Maryland, who requested the *World Book Encyclopedia* correct their error in excluding the world-class athlete. The publisher complied immediately! Wilma has also been honored with induction in both the Olympic Hall of Fame and the National Track and Field Hall of Fame. A film version of her autobiography *Wilma* starring Cicely Tyson was produced to tremendous acclaim. Her death from terminal brain cancer took place shortly after she received an honor as one of "The Great Ones" at the premiere National Sports Awards in 1993.

"I have spent a lifetime trying to share what it has meant to be
a woman first in the world of sports so that other young women will
have a chance to reach their dreams." —Wilma Rudolph

Evelyn Ashford: The Power of Persistence

"(Wilma Rudolph) inspired me to pursue my dream of being a runner, to stick with it," says runner Evelyn Ashford, whose incredible athletic staying power in a sport where the burnout rate is fast, is notable. She participated in Olympic games for nearly twenty years, returning to pick up a gold medal in 1992 as a thirty-five-year-old mother of one. Evelyn was always gifted at sports, but never took herself seriously until a male coach noticed her speed and issued the challenge for her to race his male track team. When she beat the "best guy" on the field, Evelyn suddenly got the attention and positive support that spurred her on.

By 1975, she had earned a full scholarship to UCLA. One year later, she was a member of the Olympic team, but had to wait for the next games four years later to make her mark. In 1980, in protest of the Soviet Union's invasion of Afghanistan, President Carter made the choice to boycott the Summer Olympic games. Along with her peers, Evelyn Ashford's chances to win were dashed. But her persistence paid in spades; she came back after the terrible disappointment and won a gold medal for the 100 meter sprint and another gold medal for the 400 meter relay in the 1984 Summer Olympic Games held in Los Angeles. Renowned as the perfect model of a good sport, on and off the field, she takes enormous joy in running with fellow champions Alice Brown, Sheila Echols, and Florence Griffith-Joyner, and promoting track and field as a sport. There's no doubt that Wilma Rudolph would be proud of Evelyn Ashford's accomplishments.

Jackie Joyner-Kersee:
Queen of the Field

Arguably the greatest cross category track and field star of all time, Jackie Joyner-Kersee has a string of firsts to her credit and keeps racking them up at an astonishing rate: she's the first U.S. woman to win gold for the long jump, the first woman ever to exceed 7,000 points for the heptathalon, and the first athlete, man or woman, to win multiple gold medals in both single and multiple events in track and field. Since her debut in the 1984 Los Angeles Summer Events, Jackie has been at the top of her game.

Along with her athletic prowess, Jackie's charisma and style made her an overnight sensation. In addition, she has a policy of giving back as good as she gets to the community she's from. She has a strong desire to nurture athleticism and scholarship in urban settings where access to a place to run and play is the first of many challenges ghetto kids face. Her foundation, the Jackie Joyner-Kersee Youth Center Foundation, is currently developing a recreational and educational facility for kids in East St. Louis where area kids will have access to a computer lab, library, ball fields, basketball courts, and of course, indoor and outdoor tracks.

Like several other outstanding athletes, Jackie comes from poverty, an alum of the poorest part of East St. Louis. Fortunately, Jackie received encouragement from her family to participate in sports. She discovered track and field at the Mayor Brown Community Center, and her Olympic dreams started when she saw the 1976

▲ *Jackie Joyner-Kersee: herstory-making heptathlete!*

Olympics on television. Jackie quickly emerged a veritable "sporting savant" and started breaking national records at fourteen, excelling at basketball and volleyball while maintaining a super grade point average. Soon she was courted by many tantalizing college scholarships, ultimately deciding to attend UCLA where Bob Kersee would be her coach.

Bob Kersee, whom she married in 1986, convinced both Jackie and the powers-that-be at UCLA that Jackie's career lay in multitrack events. Looking back, it's hard to imagine Jackie anywhere but in the event where she is the best in the world. Jackie's forte is the seven-event heptathalon, a previously overlooked event in which athletes earn points by running a 200-meter dash, compete in both high and long jumps, throw both the javelin and shot put, run the 100-meter hurdles, and complete a 800-meter run, all in two days. These herculean challenges alone call for super-sheroism, and Jackie has not only made the heptathlon her own, but through her prowess, made the event a track and field favorite.

She is one of the few African American athletes to get prestigious product endorsement contracts and is very aware of her opportunity to provide a positive role model, telling *Women's Sports & Fitness*, "I feel that as an African American woman the only thing I can do is continue to better myself, continue to perform well, continue to make sure that I'm a good commodity. If doors aren't opened for me, then maybe it will happen for someone else."

> *"I understand the position I am in, but I also know that tomorrow there's going to be someone else. So I try to keep things in perspective."* —Jackie Joyner-Kersee

Florence Griffith-Joyner:
Going with the Flo Jo

Jackie Joyner-Kersee's brother, Al Joyner, was an Olympic athlete too. When he saw the flamboyant Florence Griffith in 1984, the runner who made her mark on the track world as much for her long fingernails and colorful attire as for being "the world's fastest woman," she was working days as a customer service rep for a bank and moonlighting as a beautician at night. The former world-class runner had lost the gold to

Valerie Brisco in 1980 and had given up. At Al's urging, she began training again. They also started dating seriously and got married soon after. This time, Florence had the will to win and stormed the 1988 Seoul Olympics to take home three gold medals. Off the track, "Flo Jo", as the press dubbed her, has devoted herself to working with children, hoping to educate the youth of America to "reach beyond their dreams,"eat right, play sports, and stay away from drugs. After her record-setting gold medal races in Seoul, *Ms.* enthused, "Florence Griffith-Joyner has joined the immortals, rising to their status on the force of her amazing athletic achievement, aided by the singular nature of her personality and approach."

▲ *Florence Griffith-Joyner: olympic Goddess and "fastest woman in the world."*

"Looking good is almost as important as running well. It's part of feeling good about myself." —Florence Griffith-Joyner

Arlene Blum:
"A Woman's Place Is on Top"

Arlene Blum has made a success by doing what she's not "supposed" to do. Born in Chicago in 1945 and raised by her mother's parents, Arlene overcame "arithmaphobia" to go to the top of her class in mathematics and science where she developed a taste for competing academically with boys. She decided to study chemistry in Portland's Reed College, ultimately earning a doctorate in chemistry from U.C. Berkeley. In an interview with *Ms.* in 1987, she indicated that this spirit of competition still propelled her, "I know that . . . girls weren't supposed to be chemists. And it's always sort of nice to do things you're not supposed to do." Reed's location near Oregon's mountain peaks was auspicious for the young scientist. She fell in love with mountain climbing and even worked it into her academic regimen by analyzing volcanic gas from the top of Mount Hood.

More exotic ranges beckoned and Arlene soon trekked to Mexican and Andean peaks. An eye-opening event happened when she submitted an application to be a part of a team destined for Afghanistan and was turned down for being a woman. After a second rejection for an Alaskan expedition, Arlene Blum took the "bull by the horns" and put together her own all-woman team of six climbers, all of whom made the peak of Alaska's Mount Denali (formerly known as Mount McKinley) in 1970. This was just the beginning for the barrier-breaking shero who, in 1978, took another all-woman team to Annapurna, one of the highest mountains in the world. At the time, only four teams had ever made it to the top of Annapurna, a treacherous mountain known for fierce storms and dangerous avalanches. In addition to the danger, such treks are always extremely expensive. Ever plucky, Blum and her team of Sherpas and sheroes paid their way to the top of Annapurna, the world's tenth highest peak, by selling t-shirts and gaining corporate sponsorship. The t-shirts became real conversation starters with the winning slogan, "A Woman's Place is on top . . . Annapurna!'

Amazing Arlene has gone on to walk the entire Great Himalayan mountain range, crest Everest, and organize many expeditions and explorations. She has also excelled at her other profession, chemistry, and helped identify a carcinogenic flame-retardant in children's clothing. Arlene's daughter Annlise joins her mother on climbs now, part of the generation of women for whom Arlene cleared the path. Arlene Blum showed the world that, when it comes to excluding women from sports, there "ain't no mountain high enough" to keep a good shero down!

"People say I've organized all-women's expeditions to show what we can do; but it wasn't like that. It was more a rebellion against being told I couldn't do something, or... that women couldn't do something." —Arlene Blum

Other Gals Who Climbed to the Top

Fifty years earlier, Arlene Blum would not have been allowed in certain areas in the Great Himalayan range. It was an entirely different kind of explorer who helped open those gates. In 1924, spiritual seeker **Alexandra David-Neel** was the first Western woman to visit Tibet's "Forbidden City," Lhasa, in its mountain perch. Dressed as a beggar and traveling so light they didn't even have blankets, the fifty-five-year-old Alexandra and a young monk, made the perilous climb up 18,000 feet to the holy city. Her travelogue is one of the most treasured resources in Asian studies, published as *My Journey to Lhasa*.

Opera singer turned scholar, the intrepid Frenchwoman also has the honor of being the first Western woman to have an audience with the Dalai Lama in his Indian exile. Alexandra never did anything halfway and found the study of Buddhism so appealing that she moved into an ascetic's snowy cave, and undertook the studies and spiritual practice of a Buddhist nun. She became such an adept that she reportedly was able to control her body temperature through meditation, and there are legends of levitation and other psychic phenomenon. Poo-poohing "the supernatural," her explanation for these matters is simple and practical: she learned from the Tibetans that it is all a matter of the management of natural energies. One of the world's earliest scholar's in Eastern Studies and Oriental mysticism, Alexandra David-Neel's unique combination of daring and curiosity made her one of the most fascinating women in any part of the world.

Then there's **Lynn Hill**. Although many of our sportsheroes have made strides for women simply by being the best, others, like Lynn Hill, have done so with great intention. Lynn Hill is a world class climber whose stated mission is to create equality for women climbers in an admittedly steep arena. In what was previously a totally male-dominated sport requiring strength women "aren't supposed" to have, Lynn Hill has rocketed to the top, demanded to be allowed to climb the same courses as men, and proved to the world that a woman can climb as well as any man. As she says, "If extreme athletics improves you as a person, why can't that be feminine?"

And don't forget **Annie Smith Peck.** She was a classical scholar born in 1850 with a yen for heights. Wearing a suit of animal skins explorer Robert Edwin Peary had brought back from his exploration of the Arctic Circle, she climbed the Andean apex, Mount Huascaran, and went on to become the foremost female mountain climber of her day. She was fifty-eight years old at the time. She wrote about her exploits and became quite a popular travel writer. One of her most sheroic exploits involved climbing the formidable Mount Coropuna in Peru and hanging a banner at the summit reading, "Votes for Women!" She didn't stop climbing until a year before her death at age eighty-five.

Myriam Bedard:
Canadian Bi-Athlete

Well on her way to a successful career as a figure skater, Myriam Bedard hung up her figure skates as a young teenager to become a pioneer in one of the Olympic's newest sanctioned sports competitions for women: the much less glamorous and far more rigorous biathlon. A combination of cross-country skiing and sharp-shooting, the biathlon has an interesting history: for ancient Scandinavians, skiing and stalking prey were necessary for survival in their wintry climes. Infantry soldiers in World War II came to the same conclusion for completely different reasons, leading to the formation of military ski patrols in Norway, Finland, Sweden, and other parts of Scandinavia. The biathlon is a refinement of these origins but wasn't recognized as an Olympic sport for men until 1960. Women biathletes had to wait thirty-two more years to compete on the Olympic games. The young Myriam was ready.

She had been training for several years in a suburb outside Quebec City and quickly discovered the prohibition on firearms in Canada's public bus system. Resourcefully, she figured out how to tear her gun down so it could be transported in an innocent-looking violin case. Highly driven, Myriam started winning races at fifteen, even though the only ski boots she had were so big she had to stuff paper in the toes. Two years later, she became Canada's junior biathlon champion and, by the 1992 Olympics, won the bronze medal for the 15-kilometer race.

Myriam's career has been cloaked in both mystery and controversy. Upon winning her Olympic prize, she stirred debate with her abject refusal to sign Biathlon Canada's contractual agreement to cycle a portion of her other earnings back to the organization, accompanied by a "gag order" to prevent media appearances by national biathletes. Her stubbornness or independence, depending on the point of view, concluded in her suspension from Canada's team. A truce was won in time for her to rejoin the team and lead them to an exciting win in the 1993 world championships in Bulgaria. Bedard did Canada proud in Bulgaria, shooting past the Russian skier who had bested her in '92.

Her critics love to harp on her solitary ways and her secrecy with her private coach, whose name she refuses to reveal. When she performed with less than stellar speed at the 1993 winter trials, the naysayers came out in droves to predict gloom, doom, and disaster for Canada. Resolute in her own judgment and that of her "mystery coach," Myriam had simply decided to reserve her strength for the 1994 Olympic games in Lillehammer. Although her starting position for the 15-kilometer race was third from last, with the fierce concentration that has become her trademark, Bedard swept to the front and took the gold, following that victory with a second win on the 7.5-kilometer race. A fascinating footnote to the Lilehammer triumphs is that she realized after her second race that she had on mismatched skis!

The reticent Myriam Bedard has become a much sought speaker in Canada and a national shero to Canada's youth who cherish that she is one of the nation's all-time greatest Olympic champions. Bedard tries to balance all this with motherhood (she married a fellow biathete in 1994) and her love of a quiet life. She walked her own path every step of the way and carved out a destiny in what is arguably the toughest of all Olympic sports.

"I like it when I strike sparks in people . . . after all,
that's why I'm here!"—Myriam Bedard

Michele Akers: The Girl with the Golden Boot

Women's soccer is enjoying a growing popularity worldwide, and Michelle Akers has been hailed as the best soccer player in the world. The native Californian demonstrated her promise early on, earning an unprecedented place as All-American four consecutive years in high school in the 1980s. She then went on to lead her soccer team into the international spotlight as the world's first champion women's soccer team and later as the first world champion women's team. Out of eighty-seven games played for the American championship team, Michelle Akers scored a staggering eighty-two goals. Her "personal best" occurred in a historic game in China where she scored five goals in one match. Akers has parlayed her fantastic success into a professional career, mostly in Europe where she led her Swedish team to the top, scoring more goals than any other male or female player in the country in 1992. Currently, she battles Epstein-Barr, an immune deficiency virus, but continues to play the sport she enjoys despite the challenges of a debilitating disease: "I still just love to play."

Bonnie Blair:
Speed Racer

Bonnie Blair has skated her way into the hearts of America. She comes from an entire family of skaters; Bonnie is the "baby" of the family, born in 1964. She was skating with ease by the age of two and was a competitor by four! When Bonnie was

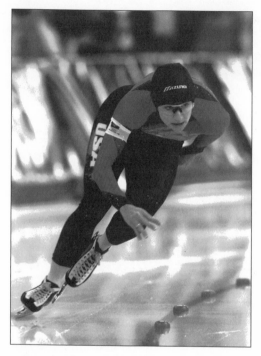

▲ *Bonnie Blair: speed-skating to olympic glory.*

seven, her family moved from her birthplace of Cornwall, New York, to the Midwestern town of Champaign, Illinois. She won the state speed skating championship for her age group that same year.

In Illinois, Bonnie was fortunate to hook up with a great coach, Cathy Priestner, an Olympic champion herself. Cathy directed her toward Olympic-style speed skating and away from the pack racing that had been her strength. Age sixteen was certainly sweet for Bonnie when she skated 500 meters in 46.7 seconds at her debut as a potential Olympian. This gave her the taste of what it could be like to be the fastest woman on skates. However, Bonnie had some bumpy ice ahead—she didn't make the cut in the actual trials later. Another stumbling block that nearly felled her was money problems; the grueling expense of travel expenses and coaching was more than the Blairs could handle. But Bonnie's hometown rose to the occasion and the local police force ran a ten-year campaign to raise funds to pay for their Olympic hopeful through sales of bumper stickers and t-shirts. Their generous spirit paid for Bonnie's training with the U.S. men's speed skaters in the Big Sky country of Butte, Montana.

Bonnie first came into global view in the Sarajevo games in 1984. She finished quite honorably, ranking eighth in the 500-meter speed skating race, but Bonnie knew she could do better. For the next Olympics, she focused even harder and increased the difficulty of her regimen—weight-training, running, biking, and roller-skating, all over and above the intense skating. Pushing herself was key for Bonnie. She started breaking world records in 1986 and took the U.S. championship every year from 1985 to 1990. In a power sport, Bonnie actually measured in as much smaller and lighter than many of her rivals from around the world.

After adopting her new style of training, 1988 was the first Olympics Bonnie participated in. She took a gold medal in the 500-meter race and set a world record of 39.10 seconds, beating out a German skater in first place who had just set a world record. Bonnie didn't stop with that and took home the bronze for the 1,000-meter sprint. Bonnie became the best speed skater in the world in Calgary that day and kept her title at the 1992 games in Albertville, France, with two more gold medals. Bonnie also started winning hearts with her friendly, open manner and lack of pretension.

Odds were somewhat against veteran Bonnie in Lillehammer in 1994, but she did what no other woman has done and took two more gold medals. The emotional highlight of the games that year was not the other drama queen figure skaters—Harding and Kerrigan—but Bonnie Blair. Half the world cried with her as she took her gold and cried while the national anthem played during what was to be Bonnie's last Olympics. Bonnie Blair: the first woman to earn gold medals in three straight Olympic games and the first American woman to win five gold medals in the history of Olympics.

"... I'm in this because I love what I'm doing."—Bonnie Blair

Susan Butcher:
The Last Great Race on Earth

New Englander Susan Butcher had an unusual upbringing; in the fifties, her parents Charles and Agnes Butcher felt girls should be treated the same as boys. With this atmosphere, their two daughters were exposed to carpentry, mechanics, shipbuilding, and anything else they cared to learn. Susan really enjoyed boat-building and restoration, and she applied to a special training school at sixteen but was turned down for being female. She also loved any activity where she could be outdoors. Every chance she got, she was outside with her beloved dog, Cabee. Her love of animals was such that her family thought she might aspire to veterinary science because she was "more comfortable with animals than she was with people." But Susan threw everyone a curve when she chose her life's work.

Moving to mountainous Boulder, Colorado, seventeen-year-old Susan opted against college to take up "mushing"—dogsled racing. Later, she moved to Fairbanks to attend the University of Alaska in order to participate in a special project helping forestall the extinction of musk oxen. Susan was definitely in the perfect setting to practice mushing; she got three dogs and moved to a remote Wrangell Mountain log cabin outside Fairbanks and lived, pioneer style, hunting for food and sledding her way around the snowy countryside. In 1977, her work with the endangered musk oxen took her to Unalakleet, the home of the "Last Great Race on Earth." Here, she met Joe Reddington, Sr., the founder of this race, more commonly known as the Iditarod Trail Sled Dog Race. Reddington immediately became a fan of Susan's who saw her talent with dogs and how hard she worked at mushing. He declared that one day Susan Butcher would be an Iditarod champion. His prescience was soon proven.

In the 1978 race, Butcher placed nineteenth as a first-timer. She then met a young lawyer and sled racer named David Monson. Although the relationship started out in a dispute over Susan's rather large, past-due debt for dog food to the company Monson represented, they fell in love, got married, and settled in Eureka, a hundred miles south of the Arctic Circle. They founded the Trail Breaker Kennels, built 120 houses for racing dogs and four one-room cabins for human visitors and fellow racers. Friends say that she has a uniquely close bond with her dogs, treating them as she does people and finding the unique qualities that make each dog different. Susan just says the dogs are her "best friends."

She has continued to race every year after getting married, winning many times. Despite blizzards and eighty mile-per-hour winds, moose attacks, and a bad sled wreck, Susan has set records for speed in the Iditarod and made headlines around the world as the woman who could outrace any man in the most extreme climate on earth.

"Alaska—Where Men are Men and Women Win the Iditarod"

> —slogan on more than one million
> t-shirts sold since Susan Butcher
> first won "The Last Great Race"

Of Cockpits, Cocks and Bulls, and Other "Ladylike" Pursuits

Adalynn (Jonnie) Jonckowski: This card-carrying member of the cowgirl hall of fame has an unusual idea of a good time—hopping on the back of an angry bull and hanging on as long as possible. Called the "Belle of Billings" (Montana), she has repeatedly proved to be the world's best bull rider. Adalynn's winning attitude is evidenced here, "Any time you have the freedom to do what you want to do and exercise that freedom, you're a champ."

While Jonnie Jonckowski clings to the backs of angry Brahma bulls, **Julie Krone** has her own wild rides. Petite and determined, Julie Krone was the first female jockey to win Triple Crown a race at the Belmont Stakes. She had shown that women can ride the winning race and has $54 million worth of purses to show for it. (Jockeys keep 10 percent of the take, quite a motivator!) Even though Julie says that "times have changed" for women, she will still occasionally be heckled with yells of "Go home, have babies, and do the dishes," when she *loses*. The wealthy winner's final comment: "In a lot of people's minds, a girl jockey is cute and delicate. With me, what you get is reckless and aggressive."

Shirley Muldowney, born Belgium Roque, took on one of the last bastions of machodom—drag racing—and came up a winner. She fell in love with cars at the age of fourteen in Schenectady, New York, racing illegally "when the police weren't looking." At fifteen, she married mechanic Jack Muldowney, and they became a hot-rodding couple. Shirley put up with enormous hostility from race fans and outright hatred from fellow drivers. In 1965, she became the first woman to operate a top-gas dragster and went on to win seventeen National Hot Rod Association titles, second only to Don Garliz. Queen of the cockpit, Shirley Muldowney became an internationally famous superstar with the critically acclaimed film about her life and achievements, "Heart Like a Wheel."

Hockey is certainly no sport for lightweights. For many, taking shots from a bunch of big men with sticks might seem like a risky business, but to French Canadian **Manon Rheume**, it's the sport she loves. She is goalie for the Atlanta Knights and, as such, is the first woman to play professional hockey in the men's leagues. At five feet six and 135 pounds, Manon is slight compared to many of her team members and opponents, but she has proven her ability to stop a puck. The world is finally taking note of women's ability to play this sport overall; in the year 1998, women's ice hockey became a full medal sport at the Winter Olympics, no small thanks to Manon and others like her.

Then there's **Angela Hernandez**, whose surely to be admired for fighting for her right to bullfight in the birthplace of macho—Spain! In the polyester-laden year 1973, she demanded to be allowed to compete in the male-only zone of the bullring. This caused quite a commotion; how dare she question the 1908 law forbidding women to participate in the sport of horseback bullfighting. Twenty-year-old Angela took her case all the way to the courts where the Madrid labor court ruled in her favor, allowing her to fight, but only on foot. But threatened males found another way to thwart her—the Ministry of the Interior wouldn't issue her a license. Would-be torero Angela refused to go quietly into the Seville sunset, loudly contesting her plight, "These damned men. What do they think they are doing? Women fly planes, fight wars, and go on safaris; what's so different about fighting bulls?"

Judi Sheppard Missett:
She Made the Connection

Not every shero's interest in physical fitness and sports results in Olympic glory. For most of us, just taking care of our bodies and ourselves is a herculean challenge in the wildly paced workaday world. One unsung shero who offers solutions for this issue is Iowa's Judi Sheppard Misset, the founder and CEO of Jazzercise, Inc., who took her own passions for jazz music and dance and created a creative and healthy way for the not-necessarily-athletic to achieve health, fitness, and fun. A pioneer for this innovative program, Judi has devoted the last thirty years to developing a program that includes comprehensive, nutrition, Children's fitness awareness as well as options for the elderly and inner-city families who have no access to playgrounds, gyms, and sports outside the streets. Judi has offered the benefit of accessible, easy, and joy-filled exercise that builds community at the same time. Obviously, in addition to "inventing" Jazzercise, Judi has also founded a very profitable empire along the way. A shero to the bone, Judi gives millions of dollars to myriad philanthropic causes. Apparently, the Misset clan is a matriarchy, as evidenced by her daughter Shanna Misset's role as Vice President and latest spokesperson for Jazzercise. Brilliant and beautiful, Shanna is poised to lead her mother's company into the new millennium!

Scholarly and Scientific Sheroes:
Breaking New Ground

Parade magazine, one of the most widely read publications in the world, features a favorite columnist, Marilyn Vos Savant. Aside from drop-dead wit, tons of common sense, and apparent omniscience, Marilyn's distinction is that she has the highest I.Q. in the world. So you could certainly say the smartest person in the world is a woman!

Women dispelled the notion that men are smarter some time ago, thanks to the tireless efforts of shero scholars, thinkers, and scientists who dealt with the issue head on. As hard as it is to imagine, it wasn't all that long ago that women and minorities were shunted aside, blocked from opportunities, political office, and employment because of the age-old smear campaign that started with Eve (the Marilyn Vos Savant of her time who quite obviously had more curiosity and chutzpah than Adam) indicting women on the charge that emotionalism lessened their intelligence and decision-making abilities.

The ground-breaking women profiled in this section changed that for us by taking former Congresswoman Pat Schroeder's comment, "I have a brain and a uterus, and I use both" very seriously. In the fields of science, medicine, astronomy, genetics, physics, anthropology, and psychology, women have made their mark. From computer pioneer and mathematician "Amazing Grace" Murray Hopper who helped engineer the first commercial computer and COBOL computer language in 1955 to today's digerati diva Ester Dyson, women are forging ahead with sagacity, savvy, and inventive, original thinking. These brainy brilliants discovered galaxies, created theory, won Nobel Prizes in science, and in general were as at home (if not more so) in the lab or the field or the classroom as in the kitchen. They are inspiration to us all.

Caroline Herschel:
Super Star

Caroline Herschel's childhood in Hannover, Germany, didn't exactly prepare her to become one of the two top astronomers of her day! Born in 1750, her education didn't extend beyond violin lessons, playing, and learning to do household chores. Indeed, though she longed for an education and her father wished her to be trained, as were her brothers, in French, mathematics, and music, her mother had other plans for her, insisting that Caroline become her domestic slave. At ten, she got typhus, which stunted her growth—she never grew taller than four foot three inches and prompted her father to proclaim that she must prepare for a life as an old maid. When she was in her early twenties, her elder brother, William, moved to Bath, England, and took Caroline along to keep house for him. An accomplished musician, William took pity on Caroline and gave her voice lessons. Soon she was the most famous soprano in the area.

William also had an advocation, which he supported with his musician's wages—he was an amateur astronomer and Caroline ended up helping him around the observatory. Together, they scoured the heavens and later built telescopes to resell so they could build the equivalent of the Hubble of their day. Caroline became an expert in grinding and polishing the mirrors they used to search the skies. William frequently traveled on business, and Caroline would fill in for him while he was gone. Soon visitors recognized her contributions, and King George III decreed that she should have a pension of fifty pounds. It was the first time a woman was recognized for her scientific contribution.

Then William discovered the plant Uranus, originally called Georgium Sidus, and soon he got the top gig as the Royal Astronomer. Meanwhile, Caroline was exploring on her own and went on to discover fourteen nebulae and eight comets, and published a catalogue of 2,500 star clusters and nebula, as well as several other seminal astronomical references for which she received medals from England, Denmark, and Prussia. To discover the nebula, she had to teach herself mathematics; because she learned so late in life, she never was able to memorize the multiplication tables. She had to carry them around in her pocket.

One of the most famous women of her day, in 1828, when she was seventy-seven, the Astronomical Society awarded her its gold medal for her contributions to the celestial science. At eighty-five, she was elected with Mary Somerville as an honorary member of the Royal Astronomical Society, the first women to receive such an accolade.

"(I am) minding the heavens."—Caroline Herschel

Sofya Kovalevsky: It Pays to Be Calculating!

Russian child prodigy Sofya Kovalevsky wasn't allow to study her favorite subject, mathematics, because of her gender. Her parents even threatened to not allow her to be educated at all if she was caught studying math. Wily and willful, Sofya found a way: working out equations on the back of old wallpaper in an unused room in her house, thus keeping her passion for numbers safely secret. She faced similar barricades when she was older and was denied admission to a university. Around 1870, Sofya married to get away from her stifling mother and an equally repressive Mother Russia and escaped to Germany, where she attended the University at Heidelberg. Soon she was calculating rings around other students and acquired a reputation as a top-notch mathematician in the elite realm of partial differential equations. By thirty-three, she received a professorial post at Stockholm's select university and was awarded the Prix Bordin from the French Academy of Sciences. A true Renaissance woman, Sofya also wrote a few novels and plays before her creativity was snuffed by an early death at a mere forty-one.

Elizabeth Blackwell:
Medicine Woman

Born in England, Elizabeth Blackwell's family moved to the United States in 1831, settling in Cincinnati when their sugar refinery in New York burned down in 1835. They were progressives, and Elizabeth's father, Samuel, had chosen to refine sugar from beets because it could be done without slave labor. However, the malaria-ridden Ohio River Valley soon took Samuel Blackwell's life and the children all had to work to support the family. Musically talented Elizabeth taught music classes and assisted her siblings in running a boardinghouse in the family home. Elizabeth had a chance to teach in Kentucky but couldn't tolerate the idea of living in a slave state.

▲ *Elizabeth Blackwell: pioneering female physician.*

Befriended by Harriet Beecher Stowe, Elizabeth became very active in the anti-slavery movement and also explored her literary leanings, joining the Semi-Colon Club at Stowe's urgings. Elizabeth needed more intellectual stimulation then even the writing club offered, however, and spurned the attention of Cincinnati's young men in order to keep her mind clear for higher pursuits. When her father was alive, she had become accustomed to the excellent schooling and private tutors Samuel provided for his brood. Children were "thinking creatures," the elder Blackwells proclaimed. Further, they made sure that the girls were taught all the same subjects as the boys, quite a rare notion for the time.

When her friend Mary Donaldson died of what was probably uterine cancer, Elizabeth Blackwell knew she wanted to become a doctor. Mary had told Elizabeth that she believed her illness would not have been fatal if her doctor had been a woman; a woman would have taken her seriously instead of being dismissed as suffering from "woman troubles" and emotionalism. Elizabeth knew in her heart that Mary was right. Her long road to becoming a physician was more difficult than she could ever know, but her unswerving dedication to reaching her goal is a testament to Elizabeth Blackwell's character.

Elizabeth Blackwell was turned down by no less that twenty-eight medical schools in her attempt to study medicine! Even her ultimate triumph at the age of twenty-six in finally enrolling at Geneva College in New York was handled insultingly. Pressured by Joseph Warrington, a noted doctor from Philadelphia who admired Elizabeth's fierce combination of smarts and pure pluck, the board at Geneva decided to give Blackwell a chance. Wimpily, they left the vote up to the all-male student body who, as a joke, voted unanimously to let her in. Blackwell had the last laugh, however, when she outperformed the lot of jokers and graduated at the top of the class. Far from taking away from her achievement, their mockery made her victory all the sweeter. But she faced more obstacles upon graduation.

Elizabeth's first worked in a syphilis ward for women where she was greeted with rancor and resentment by all the male physicians. The only job she could get was in Paris at La Maternite hospital interning in midwifery. Then Elizabeth's hopes of becoming a surgeon were dashed when she lost her left eye to disease. She also interned a year in London, meeting Florence Nightingale and forming a friendship that lasted their lifetime. Blackwell fared no better in the United States when she tried to find work in her profession, finally going into private practice in New York City where she was deluged with obscene letters and accosted on the street as a harlot and an abortionist. Her initial interest in women's health was evidenced by her opening of the New York Dispensary for Poor Women and Children, where the unfortunate could receive medical attention. There, Elizabeth welcomed two more women doctors—Emily Blackwell, her sister, and Marie Zakrewska, both of whom had entered medical school with her help.

Blackwell's pioneering works are considerable: She authored a book *The Laws of Life,* lectured on the importance of women in medicine, organized a Civil War nursing outfit, and founded a health-inspection program run by the first African American female physician, Dr. Rebecca Cole. When she moved back to England in 1869, she added sex education and birth control to her lectures, argued against the use of animal testing, co-founded the British National Health Society, was a professor of gynecology at the brand new School of Medicine for Women, and wrote several more books and tracts, including her autobiography, *Pioneer Work in Opening the Medical Profession to Women.* Elizabeth died of a stroke at the age of eighty-nine, sixty-three years after she broke down the walls barring women from medicine.

> *"I am watching, my doubts will not be subdued. (I will) commit heresy with intelligence . . . if my convictions impel me to do it."* —Elizabeth Blackwell

Women Science Nobel Prize Winners

Physics 1903: Marie Curie, with others, "in recognition of the extraordinary services they have rendered by their joint researches on the radiation phenomena discovered by Professor Henri Becquerel."

Chemistry 1911: Marie Curie, "in recognition of her services to the advancement of chemistry by the discovery of the elements radium and polonium, by the isolation of radium and the study of the nature and compounds of this remarkable element."

Chemistry 1935: Irene Joliot-Curie, with her husband, "in recognition of their synthesis of new radioactive elements."

Physiology or Medicine 1947: Gerty Theresa Cori, with her husband, "for their discovery of the course of the catalytic conversion of glycogen."

Chemistry 1964: Dorothy Crowfoot Hodgkin, "for her determinations by X-ray techniques of the structures of important biochemical substances."

Physiology or Medicine 1977: Rosalyn Yalow, with others, "for the development of radioimmunoassays of peptide hormones."

Physiology or Medicine 1983: Barbara McClintock, "for her discovery of mobile genetic elements."

Physiology or Medicine 1986: Rita Levi-Montalcini, with a male colleague, "for their discoveries of growth factors."

Physiology or Medicine 1988: Gertrude B. Elion, with others, "for their discoveries of important principles for drug treatment."

Physiology or Medicine 1995: Christiane Nüsslein-Volhard, with others, "for their discoveries concerning the genetic control of early embryonic development."

Florence Nightingale:
The Lady with the Lamp

Before Flo got in the game, nurses had little or no medical training and sported a reputation as prostitutes and drunks. The Lady with the Lamp changed all that. Born in 1820 in Great Britain, Florence was a society girl more accustomed to salons and a silver spoon than trenches and scalpels. Well-traveled and afforded a classical education, Florence heard the call of God to a higher purpose soon after her coming-out ball

at seventeen. Her family was shocked at her decision to pursue nursing—it was entirely too disreputable. Despite her parents' objection, she visited hospitals whenever she could. On a family trip to Germany, her parents finally gave in to Florence's pleas and allowed her to enroll in nurse's training at the Institute of Protestant Deaconesses in 1851. Upon graduation, Florence set about reforming the nursing profession with many important innovations and practical improvements at the London hospital for "Sick Gentlewomen" where she worked.

Florence was called to serve her country during the Crimean War when many wounded British soldiers lay dying in despicable conditions in Turkey. Instead of being greeted with gratitude, however, Florence and her brigade of trained nurses were treated with scorn and were regarded as a threat by the army doctors.

▲ *Florence Nightingale: the shero of the Crimean War revolutionized nursing and public health.*

Undeterred, Florence flew in action organizing a field hospital that treated 12,000 soldiers and saved countless lives. Florence earned her reputation as an angel of mercy the hard way, working twenty hours at a time and falling ill to many of the scourges that swept through the camp, including a terrible fever that weakened her joints, leaving her bald and emaciated. Florence Nightingale emerged as Britain's "national hero" of the war and came home to pomp and circumstance becoming the first woman to receive the British Order of Merit in 1907. Florence had no time for honors and glory, however, preferring to continue her campaign for reform in medicine and public health until her death.

> *"Never again would the picture of a nurse be a tipsy, promiscuous harridan . . . In the midst of the muddle and the filth, the agony and the disease, she had brought about a revolution."*

—Cecil Woodham-Smith, historian

Marie Curie:
Radiant Mind

The scientist Albert Einstein most admired was Marie Curie; he once enthused, "(she) is, of all celebrated beings, the only one whom fame has not corrupted." During her lifetime, Marie Curie (nee Marya Sklodowska) was the most famous scientist in the world, progenitor of the atomic age. Born in Warsaw in 1867, she rose from humble beginnings in Russian-ruled Poland as a governess to become the first person ever to earn two Nobel Prizes—in medicine and physics.

From childhood, Marya Sklodowska was known for her prodigious memory. When she was sixteen her father, a teacher of physics and math, lost his savings and she had to begin working, first as a teacher and later as a governess. In addition, she secretly took part in the "free university" movement where she read in Polish to women workers, which was strictly forbidden by the Russian powers that be. She helped finance her sister Bronia's education in France, with the provision that Bronia would then help her.

Marie's fortunes rose when she moved to Paris in 1891 and began studying at the Sorbonne, one of the few schools to admit female science students. Three years later, she had earned two degrees in physics and mathematics and met the man she was to marry, Pierre Curie, who ran the laboratories at the Municipal School of Physics and Chemistry where he also taught classes. Pierre welcomed his bride to pursue her studies and research independently at his lab. The

▲ *Maria Curie: the founder of modern physics.*

list of firsts of Marie Curie goes on and on. She was the first to determine that *radioactivity,* a term she coined, begins inside the atom, the first woman to ever win a Nobel Prize in Physics, the first woman lecturer and first woman professor in the venerable Sorbonne's 600-year history, the first mother–Nobel Laureate of a daughter–Nobel Laureate.

Marie and Pierre Curie's discoveries revolutionized science and was the founding of modern physics. Unfortunately, the Curies both suffered from symptoms now known to have been the result of exposure to radiation. But at the time, Marie was on a roll. She identified two new radioactive elements in 1898, radium and polonium, which she named for her homeland. By 1900, Marie developed a hypothesis that moving particles made up the alpha rays emitted from uranium.

The dissertation Marie wrote based on her research was deemed to be the greatest contribution to science ever made by a doctoral student. Sadly, Marie suddenly lost her husband and lab partner, Pierre, to a fatal hit-and-run by a wagon. She carried on, raising her two children, teaching and publishing her definitive treatise on radioactivity. Despite her accomplishments, Marie came under severe fire for an affair with scientist, Paul Longevin, who was married at the time. The press lambasted her, claiming that being a woman scientist and Polish, at that, certainly explained her indecency. Marie fought back, stating "nothing in my acts... obliges me to feel diminished."

In 1911, she was nominated to the Academy of Sciences and lost by two votes; it was claimed that she was unrecognized because she was a woman. However, said the Academy, the real reason was that she was only forty-three and had plenty of time to wait for another vacancy; the man they selected, was old and would not have another chance for the honor! During World War I, she devoted herself to the development of x-ray technology, with the help of her daughter Irene. As her fame grew, she lectured around the world, receiving over 125 awards. Later she developed the Curie Foundation in Paris and, in 1932, helped found the Radium Institute in Warsaw, of which Bronia was the director. She died in 1934 of leukemia, caused by the research that had made her so well-known.

"Nothing in life is to be feared. It is only to be understood."—Marie Curie

Irene Joliot-Curie: All in the Family

For Irene Joliot-Curie, it was: like mother, like daughter. During World War I, the duo started a mobile x-ray service that treated over a million patients. In 1918, Irene joined the Radium Institute in Paris, and together with her husband, Frederic Joliot-Curie, identified artificial radiation, sharing a Nobel Prize in 1935.

Margaret Sanger:
Woman Rebel

▼ *Margaret Sanger: reproductive rights freedom fighter and founder of planned parenthood.*

Unimaginably, there were laws against the use of contraceptives until the year 1965. But Margaret Sanger worked most of her life—from 1879 to 1966—to fight for women's rights to control their bodies, a battle still going on in the wake of *Roe v. Wade*. Margaret's passion for the topic was born of personal experience: She believed her mother's death at forty-nine was due to the physical hardship of eighteen pregnancies (out of which eleven children lived).

After her mother's death, Margaret disobeyed her father's wish to stay and run the household for him, instead going to nursing school. She also fell in love with a young architect, William Sanger, during this time, and they were married in 1902. She conceived during their first year of marriage and had a hard time with the pregnancy. After the birth of a son, Margaret was told she would be an invalid for the remainder of her life and admitted to a sanitarium. Margaret, showing the wilfulness of an independent mind, quickly bailed out of the sanitarium and took care of herself. This proved to be exactly the right thing to do as her health again blossomed and she produced two more children.

Full-time housewifery and motherhood bored her, however, and she soon took a job as a nurse and midwife in New York's lower east side. Margaret's activism was stirred by the pitiful sights she saw of young, impoverished mothers "destined to be thrown on the scrap heap before they were thirty-five" dealing with unwanted pregnancies, and she resolved to do something about it.

She saw clearly the connection between reproductive rights for women and women's economic and social equality, convinced that birth control was the key not only to freedom for women but to a better world. Despite censorship laws, she started writing eye-opening articles on birth control and women's sexuality. A trip to Europe to check out the birth control scene there gave Margaret an evangelical fervor to change the state of things back home in America despite enormous opposition. Founding the national Birth Control League, Margaret also began publishing *Woman Rebel,* which nearly landed her in jail when court orders shut the magazine down after the U.S. Post Office refused to deliver it for using the phrase "birth control." Unstoppable, she circumvented the post office by handing out a circular, *Family Limitation,* telling women everything they needed to know about birth control; by 1917, she had given away 160,000 copies.

In 1916, she started the first birth control clinic in the country in Brooklyn with the help of her sister and a Yiddish-speaking friend. The clinic was an immediate hit with the women of the boroughs, and 500 women visited in less than two weeks before a police raid landed Margaret in jail. All was not lost, however; the judgement handed down from the court stated that doctors could discuss birth control in the context of prevention of venereal diseases. This gave Sanger the opening she needed and her efforts began to bear fruit. During World War I, the U.S. military distributed condoms to soldiers, along with Sanger's pamphlet, "What Every Girl Should Know." She continued to lecture and founded various birth control clinics. In 1953, she founded the International Planned Parenthood Federation; there are now more than 300 doctor-staffed Planned Parenthood clinics in the country. She was also instrumental in gaining financial support for the initial research into the birth control pill.

Margaret Sanger is truly the mother of reproductive rights. She fought on behalf of the cause for more than fifty years and was jailed nine times. Her battle for voluntary motherhood was an incredibly important step in women's liberation; as historian Ellen Chesler remarked, "Every women in the world today who takes her sexual and reproductive autonomy for granted should venerate Margaret Sanger."

"No gods! No masters!"—the slogan of
Margaret Sanger *Woman Rebel*

Faye Wattleton: Footsteps to Follow

Faye Wattleton was working as a student nurse at Harlem Hospital when one particular case drew her attention to the importance of safe and legal abortion. It was "a really beautiful seventeen-year-old girl" she recalls. "She and her mother had decided to induce an abortion by inserting a Lysol douche into her uterus. It killed her." That's when Faye became a reproductive rights activist, holding various positions in public health administration and the Planned Parenthood Federation of America

(PPFA), before being elected in 1978 to the PPFA presidency. Ironically, Faye was giving birth when she won!

She carries the triple honors of being the first woman, the first African American, and the youngest person ever to head up the PPFA. Over the years, she has worked valiantly to fight the barriers constantly being put in the way—President Reagan's "squeal rule" to notify parents of distribution of birth control or information, the "gag rule" preventing abortion counseling, and the Supreme Court's challenge to *Roe v Wade*. She resigned the presidency in 1992. Pointing to her contributions, Arthur J. Kopp of People for the American Way noted, "her remarkable ability to communicate difficult issues have made her a giant in the ongoing battle to preserve Americans' fundamental liberties."

Margaret Mead:
Coming of Age in America

Margaret Mead still stirs controversy in some circles for her pioneering work in social anthropology. Like Rachel Carson, she wrote a scientific study that crossed over into the general population and became a bestseller. For this, she received derision from the academic community. But that didn't bother the free spirit, who was one of the first women to earn a Ph.D. in anthropology.

Margaret was fortunate to be born in 1901 into a family of academics who disregarded convention and put learning and involvement in the world ahead of society's rules. The firstborn of five children, Margaret's parents were Edward Mead, a professor at Wharton School who taught finance and economics, and Emily Fogg Mead, a teacher, sociologist, and ardent feminist and suf-fragist. Margaret was homeschooled by her very able grandmother, a former teacher and school principal.

Margaret didn't fall too far from the tree when she started The Minority, an antifraternity at De Pauw University, where she was attending. Bored, she transferred to Barnard College where the academic standards were more in accordance with her needs. Originally an English major, Margaret attended a class in her senior year, given by anthropologist Franz Boas, a virulent opponent of the school of racial determinism. She also met Ruth Benedict, then Boas' assistant, who encour-aged Margaret to join her at Columbia under

▲ *Margaret Mead: wonderkind anthro-pologist rocked the Ivory tower.*

Boas' instruction. Margaret agreed and went on to graduate school after marriage to a seminary student, Luther Cressman. Soon after, true to her heritage as a free-thinking Mead, Margaret went against her mentor Boas' urgings to do field work with America's Native peoples, a pet project of his; instead she followed the beat of her own different and, as it turns out, tribal drums, setting off for Polynesia to explore the island culture. She reasoned that they were better subjects because they had been less exposed and, therefore, less assimilated than Native Americans. She was absolutely right, writing up her field studies after living with and working alongside the Samoans for three years. The date was 1926. Divorcing Luther, she married Reo Fortune and a mere three years later, published *Coming of Age in Samoa,* a ground-breaking work that shocked some circles for its frank and completely objective report of, among other things, the sexual rituals and practices among the Samoans. Nearly overnight, Margaret was a superstar, fairly rare for anthropologists and even rarer for twenty-six-year-old female anthropologists!

After a stint in the American Museum of Natural History, Margaret got the jones for another field study, so she and Reo headed to New Guinea. Her resulting book, *Growing Up in New Guinea* , was another huge hit in both academic and popular circles. While in New Guinea, Margaret met and fell in love with fellow anthropologist Gregory Bateson; after her second divorce she and Gregory married and she gave birth to her daughter, Mary Catherine Bateson. They worked together in New Guinea, but ultimately Gregory claimed she was stifling his creativity and they divorced in 1943.

Margaret Mead spent the rest of her life working full-tilt in the field of anthropology, publishing forty-four books and over one thousand articles and monographs, and working as a curator at the American Museum of Natural History between trips to the field. She also sought to support and finance the work of young anthropologists. At the core of all of her work was an analysis of childhood development (she was the first anthropologist ever to study childrearing practices) and gender roles, overturning many time-worn assumptions about personality and place in society for both sexes. Over and over, her studies demonstrated that there is nothing natural or universal about particular "masculine" or "feminine" roles; rather they are culturally determined. Detractors damn her fieldwork as being "impressionistic," but Margaret Mead's success in a male-dominated scientific field was a wonderful contradiction of the typical role for an American woman of her day and age. With forty-four books, she became a household name, made anthropology available for the masses, and blazed a trail for shero scholars of future generations.

> *"I have spent most of my life studying the lives of other peoples,*
> *faraway peoples, so that Americans might better*
> *understand themselves."*—Margaret Mead

Karen Horney:
Facing the Father Complex

Freud frequently tarried overlong on theories of hysteria and other so-called female neuroses. The first critic to respond to these theories was Karen Horney who challenged his bias against women, stressing the social rather than the biological factors in feminine psychology. She also argued that neurosis is not inevitable, but arises from childhood situations that are preventable. She met with much opposition for her sensitivity toward the plight of the patient, and her peers were appalled at her cheek in daring to criticize the "Big Daddy" of psychoanalysis.

But she was no stranger to making her own way. Born in Germany in 1925, Karen Danielson surprised her blustery and abusive Norse sea-captain father by insisting on not only seeking higher education, but studying medicine whether he liked it or not. At university, Karen met a law student, Oscar Horney, and they married in 1909. While earning her medical degree from the rigorous University of Berlin—her thesis was on traumatic psychoses—she had three daughters in four years.

Undergoing psychanalytic training from 1914 to 1918, she first opened a private practice while a faculty member at the Berlin Institute where she applied a special affinity for trauma victims while working with shell-shocked veterans of World War I. Beginning around this time, Karen sought to overturn Freud's theory of penis envy, a tired theory at best, reasoning that it is not the penis women envy but the privilege modern society accords men in contrast to the suppression of women. Horney posited an alternate theory: the castration complex in young girls brought on by their inability to follow their father's path, when doors open for men are slammed shut for women. Her theory was fairly well received and established her as a force to be reckoned with.

Karen's independent streak didn't end with her neo-Freudian theorizing; she divorced her husband in 1926 and emigrating to Chicago, cofounding the Chicago Institute for Psychoanalysis. The New York Psychoanalytic Institute was next on her plate where she taught, did clinical research, and began a career as an author, publishing *The Neurotic Personality of Our Time* to high praise and *Our Inner Conflict,* a book about denial of pain that sounds like it would do fine in the popular self-help world we live in today. Karen Horney refused to agree with the accepted psychoanalytic gospel of the day and continued to emphasize the effect of environment upon the psyche. "There is no such thing as a normal psychology that holds for all people," she proclaimed.

Perhaps Horney's optimism was the biggest division between her and the rest of the psychoanalytic pack. She believed people could help themselves. She had a severe parting of the ways with her peers when she suggested that patients need not live a life of pain, a Freudian notion, and that people can work out of their neuroses. She was booted out of the New York Psychoanalysis Society and Institute in 1941 upon the publication of her book, *New Ways in Psychoanalysis,* which laid out a series of refutations and refinements of Freud's doctrine. Undaunted, she founded her own institute, taking several other free-thinkers with her.

Karen Horney was way ahead of her time. Had she lived fifty more years, she would be safely ensconced in a comfy chair across from Oprah Winfrey, where her self-help positivity would be fully embraced. Psychoanalytic pioneer and humanist, Karen Horney shows us that even the most sacred of cows need to be led off to pasture, especially if they're wrong! Here's to the shero who deep-sixed penis envy!

"Life itself still remains a very effective therapist."—Karen Horney

Anna Freud:
A Niche of Her Own

Pop culture may relegate Anna Freud to minor league status because of her associations with the two icons, papa Sigmund Freud and patient, Marilyn Monroe. But, she should be remembered for her own ground-breaking work in child analysis and developmental psychology, collected in her eight-volume *Writings*. Although she didn't overturn her father's theories, she cultivated her own, concluding that an individual's psychology developed uniquely from an influence of a number of what she called "developmental lines." This multicausal approach to therapy was very different from the order of the day, attracting many patients to her clinic, including the famous blonde bombshell actress, the divine MM.

Hannah Arendt:
A Life of the Mind

German-born Hannah Arendt was a political theorist and philosopher who climbed out of the ivory tower to take direct action against the spread of Fascism. A student of theology and Greek and the protégé/lover of German existentialist philosopher Karl Heidegger, the brilliant student was granted a Ph.D. from the University of Heidelberg at the ripe old age of twenty-two. After a brief arrest by the Gestapo (she was Jewish), she fled to Paris where she worked for a Zionist resistance organization that sent Jewish orphans to Palestine in the hopes of creating a new united Arab-Jewish nation.

By 1940, she had fled to New York where she lived among other immigrants and worked for the Council on Jewish Relations, as an editor for Shocken Books, and

▲ *Hannah Arendt: brilliant political theorist and philosopher revealed the facism.*

served at the head of the Jewish Cultural Reconstruction, which, post-war, collected Jewish writings that had been dispersed by the Nazis. With her first book, *The Origins of Totalitarianism,* she pointed out the common elements in Nazi and Stalinist philosophies as well as discussing the roots of anti-Semitism and racism through all of Europe. Her subsequent books include *On Revolution, The Human Condition,* and *Thinking and Willing,* as well as a discussion of the trial of a Nazi war criminal, *Eichmann in Jerusalem: A Report on the Banality of Evil,"* and countless articles and commentaries on such far reaching subjects as Watergate, Vietnam, and her famous attack on Bertold Brecht for his "Hymn to Stalin." The first woman to become a full professor at Princeton, she also taught at various other institutions and translated and edited the works of Franz Kafka.

A serious thinker, she became a very public and controversial figure with her beliefs that revolution and war are the central forces of the twentieth century; that there was little organized resistance on the part of the Jews in Europe; and that the Nazis were not monsters but pragmatic rational people accepting evil commands in a banal manner.

Arendt's contributions to the intellectual community are beyond calculating. She made an insular forties America and post-war world look deeply at all the possible causes of the Holocaust. According to his article in

Makers of Nineteenth Century Culture, Bernard Crick credits Hannah Arendt with "res-cue (ing) American intellectuals from an excessive parochiality."

> *"Human beings...[are] put into concentration camps by their foes*
> *and into internment camps by their friends."*—Hannah Arendt

Barbara McClintock:
Gene Genie

When geneticist Barbara McClintock presented her findings about morphing genes in 1951 after a ten-year scientific study, the result was what is commonly known as a "roof job." Her peers just didn't get it; it went right over their heads. A pack of rabid Darwinists, her colleagues preferred to keep to the accepted notions of the day that genetic change was random in the evolution of a species. Undeterred, Barbara went back to the drawing board and the sixty-hour-a-week lab schedule she set for herself. She preferred the relative peace of her lab to people, preferred corn to fruit-flies (the research subject de jour) and she preferred to not publish her work, figuring it would be too much for her uptight colleagues to handle. As it turns out, Barbara McClintock was right an awful lot of the time.

Even as a young child, Barbara McClintock was content in her own company, pursuing her interests. An avid reader, she was also quite a tomboy, preferring cards and engines to dolls and pots and pans, having no truck with other little girls and the sugar and spice routine. She quickly found her thing—science—and pursued it with a single-minded relentlessness that served her well through the years. Despite the displeasure of her parents, Barbara chose agricultural science as her field of study at Cornell. She performed brilliantly and was asked to stay on for the graduate program in genetics where she earned a Ph.D.

She then began to teach and do research, so far ahead of the pack that she became one of only a handful of scientists in the world to first realize chromosomes were the foundation of heredity and to work from this vantage point and understanding. Indeed, she was the scientist to *discover* the nucleolar organizer within the structure of the chromosome that was the indicator of order during cell division. It would be thirty years after her discovery before science was able to explain her finding in terms of molecular biology. Despite this remarkable beginning to her career and an outstanding record as a genetic researcher, Barbara was never given a promotion while at Cornell. She left for Cold Harbor Laboratory where her work so impressed everyone that she was elected to the national Academy of Sciences in 1944 and went on to become president of the Genetics Society of America. The first woman to do so!

Not one to rest on her laurels, Barbara McClintock continued with her groundbreaking work, racking up all kinds of awards, prizes, and firsts. She became the first woman to receive an unshared Nobel Prize in physiology and medicine, and has been called the most important geneticist of the twentieth century. She worked at Cold Harbor until her death in 1983 in the lab where she discovered what everyone else wasn't ready to see.

> *"It might seem unfair to reward a person for having so much fun over the years.'*—Barbara McClintock

Shirley Jackson: Black Brainiac

Shirley Jackson is a highly regarded physicist and the first black woman to earn a Ph.D. from MIT. Her doctoral research project was in theoretical particles. Shirley has gone on to not only receive numerous awards and the highest praise for her work in elementary particles, but also for her advocacy of women and minorities in the science field. In 1995, Vice President Al Gore celebrated her contributions and her drive to be the best at her swearing in as chairman of America's Nuclear Regulatory Commission. Gore told the audience that a four-year-old Shirley Ann Jackson informed her mother that one day she was going to be called "Shirley the Great." Shirley made good on her promise as she pushed down barriers of segregation and bigotry to become one of the top scientists in the nation.

"I had to work alone... at some level you have to decide you will persist in what you're doing and that you won't let people beat you down." —Shirley Jackson

SistahSheroes:
Doin' It for Themselves

The story of the civil rights movement is emblazoned with the names of many male heros, including W. E. B. Du Bois, Martin Luther King, Jr., Medgar Evers, and Malcolm X. But every step of the way, these and countless other men were accompanied by sisters, equally fearless: Sojourner Truth, Harriet Tubman, Rosa Parks, Fannie Lou Hamer, and Coretta Scott King, to name just a few.

These powerful and courageous women—and many others unnamed and unrecognized—put their bodies on the line for civil rights in the United States. They freed slaves, marched, sang, and protested until their voices were heard and laws were changed. Each fought the double demons of racism and sexism and emerged victorious. Often they faced not only emotional but physical violence; undeterred they pressed on despite the cost. They are truly an inspiration for all who struggle against limitations of all sorts—legal, social, and psychological.

Language is one of the tools of oppression. It is, therefore, wonderfully appropriate that the word sheroes emerged from within the idiom of African American women, who bore the brunt of severest subjugation. Johnetta B. Cole and Dr. Maya Angelou were the visionary pioneers who, to the best of my knowledge, began using the work "sheroes" in their speeches. Slowly and surely, the word, the mantle, if you will, of shero is beginning to crop up here and there in the common parlance. Recently, television's supreme shero Oprah adopted the word into her personal vocabulary. I can only imagine, it will spread like wildfire from here, in the truest sense of word power.

SisterSheroes are an especially amazing group—overcoming obstacles unimaginable to others. Sojourner Truth's firebrand speeches give me goosebumps as I reread them over 100 years after she first espoused her glorious independent spirit. Marian Anderson, regarded as the greatest soprano of all time was denied the stage at a concert in Washington, D.C. Based on her race until polishero Eleanor Roosevelt took up the charge and helped unleash Anderson's gift to the nation. Sheroes of color obviously have to fight the twin battles of sexism and racism. Picture young Melba Beals walking the gauntlet of white-hot hatred on that day of desegregation in Little Rock. Think of Fannie Lou Hamer being beaten within an inch of her life for daring to eat in a cafeteria with white people in Mississippi. Remember Harriet Tubman booming a gospel song in code to "carry her people" home to freedom on the underground railroad.

Women of color, starting with the Amazons of North Africa and continuing today at the cusp of the twenty-first century had to fight harder, longer and better. When you look into the very heart of sheroism, I urge you to read beyond these pages and research the lives of these great women who, unbowed and unbroken, showed the true meaning of courage.

Sojourner Truth:
"Ain't I a woman?"

S ojourner Truth's name alone suggests sheroism. It fits her perfectly—she was a fire breathing preacher, suffragist, and vigilant abolitionist. Unschooled and born to slavery, she didn't allow these disadvantages to prevent her from becoming one of the most charismatic and powerful orators of the nineteenth century. In fact, like many African Americans of the day, hardship seemed to make her only stronger, like a blade forged by fire.

She hailed from Dutch country in upstate New York and grew up speaking Dutch. Christened Isabella, she was sold away from her parents as a child and was traded many times, until finally landing with John Dumont for whom she worked for sixteen years. At fourteen, she was given to an older slave to be his wife and bore five children. In 1826, one year before she was to be legally freed, Isabella ran away from Dumont and hid with a pacifist Quaker family.

Upon hearing that one of her sons had been sold into lifetime slavery in Alabama, Isabella sued over this illegal sale of her son and, remarkably, won the case. Isabella moved to New York in the 1930s and worked as a maid for a religious community, the Magdalenes, whose mission was the conversion of prostitutes to Christianity.

By 1843, the extremely religious Isabella heard a

▼ *Sojourner Truth: firebrand preacher suffragist and abolitionist.*

calling to become a traveling preacher. She renamed herself Sojourner Truth and hit the road where her talent for talking amazed all who heard her at revivals, camp meetings, churches, and on the side of the road, if the occasion arose. She kept her sermons to the simple themes of brotherly love and tolerance. In Massachusetts, Truth encountered liberals who enlightened her on the topics of feminism and abolition. Her autobiography, as told to antislavery forerunner William Lloyd Garrison, provided a powerful weapon for the cause of abolition when published. Her story, *The Narrative of Sojourner Truth,* was one of the first stories of a woman slave to be widely known and was retold many times, including in the charmingly entitled version, "Sojourner Truth, the Libyan Sibyl" by Harriet Beecher Stowe, which was published by *Atlantic Monthly.*

Sojourner then put her religious fervor into the message of abolition, a holy mission into which she threw all her formidable will and energy. Her call to end the slavery of human beings in this country was powerful. There is a beloved story showing her quick tongue and even quicker mind and spirit, when the great Frederick Douglas openly doubted there could be an end to slavery without the spilling of blood. In a flash, Sojourner replied, "Frederick, is God dead?"

By the middle of the nineteenth century, Sojourner was preaching the twin messages of abolition and women's suffrage. She was unwavering in her convictions and made the eloquent point that "if colored men get their rights and not colored women, colored men will be masters over the women, and it will be just as bad as before." She threw herself into the Civil War efforts helping runaway slaves and black soldiers. President Lincoln was so impressed with the legend of Sojourner Truth that he invited her to the White House to talk.

Sojourner Truth worked, preached, and fought right up to her dying day in 1883. She lived long enough to see one of her fondest hopes—the abolition of slavery—be realized and, along with the estimable Harriet Tubman, is one of the two most respected African Americans women of the nineteenth century. Was she a woman? Yes, indeed. And a shero for all time!

> *"I have ploughed, and planted, and gathered into barns, and no man could head me! And ain't I a woman?"*—Sojourner Truth

Katy Ferguson: Earth Angel

Born a slave in 1779, Catherine Ferguson accompanied her mistress to church on Sundays until she was freed at sixteen by a white woman benefactor who paid $200 for Katy's emancipation. Two years later, Katy married; by the time she was twenty, her husband and two infant children were dead. Katy, a fantastic baker, made wedding cakes and other delicacies to support herself. On the way to market to sell her baked goods, she would see dozens of poor children and orphans who pulled at the strings of her heart. The indomitable Katy started teaching these waifs church classes in her home on what is now Warren Street in Manhattan until a Dr. Mason lent his church basement to her in 1814. This is believed to be the origins of what we now call "Sunday school." Katy's classes were so popular that droves of poor black and white children came to learn. Soon, many young, unwed mothers started showing up, too, whom Katy took home to care for and teach them self-reliance. Katy died of cholera in 1854, but her work carried on in the Ferguson Home for Unwed Mothers where kindness, good works, and good learning are the helping hands to a better life.

"Where Katy lived, the whole aspect of the neighborhood changed."

—from an article on her work

Harriet Tubman:
Long Train Runnin'

In her day, Harriet was lovingly referred to as Moses, for leading her people home to freedom. An escaped slave herself, she pulled off feat after amazing feat and gave freedom to many who would otherwise have never known it. Harriet Tubman was a conductor on the Underground Railroad, perhaps the best that ever was. She is best known for this activity, but she was also a feminist, a nurse and, for a time, a spy. Her keenest interest was social reform, both for her gender and her people.

Born around 1821 on a plantation in Maryland, Harriet struggled with grand mal seizures after a blow to the head as a child, but the damage from a severely fractured skull didn't stop her from the most dangerous work she could have possibly undertaken: taking groups of slaves to freedom in the north. During her slow recovery from being hit in the head with a two-pound weight by an overseer, she began praying and contemplating the enslavement of blacks, resolving to do what she could, with faith in a higher power. She married John Tubman, a free man, in 1844, and lived in fear that she would be sold into the Deep South. When she heard rumors that she was about to be sold, she plotted her escape, begging John to come with her. He not only refused, but threatened to turn her in.

Harriet escaped to freedom by herself, but immediately plotted to return for her family members, using the Underground Railroad. She ultimately rescued all her family members except John; he had taken a new wife and remained behind. She led more than two hundred slaves to safety and freedom, encouraging her "passengers" with gospel songs sung in a deep, strong voice. She also developed a code to signal danger using biblical quotations and certain songs. Harriet Tubman always outfoxed the whites who questioned her about the groups of blacks traveling with her. She lived in the constant threat of hanging with a $40,000 price on her head, with many close calls. One of the most dramatic incidents shows Harriet's resourcefulness and resolve when she bought tickets heading south to evade whites demanding to know what a group of blacks were doing traveling together. She always carried a gun to dissuade any frightened fugitives from turning tail. "You'll be free or die," she told them— and she never lost a passenger.

Harriet also started connecting with abolitionists in the North, developing a strong admiration for John Brown (she conspired with him in his raid at Harper's Ferry) and Susan B. Anthony. During the Civil War, she nursed black soldiers, worked as a spy for the Union, and even led a raid that freed 750 slaves. After the war, she lived in Auburn, New York, in a house that had been a way station for the Underground Railroad, teaching blacks how to cope

▲ *Harriet Tubman: the great emancipater who conducted the underground railroad.*

with newfound freedom; gathering food, clothing, and money for poor blacks; and founding a home for elderly and indigent blacks. Harriet's last years were spent in abject poverty despite all she had given to others, but she died at the age of ninety-three having accomplished the task she set herself as a girl. She was the great emancipator, offering her people hope, freedom, and new beginnings. Reformer and writer Thomas Wentworth Higginson named her "the greatest heroine of the age."

"When I found I had crossed that line, I looked to my hands to see if I was the same person. There was such a glory over everything." —Harriet Tubman

Mary McLeod Bethune:
A Dollar and a Dream

In 1904 Mary McLeod Bethune started a school on $1.50 and dreams on the grounds of a former dump. "I haunted the city dump retrieving discarded linen and kitchenware, cracked dishes, broken chairs, pieces of old lumber," she remembered later. That humble beginning has now blossomed into Bethune Cookman College in Daytona, Florida.

She wasn't daunted by the idea of all the hard work it would take to make her dreams come true; she was used to picking 250 pounds of cotton a day and pulling the plow when the family mule died. The fifteenth of seventeen children born to former slaves, Mary was brought up as a strict Methodist to believe in the sweat of the brow and faith in God. At the age of twelve, she was given a scholarship by the Quakers to be educated at an integrated school in North Carolina, later going on to Moody Bible College. From these experiences, she had a profound respect for education, particularly for its value in helping her people rise from poverty.

Mary's school succeeded through her combination of penny-pinching abilities and excellent fundraising skills (she even got J. D. Rockefeller to contribute). She trained the students to pick elderberries to make into ink, used burned wood for chalk, and bartered free tuition for food for her students. Soon she added an infirmary on the site when she realized blacks couldn't get medical treatment within 200 miles of that part of the Atlantic Coast; eventually that grew into a training hospital for doctors and nurses. By 1922, the school boasted 300 students and Mary stayed on as president of the college until 1942.

She had a strong commitment to African Americans, particularly women. While running the school, she led the campaign to register black women voters, despite threats from the KKK. Her civil rights activism and humanitarianism brought her into contact with many people, including Eleanor Roosevelt with whom she became good friends. Bethune ended up serving her people in many leadership roles, including as the founder and president of the National Council of Negro Women, the leading member of the "Black Cabinet" who were advisors to FDR on African American needs and interests, and Director of the Office of Minority Affairs of the National Youth Administration. When she was seventy-seven, concerned over the inability of blacks to get life insurance, she started the Central Life Insurance Company, becoming the only woman president of a national life insurance company in the entire United States.

For these and other accomplishments, Mary McLeod Bethune was regarded as the most influential black woman in America until her death in 1955. Mary's rise from poverty to national leadership is sheer sheroism!

"I leave you love. I leave you hope . . . I leave you racial dignity."
—Mary McLeod Bethune

Nannie Helen Burroughs:
The Practical Prophet

NAACP pioneer William Picken described Nannie Burroughs this way: "No other person in America has so large a hold on the loyalty and esteem of the colored masses as Nannie H. Burroughs. She is regarded all over the broad land as combination of brains, courage, and incorruptibleness." Born in the Gilded Age in 1879, Nannie Burroughs was fortunate to be born into a family of exslaves who were able to establish a comfortable existence in Virginia, affording young Nannie a good education. Nannie applied for a job as a domestic science teacher and wasn't hired because she was "too dark." Later, she was turned down for a job as a government clerk because she was a black woman.

Nannie began dreaming of a way to prepare black women for careers that freed them from the traps of gender and bias. Nannie worked for the national Baptist Alliance for fifty years, starting as a bookkeeper and secretary. In her spare time, she organized the Women's Industrial Club, providing practical clerical courses for women. Through the school she founded in 1909, the National Training School for Women and Girls, she educated thousand of black American women as well as Haitians, Puerto Ricans, and South Africans to send them into the world with the tools for successful careers. Her program emphasized what she called the three Bs: the Bible, the Bath, and the Broom, representing "clean lives, clean bodies, and clean homes."

An advocate of racial self-help, Nannie worked all her life to provide a solid foundation for poor black women so they could work and gain independence and equality. She practiced what she preached. At one point, she wrote to John D. Rockefeller for a donation to her cause. He sent her one dollar with a note asking what a businesswoman like her would do with the money. She purchased a dollar's worth of peanuts and sent them to him with a note asking him to autograph each one and return them to her. She would then sell each one for a dollar.

She founded the Harriet Beecher Literary Society as a vehicle for literary expression and was also active in the antilynching campaigns. She gave Sojourner Truth a run for her money for dramatic speech-making with stirring lectures such as her headline-making speech in 1932: "Chloroform your Uncle Toms! What must the Negro do to be saved? The Negro must unload the leeches and parasitic leaders who are absolutely eating the life out of the struggling, frightened mass of people."

One of her students once said that Nannie considered "everybody God's nugget." Nannie Burroughs' pragmatic "grab your own bootstraps" approach to racial equality offered that chance to everyone who came into her purview.

> *"The training of Negro women is absolutely necessary, not only for their own salvation and the salvation of the race, but because the hour in which we live demands it. If we lose sight of the demands of the hour we blight our hope of progress. The subject of domestic science has crowded itself upon us, and unless we receive it, master it and be wise, the next ten years will so revolutionize things that we will find our women without the wherewith to support themselves."*—Nannie Helen Burroughs

Eslanda Goode Robeson:
"Africans Are People"

Eslanda Goode Robeson was the wife of the famous singer and civil rights activist Paul Robeson. However, she was an important shero in her own right, distinguishing herself both in political activism and as an anthropologist.

The daughter of a freed slave, Essie, born in 1896, was passionately interested in Africa and the conditions that made the mother continent vulnerable. Her mother, Eslanda Cardoza Goode, was of mixed race, born among South Carolina's free blacks to an octoroon mother and a wealthy Spanish Jew, Isaac Nunez Cardoza. Essie's uncle Francis Louis Cardoza was named as "the most highly educated Negro in America" by Henry Ward Beecher. When Essie was six, her father died of alcohol abuse and the family moved to New York City just in time for the birth of the Harlem Renaissance. Essie was well educated herself, attending Teachers College at Columbia University and one year of medical school, ultimately receiving her degree in chemistry from Columbia. Her other interests included a strong proclivity for politics and the desire to fight for racial equality. Essie was on her way to becoming a model for the new equality when she became the first black person to work in the pathology and surgery departments of Columbia Presbyterian where she ran the lab. In the twenties, she met and married Paul Robeson; after hearing him sing at a party, Essie became convinced he had a future in show business. She talked him into performing and soon his career was launched. By the mid-twenties, Paul was the toast of Europe and America; Essie quit her job to travel with Paul and manage his career. However, over and over the duo suffered the sickening hypocrisy of a white society that lauded Paul as the toast of stage and screen while not allowing he and Essie to eat in the same restaurants as the white music patrons. To avoid the pain, Essie began to stay home and focus upon their shared dream of a modern black family—emancipated, educated, and enlightened.

In the thirties, the ever intellectually restless Essie developed an intense interest in anthropology and in Africa. Studying at London University and the London School of Economics, she became even more radicalized: "I soon became fed up with white students and teachers 'interpreting' the Negro mind and character to me," she wrote later. "Especially when I felt, as I did very often, that their interpretation was wrong."

She decided to make her own conclusions. She traveled to Africa several times, exploring widely, up the Congo and into the heartland by any means available. Her exploration led her to emphasize the importance of racial pride in overcoming racism, and she banded with other black people to found the Council on African Affairs. She was always extremely outspoken about the plight of her people as a result of slavery and colonialism and never backed down from a debate. She drew fire when she suggested the Soviet Union had created a better foundation for equality than the United

States. In the forties, during World War II, she was especially vocal, perceiving that the war against Fascism was an opportunity for a more racially united and equal opportunity America. Her book, *African Journey,* was published in 1945; that same year, as a representative of the Council on African Affairs, Essie participated in the conference that founded the United Nations.

In the fifties, the activity and views of the Robesons were brought to the attention of Senator Joseph McCarthy who called her before the House Un-American Activities Committee. McCarthy was no match for the brilliance and verbal dexterity of Essie, who turned the tables on him, drilling him with questions about the black civil rights issue. But McCarthy got his revenge, revoking both their passports, reducing Paul's income from international concert tours to almost nil.

This only spurred Essie on to greater activism—ultimately her passport was reinstated and she traveled to Germany to receive the Peace Medal and the Clara Zetkin Medal, a governmental award for women who have fought for world peace. She continued to write articles and give speeches on behalf of equality and justice until she died in 1965. No matter what the personal cost, Essie fought to free her people from the invisible bonds that still held them back. Her work was invaluable in the civil rights movement; her call for absolute racial equality rang clear and true: "No man can be free until all men are free."

"I believe there will never be peace in the world until people have achieved what they fought and died for." —Eslanda Goode Robeson

Rosa Parks:
The First Lady of Civil Rights

Rosa Parks gave a human face to the civil rights movement. She showed how the issues addressed in all of the speeches affected a woman's life in the course of an ordinary day. The woman was Rosa Louise McCauley Parks, the day became an extraordinary day that rocked the nation and changed history.

Born in 1913, Rosa grew up in Pine Level, Alabama, with her schoolteacher mother, Leona. She helped her mother take care of her sickly grandparents and run the household because Rosa's father had gone to work up north and effectively disappeared from their lives. Later, she moved in with her aunt Fanny and enrolled in the Montgomery Industrial School for Girls, a private school, where she was exposed to the liberal ideals of teachers raised in the north. Rosa took her teachers' lessons to heart, as well as the stories her elderly grandparents told about the evils of slavery, sparking a sense of justice that would only grow.

Rosa vacillated between following in the footsteps of her mother and becoming a teacher and pursuing her own dream of training to be a nurse. Then in 1932, she met and married Raymond Parks, who had struggled up from an impoverished background where he wasn't allowed to attend school because of his color. To augment her husband's income from barbering, Rosa dabbled in many lines of work, including maid, seamstress, and secretary.

Her involvement in civil rights grew. She was the first woman to start attending the Montgomery chapter of the NAACP and also worked in the effort to register blacks to vote. Rosa often walked home from work to avoid the "back of the bus" issue until December 1, 1955, when she was returning home from a long day of sewing at a Montgomery department store. The buses from downtown were always fairly crowded and had a section designated for blacks behind the ten rows of seats in the front for white folks. Rosa was sitting in the first row of the "blacks only" section when the white section filled up, leaving a white man without a seat. The tacit understanding was that, in such a scenario, the black person was supposed to stand and let the white person have the seat. The white bus driver called for the four black people in the front row of the black section to get up and let the white man have the row. Rosa refused and the driver called the police.

Her solitary action started a firestorm of controversy, including a bus boycott and protest march led by Martin Luther King, Jr. and Coretta Scott King. A fascinating footnote to the incident is that Rosa had been evicted by the very same bus driver twelve years before. Though there had been several incidents on Montgomery busses, Rosa stuck to her guns and became the pivotal legal case for the burgeoning civil rights movement's

▲ *Rosa Parks: fired the first shot in the civil rights victory.*

attack on segregated seating. Upon going to trial and being found guilty, she refused to pay her fine and appealed the decision. Her actions cost Rosa and her husband dearly; they both lost their jobs and were the recipients of threats to their lives. Undaunted, Rosa worked with the carpooling efforts that enabled blacks to continue their 381-day boycott of the bus system.

The sacrifices of the black community were not in vain because the U.S. District Court ruled segregated seating to be unconstitutional. However, due to the controversy, Rosa, the shero who started the battle by keeping her seat, couldn't get a job anywhere in Montgomery. Rosa, Raymond, and Rosa's mother moved to Detroit and started a new life there, Rosa working as a seamstress and for the Southern Christian Leadership Conference. She ultimately found a career in U.S. Representative John Coyner's office.

Rosa Parks' courage in that split second moment when she made her decision is at the very crux of the victorious struggle for African Americans. Rosa still works for the good of her community, traveling and speaking on behalf of the NAACP. She loves to talk to young people about the movement, for the work has, truly, only begun. Rosa Parks has become a symbol of fearlessness and fortitude. In 1980, Rosa was honored by *Ebony* magazine as "the living black woman who had done the most to advance the cause of civil rights."

"You didn't have to wait for a lynching. You died a little each time you found yourself face to face with this kind of discrimination."—Rosa Parks

Fannie Lou Hamer: Bravery Unbound

Fannie Lou Hamer grew up a sharecropper's daughter in Montgomery, Mississippi, where she was exposed to the worst face of racial injustice. Forced to quit school in the sixth grade to work in the cotton fields to help support her family, she got involved in the effort to register blacks to vote in 1962. At the time, a literacy test was required in order to secure the right to vote, and Fannie helped teach people so they could pass the test. One day, Fannie was on a bus with a group of fellow African American youths who were challenging the "whites only" policy at the bus terminal diner. When they were attacked by state troopers called in to deal with the "insurrection," Fannie was hurt badly and jailed with everyone else from the bus. Her sufferings had only begun, though. Hamer was incarcerated in a cell with two black men who were ordered to beat her with a metal-spiked leather billy club. Fannie was permanently blinded in one eye by this beating and suffered kidney damage, but she emerged with even more inner resolve to put an end to racial injustice. Fannie worked without cessation for many related causes: Head Start for black schools, jobs for poor blacks, and against the Vietnam War because she felt black soldiers were being sent to protect rights they themselves didn't have at home. Fannie Hamer risked her life over and over to improve the lot of her people until her death in 1977, never receiving the attention that was her due. A true unsung shero, her essential belief was, "We serve God by serving our fellow (human beings)."

Coretta Scott King:
Unshakable Faith

Like the Robesons, the Kings had a marriage based on love—for each other and for racial equality. After the assassination of Martin Luther King, Jr. Coretta gained recognition in her own right as a pillar of the civil rights movement. A talented musician, Coretta was born in Alabama in 1927 and was educated at Antioch, where she got a degree in music and elementary education, and was exposed to whites in a very different environment than the South, learning a great deal about techniques to foster

▲ *Coretta Scott King: carrying on "the dream."*

interracial communication. In 1953, she married Martin Luther King Jr. while they were both college students, and they pursued a life together, her music—she got a higher degree at the New England Conservatory of Music—and his theological degree. From a long line of ministers, Martin felt a call to become a pastor, a decision that found the young couple moving to Montgomery, Alabama, after their education. They had their first of four children in the first year at the Dexter Avenue Baptist Church and became deeply involved in the actions of the civil rights movement. Martin Luther King Jr. led the bus boycott after Rosa Parks' historic bus ride. As the footage shows, Coretta was right beside Martin at every protest, fighting for the rights of all African Americans. She also participated in fundraising for the movement by giving more than thirty concerts in Europe and the United States to raise money for Martin's organization, the Southern Christian Leadership Conference (SCLC).

The Kings traveled extensively in their work—to Ghana, to India, to Nigeria, and, in 1964, to Norway to receive Dr. King's Nobel Peace Prize. Four years later, the world watched in horror as Martin was gunned down in Memphis, Tennessee, during a garbage workers strike. Coretta didn't shrink from the work at hand and led a protest in Memphis four days later with her children at her side. Her quiet dignity captured the nation; that year she was voted Woman of the Year and Most Admired Woman by college students.

Since that fateful day, Coretta stepped forward and took up the mantle of leadership in the civil rights movement, which she shared with the young Jesse Jackson. Coretta amazed everyone with her stamina and heart as she made speech after speech and led march after march. She has received innumerable awards for her tireless efforts in her lifetime. She founded the Martin Luther King, Jr. Center for Nonviolent Change and has also led the attention of the nation into new directions, organizing antiwar protests, antinuclear and antiapartheid lobbies, and employment for African Americans. More than 100 colleges have given her honorary doctorates. Coretta Scott King has never hesitated to give of herself to the struggle for freedom and justice, viewing it as both "a privilege" and "a blessing."

Yolanda King and Attallah Shabazz: Passing On the Torch

The daughters of two very different civil rights warriors, Martin Luther King, Jr. and Malcolm X, have recently paired up to represent the next generation of activism. Although Yolanda King and Atallah (Arabic for gift of god) Shabazz were raised in different faiths and from different philosophical points of view, the commonalities override the dissimilarities. Both lost their fathers to assassins as children under the public eye and both desired to escape the attention and live their own lives. Yolanda and Attallah are two creative spirits for whom the arts provide release, solace, and strength. They were wary of each other upon meeting in New York City where they were both trying to start acting careers. It wasn't long, however, before a bond forged and they started working on a play together, "Stepping into Tomorrow," a musical dramady with a powerful message of empowerment for youth. The play began a career of collaboration and activism in which both Yolanda and Atallah travel extensively lecturing on civil rights, the importance of the arts, and the legacy of their fathers. In Yolanda King's words, "I see these responsibilities not as a burden, but as an extension of who I am."

Daisy Bates:
Fighting the System and Winning!

T he image of an eight-year-old black girl in her perfectly starched blouse and skirt, walking through a gauntlet of hatred to go to school was etched in the minds of every American alive in the sixties. Everyone was touched by the grace and dignity shown by the young girl who was spat at and heckled, as cameras shoved in her face recorded it all for posterity. Activists for integration won a huge victory that day and with an even greater strength and resolve went on to flatten every segregationist wall that presented itself.

Daisy Bates was one of the civil rights warriors first called into action in the fight for desegregation. Born in 1920, Daisy was adopted into a loving family in Little Rock, Arkansas, and never knew what had happened to her birth mother until the taunts of schoolchildren made the eight-year-old question her adoptive mother. On that day, she found out that her mother had been raped and murdered by three white men who then dumped her body in a pond. Her father left town to escape having the crime pinned on him.

When Daisy was twenty-one, she married L. C. Bates, a black man who had been educated as a journalist. Together, they took over a Little Rock newspaper, the *Arkansas State Press,* and turned it into a platform for "the people," reporting crimes committed against blacks that the white paper ignored. Daisy worked as a reporter, covering with complete honesty, for example, the cold-blooded murder of a black soldier by military police. The white business community was outraged over the *State Press'* coverage: They feared the army would leave their town and withdraw all advertising. However, the Bates' brave coverage of brutality to blacks curtailed these crimes, and Little Rock became a more liberated town despite itself.

Then the movement toward desegregation heated up, with Daisy Bates right in the thick of things. The Supreme Court had declaimed segregation of schools unconstitutional in May of 1954, giving Southern schools the chance to describe how and when they would make the required changes. The local school board had responded by saying that they would take on the notion of integration "gradually." Little Rock's black community was up in arms about the foot dragging and, after butting their heads in many stony-faced meetings, opted to take matters into their own hands. The state and local NAACP decided that they would try to enroll the students into the segregated schools and build up cases of denied admission in order to create a true challenge to the policy of gradualism. Daisy Bates, as president of the NAACP in Little Rock, worked with the *State Press* and other papers to publicize this flouting of the Supreme Court's ruling. Finally, in 1957, they decided to integrate the high school, come hell or high water. The children who would put their bodies on the line would became famous overnight as "Daisy's children" and suffer personal agony for the cause of racial justice.

When nine children were selected to attend the "whites only" Central High School, Daisy acted as their escort and protector. Answering a poll and screened by school officials, the group of young heroes and sheroes consisted of: Carlotta Walls, Thelma Mothershed, Melba Patillo, Ernest Green, Terrence Roberts, Gloria Ray, Minnijean Brown, Jefferson Thomas, and Elizabeth Eckford. When Little Rock school superintendent, Virgil Blossom, decreed that no adults could accompany the black students, Daisy called all of their homes and told them there would be a change of plans.

Elizabeth Eckford's family had no telephone, so she showed up on opening day—to be faced by an angry white mob who also attacked the reporters and photographers. The mob siege lasted seventeen days until 1,000 paratroopers showed up in response to orders from the White House to carry through the order of legal integration of the school.

However, the students were on their own once inside, prey to taunts, shoving, and threats of violence. Daisy Bates continued to protect and advise the children throughout the ordeal, accompanying them to every meeting with a school official when racial incidents happened. The struggle at Little Rock was only the first in a round of actions that ultimately led to full legal desegregation. Though difficult, the victory was entirely to Daisy and her "children" who showed the nation that you could stand up to hatred and ignorance with honesty and dignity. You can fight a losing battle and win!

To Learn More

The National Archives for Black Women's History is the largest repository solely dedicated to the collection and preservation of material relating to African American women. The collection includes correspondence, photographs, and speeches. For further information, please contact 202-673-2402.

PoliSheroes:
Stormin' the Halls of Power

The women's movement is, in essence, a social and political movement. Make that *very* political! While sheroes have been blazing trails in every field, some of the work that has made for the most meaningful changes has taken place in the political arena for women's rights, civil rights, and rights for workers. Often, the first women that come to mind are Susan B. Anthony and Elizabeth Cady Stanton who organized the first women's convention 150 years ago. But women all over the world have sacrificed and soldiered in the trenches of bureaucracy and policy to open up the world up for all women.

Although "breaking the chains" that oppress and limit women's lives might be a notion that is a bit hackneyed now as we head for the new millennium, the laws did bind. Women couldn't vote by law! Women were paid less than half of men's wages! Women couldn't inherit property by law! A woman didn't have rights over her own body, birth control, or pregnancy until January 22, 1973 with *Roe v. Wade* ("We recognize the right of the individual, married or single, to be free from unwarranted government intrusion into matters so fundamentally affecting a person as the decision whether to bear or beget a child. That right necessarily includes the right of a woman to decide whether or not to terminate her pregnancy"), a heated battle in the courts even now. Until the 1970s, a woman could be committed to an asylum with a mere piece of paper signed by her husband. Imagine! There are many cases of a woman being hauled off to the nuthouse so hubby could trade her in for a new, younger model. The work done to change these laws can never be forgotten. We're now free to pursue any dream, any career, even political power thanks to the sheroic foremothers who dismantled the walls brick by brick.

With a few born-to-the-throne exceptions, women have only begun to rule the world in the second half of the twentieth century. But as these gals prove, we're making up for lost time! And when we can't get inside the seats of power, we rouse a great deal of rabble around the edges.

Queen Isabella:
More than an Armchair Traveler

Popular history has defined Queen Isabella's main achievement as bankrolling Christopher Columbus. But, that is only one of her remarkable achievements. Isabella should also be remembered for the unification of a splintered Spain and as the monarch who forged the newly unified country into a colonial superpower. Isabella had plenty of strikes against her including a nasty pair of brothers, Alfonso and Enrique, with a penchant for exiling their only sister to keep her out of court.

Isabella had staying power, however, brokering her own marriage to Ferdinand, the prince of Aragon, one of the three kingdoms that made up fifteenth-century Spain along with Castile and Granada. Upon the deaths of Ferdie's brothers, Isabella declared herself Queen. The new queen was smart enough to know that the first order of business was to destroy the power base of the petty nobility in Castile. To this end, she resurrected the "brotherhood", an order of peacekeepers and judicial tribunals, which cooperated with the throne. Her savvy moves also included naming Ferdinand grand master of the religious armies, creating a powerful enough base to successfully overthrow the kingdom of Granada and kick the Moors out of Spain, as well as uniting Spain for the first time in 800 years! This occurred in 1492, the same year Columbus "sailed the ocean blue."

▲ *Queen Isabella: in 1492, she united Spain and underwrote Columbus.*

And Don't Forget These Early Rockin' Rulers . . .

Elizabeth I, daughter of Henry the Eighth, who vowed never to lose *her* head in love and reigned alone for forty-five years;

Margaret, who united three Scandinavian countries in 1387 and ruled for twenty-five years;

Sonduk, who presided over a war-torn Korea in the seventh century and sent her countrymen to China to be educated;

Eleanor of Aquitaine, who really knew how to get around—she was queen of France for fifteen years and queen of England for fifty (and she managed to have ten kids as well!);

Catherine the Great, who reigned over Mother Russia with an iron fist and unparalleled brilliance. *His*tory has attacked her for her unabashed lust for life; herstory shall, finally, acknowledge her as an extraordinary politician and pragmatist.

Anne Marbury Hutchinson:
Banished for Having a Brain

One of the earliest American sheroes is Anne Hutchinson, who was banned from the Massachusetts Colony in 1637 for daring to have her own theological interpretations of the religious teachings of her day. Born in England, the daughter of an Anglican minister, she grew up in a household where religious discussion was encouraged. As an adult, Anne and her husband, William, heard the sermons of Cotton Mather in England (whose refinement of the Puritans' Covenant of Works)—that living "right" was the key to salvation of the soul—(which he called the Covenant of

126

Grace)—and that redemption or salvation of the soul was possible only through God's grace.

Mather's "heresy" got him booted out of England. Declaring that God had told her to follow Mather, Anne and her henpecked hubby and their brood (they had fifteen children, twelve of whom survived) decamped to Massachusetts where they were soon embraced by the monied set and started going to the right church and living in the right part of the colony. The trouble started when Anne made the mistake of displaying her deep understanding of various doctrines and started holding theological salons for women. Anne's parlor preachments were very popular, but when men began attending the chauvinist colonial clergy got teed off. Anne was "ministering" and, therefore, breaking the law in Massachusetts against women having such authority. Hutchinson was tried for the "sin of traduction," branded a heretic, and banished from the colony with high drama: "The Church consenting to it we will proceed to excommunicate. Forasmuch as you, Mrs. Hutchinson, have highly transgressed and offended . . . and troubled the Church with your Errors . . . I do cast you out . . . and deliver you up to Satan . . . I command you in the name of Christ Jesus and of this Church as a Leper to withdraw yourself out of the Congregation."

Most people would have slunk away in shame, but Anne defended her philosophies: "I bless the Lord, He hath let me see which was the clear ministry and which the wrong," and told her prosecuting persecutors they would all "go to hell!" She so scared the church fathers that they ordered her supporters to turn in their guns. She then hooked up with a freethinking Samuel Groton outside the colony and started a religious rebellion. Then Groton got banished. Anne Hutchinson established a religious settlement in Rhode Island, emphasizing a personal relationship with God rather than obedience to church doctrine. After the death of her husband, she and her children moved to a remote colony in the New Netherlands (now the location of Pelham Bay Park in the Bronx!). Doubtless the itinerant religious reformer would've stirred up yet another congregation among the Dutch settlers, except Anne Hutchinson and five of her children were killed in an Indian attack.

Although she is now credited with spearheading the first salvo in the development of religious tolerance, the few history books of the time that included information on Anne branded her as a wicked "New England Jezebel." A plaque at the former Old Corner Bookstore in Boston, now the site of the *Boston Globe*, reads "On this site stood the house of Anne Hutchinson, a religious leader, brilliant, fearless, unfortunate. Banished to Rhode Island 1637. Killed by Indians 1643."

Belva Ann Bennett McNall Lockwood:
See How She Ran!

Victorian powerhouse Belva Lockwood was the first woman to plead before the U. S. Supreme Court and the first woman to run for president of the United States. After being blocked from the law department of Columbian College (now George Washington University) for fear that her presence would distract the male students, this widow and former school teacher applied to the brand new National Law School. Upon her graduation in 1869 at the age of forty-three, Belva was refused her degree and took this affront to the attention of President Ulysses S. Grant, who arranged for the due delivery of Belva's diploma.

This was just the beginning of her struggles to be allowed to practice law. Admitted to the District of Columbia bar, Belva was barred from speaking to federal courts due to her gender. Not willing to take the exclusion lying down, she then rammed a bill through Congress allowing women lawyers in the federal courts, becoming, in 1879, the first woman admitted to the bar of the Supreme Court. Proving that Belva wasn't just in it for herself, she took up many cases for the underdog—

championing, for example, the first southern black lawyer to argue before the Supreme Court. And in her most spectacular case, won a famous $5 million judgement (an unheard of amount in the nineteenth century) for the Cherokee Indians, forcing the U.S. government to pay them for their land. This spectacular victory prompted opposing lawyer Assistant Attorney General Louis A. Pratt to designate her, "decidedly the most noted attorney in this country, if not in the world."

With her brilliant legal mind, Belva figured that, "If women in the states are not permitted to vote, there is no law against their being voted for, and if elected, filling the highest office in the gift of the people" and decided to run for president as the candidate of the Equal Rights Party in 1884 and 1888, with a hefty platform espousing rights for all minorities (including voting rights for women) along with temperance, peace, and universal education. Interestingly, she was opposed by Susan B. Anthony and Elizabeth Cady Stanton who urged her to endorse the Republican candidate, James Blaine (he was in favor of women's rights). Both Blaine and Lockwood lost out to Grover Cleveland, but Lockwood surprised everyone by getting thousands of votes! Throughout her life, she continued to work and speak on behalf of her favored causes—women, peace, and minority rights—attaining a national reputation as a brilliant and powerful speaker. In her later years, she threw her energies into the Universal Peace Union, a precursor to the United Nations that advocated arbitration as a solution to international conflicts. In 1912, she reflected back on her lengthy career and remarked, "I never stopped fighting. My cause was the cause of thousands of women."

"Were I a voice—a still small voice—an eloquent voice, I would whisper into the ear of every young woman, improve and exercise every talent that has been given to you; improve every opportunity, obey your inspiration, give no heed to the croakings of those narrow minds who take old hide bound and musty customs for religion and law, with

which they have no affiliation, and who tell you with remarkable
ease that these professions were never intended for women."
—Belva Ann Bennett McNall Lockwood

Outside the Law

Women had a long journey to gain entry to the courtroom. Here are
some of the important steps along the way:

- The first known woman lawyer ever was a Babylonian who brought
  suit against her husband's brother, pleaded her own case, and
  won—in 550 B.C.!

- Biblical plaintiffs **Mahlah, Noah, Hoglah, Milcah,** and **Tizra** were
  five sisters who tried to fight the unfair treatment they were receiving
  after their father's death. In Numbers 27:1–8, they waxed eloquent,
  "Why should the name of our father be done away from among his
  family, because he hath no son? Give unto us therefore a possession
  among the brethren of our father." The judge, in this case God,
  ruled in their favor according to his spokesperson Moses, "The inheritance of their father (was) to pass unto them . . . If a man die, and
  have no son, then ye shall cause his inheritance to pass unto his
  daughter."

- In 1239, **Bettista Gozzadini** sat in the juridical chair at the
  University of Bologna, highly unusual for the Dark Ages.

- America's first lawyer was **Margaret Brent**, one of the largest land-holders in colonial Maryland and the most active attorney of her day; her name is in the court records 124 times for the years 1642 to 1650!

- Among Belva's contemporaries, **Arabella Mansfield**, in June 1869, became the first woman in the United States to be admitted to the bar, but for reasons we don't know (but can easily guess) never practiced. Ada H. Kepley was the first American woman to actually receive a law degree—from Union College in 1870.

- In the 1860s, **Myra Colby Bradwell** tried to get into the legal profession, but was barred, even by the Illinois Supreme Court who stated "this step . . . would mean . . . that it is in harmony with the Constitution and laws that women should be made governors, judges, and sheriffs." Myra tried to take it higher, but the appeal didn't get off the ground. Such a hue and cry erupted over Myra's case, the state of Illinois passed a law in 1872 forbidding sex discrimination in employment. Bradwell gained admittance to the bar in 1890, but by then was more interested in her new profession—working full time for women's civil rights!

- **Charlotte Ray** was the first black woman in America to be allowed to practice law in 1872, but couldn't because of threats from bigots.

Angelina Emily and Sarah Moore Grimké:
Sister Soldiers

The Grimké sisters were raised like Scarlett and her sisters in *Gone With the Wind,* but, unlike the fictional characters, grew up hating slavery. The privileged duo, two of twelve children, had all the southern advantages of private tutors and training in the arts at their palatial Charleston, South Carolina, home and were brought up to be good, high church Episcopalians. But they first showed their abolitionist spunk when Sarah was twelve; she was caught teaching a slave to read and write, a criminal offense. Because Angelina supported her, they were both punished.

As soon as they could, they high-tailed it out of there. Sarah bailed in 1821, moving north to The City of Brother Love and converting to Quakerism because of its anti-slavery beliefs. Angelina followed eight years later and repeated her sister's religious switch and "lefty" leanings, going so far as to joining the Philadelphia Anti-Slavery Society.

Angelina had a nose for publicity and got her passionate condemnation of slavery published in William Lloyd Garrison's magazine *The Liberator.* Spurred by this break, Angelina followed up with a pamphlet entitled "An Appeal to the Christian Women of the South," which tried to appeal to women's consciences in opposing slavery: "But, perhaps you will be ready to query, why appeal to women on this subject? We do not make the law which perpetuates slavery. No legislative power is vested in us; we can do nothing to overthrow the system, even if we wished to do so. To this I reply, I know you do not make the laws, but I also know that *you are the wives and mothers, the sisters and daughters of those who do;* and if you really suppose *you* can do nothing to overthrow slavery, you are greatly mistaken . . . 1st. You can read on this subject. 2nd. You can pray over this subject. 3rd. You can speak on this subject. 4th. You can *act* on this subject."

Her appeal created a storm of controversy. In her hometown of Charleston, the postmaster burned all copies and put out a warning that Angelina better never show her face again in the South. At that point, sister Sarah took up the charge and attacked the slavers with a shot below their biblical belts with a refutation of the lame excuse that slavery was "OK" according to the Bible in her "Epistle to the Clergy of the Southern States."

The fearless siblings took their abolitionist act on the road, speaking to mixed crowds of both men and women. This really raised the dander of so-called "proper" society—ladies were not supposed to appear in public with men who were not their husbands and women were not supposed to lecture or preach—and they returned fire with a printed attack from the Massachusetts's clergy that was preached to every available congregation in 1837. The clergy condemned women reformers and preachers, issuing a caution regarding any female who "assumed the place and tone of man as public reformer... her character becomes unnatural." This was followed by other pious publications assaulting the Grimké sisters for overstepping their place.

As a result of the churches' attack, the sisters found themselves in the middle of the women's rights movement and are generally credited with being the first to make a link between the abolitionist cause and women's rights. The irrepressible duo fired back in grand style with letters in the *Spectator* and in Sarah's book, published in 1838, *Letters on the Equality of the Sexes and the Condition of Women* where she took the panty-waisted preachers down with her brilliant manifesto declaring women as absolutely and naturally endowed with equal rights, and that the only "unnatural" behaviors being performed in American society were those of men suppressing women!

Later, Angelina became the first woman in America to speak to a legislature with the presentation of her antislavery petition signed by 20,000 women to the Massachusetts state legislative body. The Grimkés were ahead of their time in many other ways as well, embracing new health fads and intellectual movements and running with a pretty arty crowd including Henry David Thoreau who was intrigued by their up-to-the-minute fashion sense, describing them as "two elderly gray-headed ladies, the former in extreme Bloomer costume, which was what you might call remarkable." Go Grimkés!

> *"I ask for no favors for my sex. I surrender no claim to equality. All I ask our brethren is, that they will take their feet from off our necks and permit us to stand upright on the ground which God designed us to occupy."*—Sarah Moore Grimké

Amelia Bloomer: Free Your ✳✳✳ and Your Mind Will Follow

"Drag" had a whole different meaning for nineteenth-century fashion plates! Women were wearing fifteen pounds worth of skirts and petticoats until, in the 1850s, Amelia Bloomer started advocating a radical new undergarment in her circular, *The Lily*, the first journal by and for women. Amelia was inspired to try this liberating new costume when she was visited by Elizabeth Cady Stanton and her cousin, Elizabeth Miller. While abroad, Miller was motivated to unburden herself of several pounds of

▲ *Amelia Bloomer: inventor of pantaloons and published the Lily, America's first feminist magazine.*

skirts and created a Turkish-inspired short skirt and pantaloon combo that offered much comfort and freedom of movement. Stanton and Bloomer jumped into pairs of drawers with both feet, and Bloomer sang the praises of their new couture option in her magazine, "Fit yourselves for a higher sphere and cease groveling in the dirt. Let there be no stain of earth upon your soul or apparel." The pantaloons proved an overnight sensation with scores of women sending in requests for patterns. The regular press lampooned the 'loons as "Bloomerism" and thus were born "bloomers."

Susan B. Anthony and Elizabeth Cady Stanton:
Feminist Foremothers

The pioneer crusader for women's right to vote was a precocious child. Raised in the 1820s by a Quaker father who believed in independent thinking and education for women, Susan learned to read and write by the time she was three. Her first career was as a schoolteacher, but she soon found her niche as a political reformer, taking up the cause of temperance, then abolition. In 1869, she and Elizabeth Cady Stanton organized the National Women's Suffrage Association and put out a profeminist paper, *The Revolution.*

When the Fourteenth Amendment to the Constitution was passed in 1872 guaranteeing equal rights for African Americans including the right, as citizens, to vote, Anthony and Cady Stanton kicked into action demanding the right to vote for women as well. Susan and a dozen other suffragists were jailed for trying to vote in the presidential election of that year. Undeterred, they began to work for a separate amendment

▲ *Stanton and Anthony founded the first formal women's movement in the 1840's.*

giving this right to women. However, Congress patently ignored the amendments put before them each year on the vote for women until fifty years later.

Both Stanton and Anthony were real hell-raisers. Stanton, along with Lucretia Mott, organized the first women's rights convention in 1848 with a platform on women's rights to property, equal pay for equal work, and the right to vote. Stanton was introduced to Susan B. Anthony three years later. They were a "dream team" combining Elizabeth's political theories and her ability to strike people's emotions, with Susan's unmatched skill as a logician and organizer par excellence. They founded the first temperance society for women and amazed everybody with their drastic call for drunkenness to be recognized as a legal basis for divorce.

Reviled during her lifetime, she learned to live with the taunts and heckles; critics claimed, among other traits, that she had "the proportions of a file and the voice of a hurdy-gurdy." Nonetheless, the "Napoleon" of the women's rights movement as William Henry Channing called her, tirelessly lectured around the country for women's rights until her dying day, in 1906. Although she didn't get to realize her dream of voting rights for women, the successors she and Stanton trained did finally win this landmark victory for the women of America. Of the 260 women who attended the foremothers' historic first women's rights convention in 1848, only one woman lived long enough to see the passing of the victorious 1920 amendment granting women the right to vote—Charlotte Woodward. She declared at the time, "We little dreamed when we began this context that half a century later we would be compelled to leave the finish of the battle to another generation of women. But our hearts are filled with joy to know that they enter this task equipped with a college education, with business experience, with the freely admitted right to speak in public—all of which were denied to women fifty years ago."

"Failure is impossible."—Susan B. Anthony

Breaking the Concrete Ceiling

Lucretia Mott worked with Elizabeth Cady Stanton in planning the Seneca Falls Convention. Mott was an electrifying speaker, coming from Europe where she was a well known Quaker preacher. She didn't mince words and spoke powerfully and directly to women's rights, adding the radical note needed to light the fires of equal rights and abolition, "the world has never seen a truly great nation because in the degradation of women the very fountains of life are poisoned at the source."

Women legislators worked for years to get a statue of Susan B. Anthony, Lucretia Mott, and Elizabeth Cady Stanton in the Capitol rotunda. In spring of 1997, they finally succeeded. At the dedication ceremony, Representative Louise Slaughter (D., N.Y.) quipped to the statue, "Well sisters, it's going to be very hard to put you back in the basement now."

Political Correction

At the Seneca Falls suffragette convention on July 19, 1848, the Declaration of Independence was rewritten to include women and passed a slew of resolutions designed to promote gender equality. Among them are:

"Resolved, That all laws which prevent women from occupying such a station in society as her conscience shall dictate, or which place her in a position inferior to that of man, are contrary to the great precept of nature, and therefore of no force or authority.

"Resolved, That woman is man's equal—was intended to be so by the Creator, and the highest good of the race demands that she should be recognized as such.

"Resolved, That the women of this country ought to be enlightened in regard to the laws under which they live, that they may no longer publish their degradation by declaring themselves satisfied with their present position, nor their ignorance, by asserting that they have all the rights they want.

"Resolved, That it is the duty of the women of this country to secure to themselves their sacred right to the elective franchise.

"Resolved, That the equality of human rights results necessarily from the fact of the identity of the race in capacities and responsibilities.

"Resolved, That . . . [these] being . . . self-evident truth[s] growing out of the divinely implanted principles of human nature, any custom or authority adverse to it, whether modern or wearing the hoary sanction of antiquity, is to be regarded as . . . self-evident falsehood[s], and at war with mankind."

Mother Jones:
Mojo Rising

]n the 1960s, big business came to be known as "The Man." A hundred years before the hippie revolution, Mother Jones was giving The Man a kick in the wallet every chance she got. She organized her first labor strike at the midpoint of her life, forty-seven, and devoted the rest of her life to establishing unions in coal mines, breweries, factories, and cotton mills over a span of forty years. Armed with steel-trap smarts, a tough, no-nonsense manner and endless courage, she fought her way to the forefront of the labor movement and paved the way for safer, more humane conditions for workers, including child labor laws and the eight-hour work day.

A charismatic leader who helped the underpaid and overworked laborers of America fight for their rights, Mary Harris Jones came to be known as Mother Jones because of her concern for the workers she came across. Portrayed in the many photos taken, as the sweetest of grandmothers in her proper Victorian gowns, hats, and spectacles, she was however, in her own words, "a hell-raiser." Doubtless, she enjoyed the epithet once hurled at her by a prosecutor in West Virginia—"the most dangerous woman in America."

She was born into a working-class family of revolutionaries. Her father and his father before him were both soldiers in the battle for Irish independence. Her grandfather was hanged for his participation in the revolution; her father escaped to North America to avoid arrest. Young Mary attended public school and trained both as a seamstress and a teacher. She taught at a convent in Monroe, Michigan, for a year before deciding to set up a dressmaker's shop in Chicago. The year 1860 found her in Memphis teaching where she met and married George Jones, an ironworker, union member, and labor organizer, who died seven years later of yellow fever. This was enough to send her back to Chicago where she applied her skill as a seamstress, making fancy dresses for the wealthy of Lake Shore Drive. Anger welled up inside her at the selfish wealthy folks she sewed for who blithely ignored the needy and basked in their sumptuous comforts.

Four years after losing George to yellow fever, Mary lost her shop to Chicago's great fire, and she joined the ranks of the homeless. Her anger at the selfish wealthy class incited her to attend Knights of Labor meetings where she quickly became admired for her orations and argumentation. Mary Harris had found her true calling—as a labor activist, agitator, and activist. She was nothing short of brilliant. Her passionate calls to action were heard by thousands of Americans who were inspired by her to fight for basic human rights and respect as workers. She had an almost magical ability to band people together to fight against incredible odds.

"Women are the foundation of the nation," she declared as she put her heart and soul into helping the condition of working women in rural areas and mountainous towns of West Virginia, Pennsylvania, Illinois, Ohio, and as far west as Colorado, Utah, and Arizona. She forged a powerful sisterhood with these women and saw behind the shy faces, a steely strength she helped them tap. "Women have great power, if only they knew how to use it," she would declare often, urging women to focus their eyes on the prize of better pay, decent working conditions, and reduction of the soul-killing hours. "This is the fighting age. Put on your fighting clothes. You are too sentimental!"

Mother Jones labored in the trenches alongside the workers, sleeping on their floors in cold mountain shacks and sharing their scant food. While intellectuals theorized about class struggles and economic ideals, Mother Jones worked in the gritty reality of these people's daily lives. She saw herself as one of the struggling, too, and babysat, cared for the sick, held the dying, and scavenged for food, clothing, coal, and money during strikes. Her distrust of the suffragette movement came from her total allegiance to the uneducated working poor; many of the suffragists were of the monied, educated, upper-class she so resented. She let them worry about getting the right to vote for women; she was making sure they could survive the business of making a living.

A victim of sexism, Mother Jones was never allowed to participate in the United Mine Workers of America she fought so hard for. Men completely ran the union; she was allowed no part of it. From the sidelines, she tried her best to advise in impassioned letters these men for whom she had built a powerful membership. Late in life, she was saddened by the infighting and corruption she was powerless to prevent.

Mother Jones championed the underdog at her own expense and often at enormous personal risk. Ahead of her time, she amazed West Virginia mine workers she had organized when she implored them to be more understanding of the foreign-born "scabs" who were sent to work the mines during strikes. She also lobbied on behalf of African American workers who suffered bigotry from the unions.

Born in the Victorian Age and brought up to be subservient, Mother Jones was a first generation Irish American who fought the good fight and left the world a better place for her class, for women, and for the ethnic groups trying to find their place among the workers of America. Mary Harris Jones was fortunate to live long enough to see many of the great changes she fought for in improving the lot of the working class. Iron-willed and lion-hearted, Mother Jones lived by her principles. A shero in both words and action, she reminds us all "it is the militant, not the meek, who shall inherit the earth."

> *"The Jeanne d'Arc of the miners was a benevolent fanatic, a*
> *Celtic blend of sentiment and fire, of sweetness and fight . . . (who)*
> *captured the imagination of the American worker as no*
> *other woman—perhaps no other leader—ever has."*

—Dale Fetherling on Mother Jones

Emma Goldman:
Radical Rhetorician

Teenage immigrant Emma Goldman had escaped from Russia in 1885 after witnessing the wholesale slaughter of the idealist political rebel anarchists who called themselves the Nihilists. Two years later in America, the young woman "born to ride whirlwinds" as someone once said, saw it happen again with the trial and killings of the Haymarket anarchists who had opposed Chicago's power elite. Rather than scare her off the politics of idealism forever, young Emma was drawn even more toward the kind of political passion that risked death for principles. She "devoured every line on anarchism I could get," she notes in her autobiography *Living My Life*, "and headed for New York City, command central in the 1890s for radicals of many stripes."

In New York, Emma met one of the anarchists whose writing she'd been devouring, Johann Most, who encouraged her to develop her gift for public speaking. Emma worked as a practical nurse in New York's ghettos where she saw the price women paid for want of any birth control. Soon she was taking to the soapbox to air her views on this lack of available contraception and the resulting reliance on back-room abortions: "Thanks to this Puritan tyranny, the majority of women soon find themselves at the ebb of their physical resources. Ill and worn, they are utterly unable to give their children even elementary care. That, added to economic pressure, forces many women to risk utmost danger rather than continue to bring forth life." Her campaign reached the ears of Margaret Sanger and influenced the development of a national birth control campaign.

But birth control was only one of her bailiwicks; what she was really advocating was anarchism: a classless, governmentless society made up of small groups in free, humanistic cooperation with one another. She had a tremendous gift for verbal rhetoric. Nicknamed "Red Emma," she traveled the United States lecturing—often six months of the year five nights a week—making frequent stops at Mabel Dodges' infamous salon, and publishing her monthly magazine, *Mother Earth,* a vehicle for her twin concerns of women's liberation and the rights of the working class. Reporter Nellie Bly was delighted to note that "Red Emma" was very pretty "with a saucy turned-up nose and very expressive blue-gray eyes . . . (brown hair) falling loosely over her forehead, full lips, strong white teeth, a mild, pleasant voice, with a fetching accent."

In 1893, she was jailed for a year for exhorting a crowd of unemployed men who believed "it was their sacred right" to take bread if they were starving. Later she came to believe that the ends do not always justify the

▲ *"Red" Emma Goldman fought for workers rights and women's "sacred rights".*

means, and she repudiated violence as a tool to create change. She continued to mesmerize crowds with her impassioned speeches until 1917 when her opposition to World War I led to a two-year imprisonment. She was subsequently deported, the Justice Department fearful of allowing her to continue her antiwar campaign: "She is womanly, a remarkable orator, tremendously sincere, and carries conviction. If she is allowed to continue here she cannot help but have great influence."

She continued to exercise influence from abroad; in 1922 *Nation* magazine proclaimed that she was one of "the twelve greatest living women." She was allowed back into the country after her death when the government decided that her silenced corpse posed no risk, and she was buried in Chicago with the Haymarket martyrs.

"The more opposition I encountered, the more I was in my element and the more caustic I became with my opponents."—Emma Goldman

The Mabel Dodge Salon

Anybody who was anybody in the intellectual and art worlds of the early twentieth century hung out at Mabel's salon, among them: D. H. Lawrence, Gertrude Stein, Alice B. Toklas, Andrew Dassburg, Georgia O'Keefe, Leon Gaspard, Ansel Adams, and Robinson Jeffers. Beginning in New York's Greenwich Village after a stint in a Medici villa in Florence, Mabel Dodge worked for her vision of a "New World Plan" to bring the world's greatest thinkers, writers, artists, musicians, and social reformers together to whet each other's minds and create a second renaissance. Lois Palken Rudnick, a historian specializing in this era, says this about Mabel, "When she came back to the States, she landed in New York City amidst America's first great social and political revolution. She became one of the rebels of Greenwich Village and was involved with the Armory Show, the first show of post-impressionist art to come to the states. She supported anarchists and socialists and their projects, Like Emma Goldman and Margaret Sanger . . . She was an artist of life."

Dolores Ibarruri:
La Pasionaria

The shero of the Spanish Civil War, Dolores Ibarruri was born in 1895 to a Basque miner. She worked as a servant unil she joined the Partido Socialista and began writing incendiary political diatribes under the pseudonym, *La Pasionaria*: "The Passion Flower". She and her husband Julian Ruiz helped found the first Communist parties in Spain in 1920. The mother of six children with Ruiz, Ibarruri didn't let motherhood slow her down; not only did she continue writing for the *El Mundo Obrero* workers' newspaper, in 1934, she organized a women's group called *Agrupacion de Mujereres Antifascistas.*

Noted for her keen political mind, fearlessness, and charisma, Ibarurri was elected to Parliament in 1936 and was freed from a stint in jail so that she could serve. She began making speeches on behalf of the Popular Front Government, rousing audiences with her impassioned pleas to halt the tide of Fascism. When full-scale civil war broke out in Spain, La Pasionaria exhorted her fellow loyalists to remained steadfast with cries of *"No Pasaran!"* (They shall not pass!) When Franco grabbed the power seat, she left the Spain she had fought for to live in the USSR. During the mass exodus of Communists from Spain, the great Spanish matriarch met photographer Tina Modotti. Modotti was so trusted by the exiled Spaniards, she was one of two people guarding Ibarruri's hospital room when she fell ill with a bad case of hepatitis.

In Soviet Russia, Ibarruri served as Secretary-General of the Spanish Communist Party from 1942 until she assumed the presidency in 1960, a post she held until 1977. When Franco died that year, La Pasionaria moved back home to Spain and, in Spain's first elections in forty years, was reelected to Parliament. She was eighty-one years old, fierce as ever, and accorded a shero's welcome back to the country that lionized her.

La Pasionaria, whose career was based on dedication to her crusade for freedom, received much recognition for her incredible courage and self-sacrifice; she won the Lenin Peace Prize and was named honorary vice president of the International Democratic Federation of Women. She will always be remembered for her valor in the face of great danger and for her belief that, "It is better to die on your feet than live on your knees!"

Rosa Luxemburg: Red Rosa

"Emancipate!" That was the cry of socialist revolutionary Rosa Luxemburg who was born a Polish Jew and devoted her life to improving the plight of workers around the world through her political theories. She helped found the Spartacus League in Germany and worked ceaselessly toward change, cranking out more than 700 books, pamphlets, and treatises. She dazzled everyone she encountered with her fierce intelligence, Lenin himself coming to be one of her biggest fans even though she publicly disagreed with him. In 1905, Rosa staged a worker's revolt in Poland and protested World War I very vocally, prompting the authorities to throw her in jail for the entire war. Shortly before her fiftieth birthday, Rosa Luxemburg was murdered in 1919 by political opponents during the German revolution she helped create.

Rosa Luxemburg's standing as one of the great intellectuals of the turn of the century is in danger of obscurity. The Nazis set about to obliterate her writings and Stalinists undertook a smear campaign to distort Luxemburg's theories. But she was a great political theoretician, one who sought to bring equality to the working class.

International Warrior Women Taking Charge!

Hawaii's last queen was **Lili' uokalani**. She was raised by American missionaries in the nineteenth century and married an Englishman before taking up her role as the ruler of the beautiful island chain. She was quite accomplished as a stateswoman and singer who treasured her island's culture and feared the loss of it with the Western invasion. It is daunting to realize she was imprisoned and held in isolation after her brother King's Kalakaua's death so white annexationists could taker over Hawaii and incorporate it into the United States. Think about that the next time you hear somebody complain about what a tourist trap the once pristine paradise has become!

Maria de la Mercedes Barbudo was a Puerto Rican rebel who fought for emancipation and abolition circa 1800 and was exiled and murdered for her efforts toward her country's independence.

Nana Yaa Asantewa was born in 1863 and went on to become the national shero of Ghana known as the Queen Mother. British colonists stole Ghana's sacred treasure, the Golden Stool, the symbol of the Ashanti nation. While the Ashanti men waffled about going to war against the Brits, Nana (at the age of fifty) led an uprising to take back the Golden Stool. Nana and her army of women were defeated, but her sheroism and that of her women warriors was legendary. She died in prison at seventy after being a captive exile for twenty years.

Sorjini Chattophyaya Naidu was a nineteenth-century Indian-born Brahmin, the highest caste, and rebelled by marrying a man from a lower caste. This was just the beginning of her activist actions; she went against her family's orders by discarding the academics of math and science her father had chosen for her, becoming a poet instead. She joined Gandhi's movement for peaceful independence and was jailed many times ("I was born a rebel and I expect to die a rebel unless I free India!")

for civil disobedience, and later ran a salon in Bombay open to all races, castes, and religions. Upon India's independence in 1947, she became governor of her province and worked for women's rights.

In March 1928, **Chen Tiejun** was arrested, jailed, tortured, and executed at the age of twenty-four for her radical feminism. A founding member of the Chinese Communist Party, she organized a women's underground army of rebels and weapons smugglers. Forced to marry by her provincial parents, she left her husband immediately and attended college to become a teacher. Betrayed by a fellow Red Guard, her courageous refusal to divulge any information to her captors made her a shero of the Communist movement and Chinese feminists.

Founder of the Egyptian Feminist Union, **Huda Sha'Rawi** was part of the last generation of Egyptian women to come of age under the harem system in the late eighteenth century. Born to a wealthy family, she was at the forefront of Egyptian feminism and led the movement to free Egypt from British colonial rule.

Eleanor Roosevelt:
The Greatest of All?

No book on sheroes would be complete without a profile of Eleanor Roosevelt, named by historian Deborah G. Felder as the most influential woman in history. Though she was born to the privileged class, Eleanor reached out to all women, regardless of economic status, and they responded, knowing she was a kindred soul.

Eleanor was born Anne Eleanor Roosevelt and came from colonial Roosevelt stock on both sides of her family. Eleanor remembered being "like a little old woman" and was, for all of her life, keenly aware of what she called "a lack of beauty". She seems to have survived the pre-*Reviving Ophelia* batterings to her self-esteem fairly well, despite a vain and selfish mother who nicknamed Eleanor "Granny" and never passed up the opportunity to remind her that she didn't inherit her mother's beauty. Fortunately, her dashing humanitarian father, Elliott, loved her dearly and instilled in his "little Nell" a strong sense of the importance to give to others.

By the age of ten, Eleanor was an orphan and was made to live with her stern matriarch of a grandmother, then sent to the very exclusive Allenswood girls school in London. Allenswood was run by a forthright liberal activist, Marie Souvestre, who took Eleanor under her wing and lavished affection and attention on her. Eleanor recalled these days as the best of her life.

Returning home in 1902, she had the obligatory debutante ball, but preferred to do good works at settlement houses among the working class than party at snooty, upper-class salons. She also sneaked in an engagement to her fifth cousin, political aspirant Franklin Delano Roosevelt; the blushing Eleanor's hand was given in marriage by then-President Roosevelt, otherwise known as "Uncle Teddy." Eleanor and Franklin quickly had six children, losing one baby shortly after birth. Eleanor was painfully shy, a terrible issue to deal with when she had to constantly entertain to advance her husband's political career, even harder to do with a bossy mother-in-law hovering over the children and trying to take over the household.

The burgeoning young Roosevelt clan soon found themselves in the District of Columbia while FDR served as Assistant Secretary of the Navy. It is there that Eleanor found out about his affair with Lucy Mercer, Eleanor's social secretary. Eleanor was devastated, but found an inner resolve to withstand the pain and became even more dedicated to positive social change. She joined the League of Women's Voters and the Women's Trade Union League, working toward reform for women's pay and limiting the hours of the working day. In 1921, FDR fell ill with polio. Leaving the tending of him to others, Eleanor served as FDR's eyes and ears out in the world, traveling all over the country listening to people, discerning what Americans of all walks of life wanted and needed. For the rest of her life, she strove tirelessly to advance the cause of getting more women into government office and was deeply concerned with unemployment, poverty, education, housing, day care, health care, and civil rights. (Of her, Franklin once prayed, "Dear God, make Eleanor a little tired." But he never ceased relying on her sage advice.)

When FDR was elected president, Eleanor was less than thrilled with her status as First Lady: "Now I'll have no identity," she proclaimed. But she took on the job and made it her own. She held a press conference in 1933, the first First Lady to do so, and regularly spoke with a corp of women reporters. While FDR had his fireside chats, Eleanor had "My Day," a newspaper column and radio show that she used as a pulpit for many social justice issues, including the time Marian Anderson was blocked from singing in D.C. by the Daughters of the American Revolution because she was black. When Eleanor announced her resignation from the DAR in protest, their ranks dwindled in shame.

After her husband's death, she continued on with her work, including becoming a delegate to the United Nations, where she is credited with drafting and pushing through to adoption the *Universal Declaration of Human Rights* and launching UNICEF. For all the good she did, this humanitarian whom Harry Truman dubbed "The First Lady of the World" is still, nearly fifty years after her death, one of the most cherished figures in herstory.

> *"You get more joy out of the giving to others, and should put a*
> *good deal of thought into the happiness you*
> *are able to give."*—Eleanor Roosevelt

Frances Perkins: Dear to Her Heart

Frances Perkins joined Franklin Delano Roosevelt's cabinet in 1933 as secretary of labor when America was reeling from The Great Depression. She remained in this office as long as FDR himself did, serving her country well during its worst-ever economic crisis. Frances also worked on behalf of reform for workers and on many other issues dear to the First Lady, Eleanor's, heart. She was responsible for the creation of many jobs and work corps, for the development of better minimum wages, and for benefits such as Social Security and unemployment insurance. Frances' zeal as an industrial reformer came from a tragedy she witnessed in 1911 when 146 women working at the Triangle Shirtwaist company died in a fire because there were no fire escapes. This was a real turning point for Perkins, "I felt I must seal it not only on my mind but on my heart as a never-to-be-forgotten reminder of why I had to spend my life fighting conditions that could permit such a tragedy."

Clare Boothe Luce:
Luce Cannon

Clare Boothe Luce, "the woman with the serpent's tongue," was the anti-Eleanor Roosevelt, a sort of alternate universe doppelganger who used her razor-sharp wit to oppose while "faintly praising" the First Lady and other unrepentant New Dealers. A virulent Republican and FDR basher, Clare was a both a smart and tough cookie, albeit not to everyone's taste. Clare, however, had a wholly unique way of asserting her woman power. As a young woman, one of her summer jobs during college was dropping feminist tracts out of an airplane for some elderly but unstoppable suffragists. Her next job was writing photo captions for *Vogue;* there the renowned beauty quickly ascended to the position as *Vanity Fair's* managing editor. She was the first woman to hold this post for the glamour glossy and soon proved she could hold her own with the boys, even managing to be welcomed in to their cigarettes and brandy ritual.

Then she met *Time* and *Fortune* magnate Henry R. Luce, married, and quit the day job to write plays, starting with the stinker *Abide with Me* and then surprising everyone with the all-female *To the Women,* a take-no-prisoners satire of snooty society ladies, which went on to become a very successful movie. Clare became an international cause celebre with the success of *To the Women,* penning a few more stage plays including *Kiss the Boys Goodbye* before she pulled another switcheroo: war correspondent for *Life* magazine on the battle fronts of Burma, India, and China during the early years of World War II. She even interviewed Madame Chiang Kai-shek and Prime Minister Nehru.

Clare's next incarnation was politician and she went on the stump, dissing FDR, Winston Churchill, and a herd of other such sacred cows. She stunned everyone with her gift for rhetoric of the biting, stinging sort. Her next move was to run for a seat in Connecticut's Congress with a very hawkish platform—her slogan was "Let's Fight a Hard War Instead of a Soft War"—and she campaigned for the rights of women, blacks, and workers. Easily winning a seat, she served for four years and then retired while she was ahead. Clare then took her domestic campaigns abroad, convincing the Italian Prime Minister to give Italian women the vote! Her good relations with Italy garnered a post for Clare as the ambassador to Italy in 1953, becoming the United States' second woman ambassador and the first woman chief of mission to a major European power. In 1953, she was fourth in the Gallup poll of the most admired women in the world.

Clare became the grande dame of the Grand Old Party from the Goldwater sixties until her death of cancer in 1987. Clare will be best remembered for her quick wit and verbal virtuosity. She was absolutely one of a kind; she never luxuriated in her husband's great wealth, but instead worked her behind off for many causes and made great strides for women in her wake.

"Because I am a woman, I must make unusual efforts to succeed. If I fail, no one will say 'She doesn't have what it takes.' They will say, 'Women don't have what it takes'."—Clare Boothe Luce

Luce Lips

- From the diary Clare kept her psychedelic-inspired musings in when she and hubby Henry dropped acid in 1960: "Capture green bugs for future reference," "Feel all true paths to glory lead but to the grave," and "The futility of the search to be someone. Do you hear the drum?"

- On Veep Henry Wallace, "his global thinking is, no matter how you slice it, globaloney!"

- On Franklin Delano Roosevelt, "Now I do not for a moment believe that Mr. Roosevelt is a real dictator. Rather, he is a sort of super-duper, highly cultured political boss."

- On Harry Truman, "A gone goose."

- On Eleanor Roosevelt, "No woman in American history has ever so comforted the distressed or so distressed the comfortable."

- On Mississippi senator Theodore Bilbo, "the high muckamuck in America of that muckiest and most vulgar of all modern pagan cults: racism!"

- On the environment, "I am bewildered by the paradox presented by a nation that can land on the moon, orbit satellites 190 million miles from earth, but can't find a way to rid its own landscape of broken-down automobiles."

Betty Friedan:
Mad Housewife

When Betty Friedan submitted her article in 1956 about the frustrations women experience in their traditional roles as housewife and mother, she received rejections from *McCalls, The Ladies's Home Journal,* and every other publication she approached. The editors, all men at that day and age, were pretty disapproving, too, going so far as to say any woman would have to be "sick" to not be completely satisfied in her rightful role!

But Betty knew that she and the millions of women like her were not sick, just stifled. Betty *neé* Goldstein Friedan put aside her dream of being a psychologist for fear of becoming a spinster, instead choosing to marry and work for a small newspaper. She was fired from her job when she got pregnant for the second time, and began, like most middle-class women of her day and age, to devote herself full-time to the work of running a home and family, what she called "the dream life, supposedly, of American women at that time." But after a decade of such devotion, she still wasn't happy and theorized she wasn't alone. A graduate of Smith College, she decided to poll her fellow alumnae. Most of her classmates, who had given up promising careers to devote themselves to their families, felt incomplete; many were deeply depressed. They felt guilty for not being completely content sacrificing their individual dreams for their families, each woman certain that her dissatisfaction was a personal failing. Betty called this "the problem that has no name" and so she gave it one, "the feminine mystique".

Over the next five years, her rejected article evolved into a book as she interviewed hundreds of women around the country. *The Feminine Mystique* explored the issue, criticizing American advertisers' exclusively domestic portrayal of women and issuing a call to action for women to say no to the housewife role and adopt "a new life plan" in which they could have both families and careers. With its publication in 1963, *The Feminine Mystique* hit America like a thunderbolt; the publisher W.W.I. Norton had printed only 2,000 copies, never anticipating the sale of 3 million copies in hardcover alone!

▲ *Betty Friedan's* The Feminist Mystique *kick-started "second wave feminism."*

Unintentionally, Betty had started a revolution; she began to be flooded with letters from women saying her book gave them the courage to change their lives and decry equal access to employment opportunities and other equality issues. Ultimately, the response to Betty's challenge created the momentum that led to the formalization of the second wave of the U.S. women's movement in 1966 with the organization of NOW—the National Organization for Women.

Betty was NOW's first president and took her role as a leader in the women's movement seriously, traveling to lectures and campaigns for change, engendering many of the freedoms women now enjoy. She pushed for equal pay for equal work, equal job opportunities, and access to birth control and legalized abortion. In 1970, she quit NOW to fight for the Equal Rights Amendment and, in 1975, was named Humanist of the Year. Of her, author Barbara Seaman, wrote, "Betty Friedan is to the women's movement what Martin Luther King was to blacks."

In 1981, responding to critics who claimed feminism ignored the importance of relationships and families to most women, she penned *The Second Stage*, in which she called on men and women to work together to make both the home and the workplace havens for both genders. These days, Betty is making another revolution with her latest book, *The Fountain of Age*, raising consciousness about society's stereotypes about aging thirty years after she, as futurist Alvin Toffler so aptly put it, "pulled the trigger of history" with *The Feminine Mystique*.

"It's been a lot of fun making the revolution."—Betty Friedan

Betty's Personal Sheroes

From a 1984 radio interview: "I admire Barbara Jordan [and] Martha Griffiths, the lieutenant governor of Michigan . . . I have in some ways, great admiration for Indira Gandhi . . . After the winning of the vote in 1920, until my *Feminine Mystique* in 1963, women's history was almost blotted out of the national consciousness. We didn't study it in school. So, the women that are now, in my opinion, heroines of history before me: Mary Wollstonecraft in England, Elizabeth Cady Stanton, Margaret Fuller, Susan B. Anthony, [and] Charlotte Perkins Gilman in the United

States, and their like in other countries . . . Eleanor Roosevelt, of course . . . I criticized, but also admired a great deal; Margaret Mead, Abigail Adams, the wife of John Adams, one of the first presidents of the United States. . . . I always adored Collette, and the idea of Collette and the writings of Collette. I love the imagery of Madame de Stael, who would be doing all the things at once the way women have to do them. She would be having a pedicure, having her nails polished, nursing her baby at her breast, dictating a menu to her cook, waving goodbye to her lover going off to the Napoleonic Wars and writing at the same time, writing her stories, her memoirs. . . . I love that image. But the images of women we are beginning to have now, we are only [now] discovering that are as result of the women's movement. We, who have made the women's movement, had to create ourselves and help each other create ourselves as a new kind of woman."

Bella Abzug:
Battling Bella

When brilliant young attorney and editor of the *Columbia Law Review* Bella Abzug graduated from Columbia in 1947, she headed straight back home to New York City to represent labor interests and civil rights. The daughter of a Bronx butcher, Bella credits her interest in social change to her grandfather, a Russian Jewish immigrant. In the fifties, she got ample opportunity to pursue her passionate causes during the McCarthy hearings, defending many on trial for leftist leanings.

For decades, if there was action to be taken or change to be made, Bella Abzug was

▲ *"Battling Bella" Abzug fought the system from within a congresswoman.*

in there with her considerable charisma, impressive rhetoric, and intense desire to make the world a better place, particularly for women and minorities. She was regarded to have been influential in the passage of the 1954 Civil Rights Act and the Voting Rights Act of 1965. Unstoppable Bella also took on the Vietnam War issue in the sixties and founded Women Strike for Peace.

In 1969, the die-hard Democrat jumped into politics herself, running for New York City's 19th Congressional District with the catchy slogan, "This Woman Belongs in the House!" and winning a showdown against Barry Farber. Bella Abzug didn't disappoint her backers one bit when she started in, hammer and nails, constructing her platform of change. Her very first day, Bella put out a call for withdrawal of all troops from Vietnam by July, 1971, and went on from there with dramatic pursuits of her ultraliberal agenda. Almost as famous for her hats as her flamboyant rhetoric, she never backed away from the chance to fight for one of her causes, a trait that earned a number of nicknames: Battling Bella, Hurricane Bella, and Mother Courage to name three.

In her signature large hats, she was easily recognized as one of the preeminent feminists among a core group including Betty Friedan, Shirley Chisholm, and Gloria Steinem with whom she founded the National Women's Political Caucus in 1971 whose mission was the dispersement of political power to include the women, the poor, the working class, racial minorities, and other groups previously shut out from politics.

She lost a bid for the Senate by a narrow margin in 1976 and lost the chance to become the mayor of New York City the following year. In the ninties, she was the co-chair of the Women's Environment and Development Organization, an international network dedicated to protecting the planet, as well as furthering the causes of social justice and women's rights. Until her death in 1998, this plain-spoken strong-headed shero never backed away from a chance to fight for one of her causes.

Bella, who insisted on being called "Ms.," continued to attract considerable controversy as well as virulent defenders and supporters thoughout her life. One thing for sure, is that she never failed to put everything she had on the line for the pursuit of a better world for women and minorities. In her autobiography, *Bella! Ms. Abzug Goes to Washington,* she says, "There are those who say I'm impatient, impetuous, uppity, rude, profane, brash, and overbearing. Whether I'm any of those things or all of them, you can decide for yourself. But whatever I am—and this ought to be made very clear at the outset—I am a very serious woman."

"We were meant to advise, not just consent."—Bella Abzug

Kate Millett:
The "Lavender Menace"

The second wave of feminism had many facets. While Betty Friedan argued for economic equality, in her 1970s book *Sexual Politics,* Kate Millet advocated a more militant revolution and boldly decried patriarchy with a call for a radical revision of roles for women. Millet represented the "lavender menace" uptight Americans feared—lesbians! Wild woman politico, Millett minced no words in her crusade against sexism, even criticizing missionary style intercourse as one of the evils of keeping women down. She has gone on to write several more books, guaranteed to shock in some form or fashion: *The Prostitution Papers*, an exploration and defense of hooking, *Flying*, a frank account of her love life, and *Sita*, about the death of a lesbian affair. She has also made a well regarded film, *Three Lives*, and revealed her institutionalization for mental illness in an eye-opening account. According to Gayle Graham Yates in *Makers of Modern Culture*, Kate Millet is the best known American feminist outside America because of her newsmaking trip to Iran to work on behalf of Iranian women's rights ending in her expulsion from the country by the Ayatollah Khomeni.

> *"Patriarchy decrees that the status of both child and mother is primarily or ultimately dependent on the male."*—Kate Millett

Gloria Steinem:
Wonder Woman

Gloria Steinem's name is synonymous with feminism. As a leader of the second wave of feminism, she brought a new concern to the fore—the importance of self-esteem for women. Her childhood did little to bolster her sense of self or predict the successful course her life would take. Her father, an antique dealer, traveled a lot for work, and her mother suffered from severe depression and was often bedridden and self-destructive. Because they moved so often, Gloria didn't attend school until she was ten, after her family was deserted by her father and Gloria assumed the roles of housewife and mother to her mother and sister. Escaping through books and movies, Gloria did well at school and eventually was accepted to Smith College, where her interest in women's rights, sparked by her awareness that her mother's illness had not been taken seriously because "her functioning was not necessary to the world" began to take hold.

After a junket in India, she started freelancing; her goal was to be a political reporter. Soon she hit the glass ceiling; while she made enough money to get by, she wasn't getting the kind of serious assignments her male colleagues were—interviewing presidential candidates and writing on foreign policy. Instead she was assigned in 1963 to go undercover as a Playboy Bunny and write about it. She agreed, seeing it as an investigative journalism piece, a way to expose sexual harassment. However, after the story appeared, no editors would take her seriously; she was the girl who had worked as a Bunny.

But she kept pushing for political assignments and finally, in 1968, came on board the newly founded *New York* magazine as a contributing editor. When the magazine sent her to cover a radical feminist meeting, no one guessed the assignment would be transformational. After attending the meeting, she moved from the sidelines to stage center of the feminist movement, cofounding the national Women's Political Caucus and the Women's Action Alliance.

The next year, Steinem, with her background in journalism, was the impetus for the founding of *Ms.*, the first mainstream feminist magazine in America's history. The first issue, with shero Wonder Woman on the cover, sold out the entire first printing of 300,000 in an unprecedented eight days, and *Ms.* received an astonishing 20,000 letters soon after the magazine hit the newsstands, indicating it had really struck a chord with the women of America. Steinem's personal essay, "Sisterhood," spoke of her reluctance to join the movement at first because of "lack of esteem for women—black women, Chicana women, white women—and for myself."

The self-described "itinerant speaker and feminist organizer" continued at the helm of *Ms.* for fifteen years, publishing articles such as the one that posited Marilyn Monroe as the embodiment of fifties women's struggle to keep up the expectations of society. She penned *Outrageous Acts and Everyday Rebellions* in 1983 urging women to take up the charge as progenitors of change. This was followed by *Revolution from*

Within in 1992, illuminating her despair at having to take care of her emotionally disturbed mother as well as her struggles with self-image, feeling like "a plump brunette from Toledo, too tall and much too pudding-faced, with . . . a voice that felt constantly on the verge of revealing some unacceptable emotion." Steinem stunned her reading public with such self-revelatory confessions. Who would have guessed that this crack editor and leading beauty of the feminist movement had zero self-image?

Gloria Steinem's real genius lies in her ability to relate to other women, creating the bond of sisterhood with shared feelings. Her latest book, *Moving Beyond Words*, talks about "doing sixty" and the challenges of aging in third-wave America. Still a phenomenally popular speaker and writer, Gloria Steinem crystallizes the seemingly complicated issues and challenges of her work by defining feminism as simply, "the belief that women are full human beings."

> *"The sex and race caste systems are very intertwined and the revolutions have always come together, whether it was the suffragist and abolitionist movements or whether it's the feminist and civil rights movements. They must come together because one can't succeed without the other."*—Gloria Steinem

Steinem's Sheroes

- The Grimké sisters whom she sees as the roots of "new feminism"
- Shirley Temple
- Louisa May Alcott

Katherine Graham:
Katherine the Great

Although Katherine Graham was not a politician, she wielded enormous power in the political arena as owner of the *Washington Post,* still one of the most important and respected newspapers in the world today. Born Katherine Meyer, she was the daughter of Eugene Meyer, a brilliant French Jew who moved to America and attended Yale, made a fortune in banking and on the stock exchange, and retired a multimillionaire before he was thirty years old!

Katherine's childhood is a classic silver spoon story, raised by domestic help while her parents maintained the lifestyle of the glittery successes they were. A staunch Republican, Eugene Meyer took on a second career as a public servant and served as advisor to seven presidents. Katherine, an independent thinker, swung to the opposite pole on the left and earned a degree in journalism. After a brief stint in San Francisco reporting for the now defunct *News,* Katherine accepted an offer of $29 dollars a week to go and work for the paper Eugene Meyer had bought five years before—the *Washington Post.*

Katherine fell in love with the publisher of the *Post,* Philip Graham, and after they wed, they bought the paper from her father for a million dollars. Philip was brilliant and bipolar. He was keenly interested in building a publishing empire, and soon they added the

▼ *The Washington Post's Katherine Graham held her ground against the White House in Watergate.*

magazine *Newsweek* to their holdings. Philip dabbled in the high stakes game of politics, also, and became involved in the very inner circles of power on Capitol Hill, convincing the young John Fitzgerald Kennedy to go with Lyndon Johnson from Texas as his running mate for the presidency. Then, in 1963, he committed suicide after a manic depressive episode. Katherine became a widow and responsible for both *Newsweek* and the *Post* in one day.

Katherine battled her shyness and rose to the occasion, becoming the publisher of the *Post*. Diving in feet first, she saw that the *Post* had been drifting along listlessly. It needed, Katherine believed, a charismatic editor to become a first-rate example of journalistic excellence. She found him in Ben Bradlee, a hard charging investigative reporter whom she quickly named managing editor.

In 1971, the *Post* received worldwide attention when President Richard Nixon slapped a restraining order on the paper for the publishing of the Pentagon Papers, revealing the United States government's involvement in the political machinery of Southeast Asia. Graham refused to back down and later emerged the victor in that skirmish when the Supreme Court decided in the *Post*'s favor.

One year later, the *Post* took the spotlight again for breaking the story of the Watergate scandal. Graham financed the Watergate investigation and stood firmly behind her editor and reporters against the White House's retaliatory measures. Her sheroism in the face of enormous pressure from friends and political players to back off from Watergate is simply astounding. She remained steadfast while the *Post*'s stock plummeted and so-called friends disappeared rather than be associated with the woman who challenged Richard Nixon and, ultimately, brought him and his house of cards down. When she retired in 1991, she was one of only two women heads of *Fortune* 500 companies.

Shirley Chisolm:
"Unbought and Unbossed"

Shirley Chisolm was a nonstop shero whose own sense of empowerment spread to everyone who came in contact with her. In 1968, Shirley Chisolm was the first black woman to be elected to Congress, a historic triumph for her gender and race. Four years later, she ran for president in the primaries.

Born in the borough of Brooklyn, New York, in 1924, she spent seven years in Barbados with her grandmother, Emily Seale. She credits the stiff upper lip, yet excellent education she received in Barbados as giving her an advantage when she returned to the United States. Shirley garnered many scholarship offers upon high school graduation, choosing Brooklyn College to study psychology and Spanish with the intention of becoming a teacher. She got involved with the Harriet Tubman Society where she developed a keen sense of black pride. Acing every course, she received a lot of encouragement to "do something" with her life. A Caucasian political science professor urged her to pursue politics, a daunting idea at the time. But the seed was planted.

After an arduous job search, Shirley finally found work at the Mount Calvary Child Center; her magna cum laude degree didn't seem to offset her color for many potential employers. She also took night classes at Columbia where she met Conrad Chisholm. They married soon after, giving her a stable foundation upon which to build her house of dreams. She continued to work in early childhood education, becoming director of several day care centers and private schools.

In the sixties, Shirley stepped into the political arena, campaigning for a seat in the state assembly in her district. She won the Democratic seat in 1964 and began the first step in a history-making career, winning again in '65 and '66. Then she decided to run for the U.S. Assembly. Even though she was up against a much more experienced candidate with deep-pocketed financial backing, Shirley prevailed; she was aware that there were 13,000 more women than men in the district and quickly mobilized the female vote. She also underwent surgery for a tumor at this time, but went back to work immediately, quickly earning a reputation as one of the most hard charging black members of the Assembly.

Even in Congress, the race issue reared its head. She was assigned to the Agricultural Committee to work with food stamp distribution because she was a black woman. Shirley didn't take this lying down and fought to get off that committee, moving on to Veteran's Affairs and, finally, Education and Labor where, she believed, she could really do some good. Known for her straight-shooting verbal style and maverick political ways, she always saw herself as an advocate for her constituency, seeking to be the voice of those traditionally overlooked by politics: Hispanics, Native Americans, drug addicts, and gay activists.

As a presidential candidate for the 1972 Democratic nomination, she placed women's rights at the center of her campaign, claiming that she was not a "gimmick" candidate, but a serious contender. Although she failed to get the nod, it did make her a national spokesperson for the civil and women's rights movements. Since then, she has helped create the National Political Congress of Black Women and has taught, lectured, and authored two books, *Unbought and Unbossed* and *The Good Fight*. Shirley Chisolm was at the forefront of obtaining real political power for African American woman.

> *"I'm the only one among you who has the balls to run for president."*
> —Shirley Chisolm to the Black Caucus members
> at the Democratic convention

Yvonne Brathwaite Burke: Political Standout

Yvonne Burke was the first black woman elected to the U.S. House of Representatives from California, serving from 1973-1978. The daughter of a janitor and a real estate agent, the Angeleno native was noted as exceptionally bright by her teachers and was sent to a "model" UCLA college prep school. The only African American student at the school, Yvonne was treated viciously by the other students, but didn't let that stop her from turning in a stellar performance. Everywhere Yvonne went, she encountered more bigotry, including the women's law sorority she was turned down by, compelling her to form an alternative women's law sorority with two Jewish law students. Starting with her election in 1972, Yvonne Brathwaite's career in Congress was equally outstanding; she was unfailingly supportive of the causes of desegregation, equal employment, and better housing. In '78, she chose to run for California State Attorney General rather than seek reelection. She currently practices law in Los Angeles. Yvonne is a visionary with the smarts and dignity to rise above the hatred she has personally experienced just for being black saying, "It's just a matter of time until we have a black governor and, yes, a black president."

Indira Gandhi:
Daughter of Destiny

]ndira Nehru Gandhi's life mirrors the divided country she governed as the first woman Prime Minster of India. She inherited a political consciousness from her nationalist grandfather Motilal Nehru and her father, India's first prime minster, Jawaharlal Nehru. The Nehrus are sometimes called India's royal dynasty, but this is a contradiction to the very ideals the Nehru family and the peaceful revolutionary Mohandas K. Gandhi believed in as they worked to end England's colonial rule over India.

As a girl, Indira witnessed up close the birth of modern, independent India under the leadership of Gandhi and her relatives. The Nehrus were a wealthy family who were moved by meeting Mohandas in 1919 to give up all their possessions and join in the struggle for independence. Indira endured the frequent jailings of Jawaharlal (and later, her mother) for nationalist activities. The young girl's role model was Joan of Arc; later she told of playing with dolls to whom she assigned patriotic roles in the fight to free India from their foreign rulers. Indira's childhood was unusual, by any means, often accompanying her father in his travels and meeting luminaries such as Albert Einstein and Ernst Toller. Indira also organized The Monkey Brigade for pre-teen revolutionaries and was, later, beaten cruelly for marching carrying India's flag. She and her family often visited Gandhi who was "always present in my life; he played an enormous role in my development."

Indira suffered depression, anxiety, and illness from her unsettled life, and at age twenty-two married Feroze Gandhi, a family friend who was a Parsee, a member of a small religious sect, and not considered appropriate for Indira, who was of the Brahmin, or priestly, caste. Arrested for their nationalist activities, both Indira and Feroze spent nine months in jail, which, Indira claimed, was the most important event of her life, strengthening her political resolve.

Upon the deaths of their great leader Gandhi and the continued bloodshed during the Partition dividing India into Hindu India and the new Muslim state of Pakistan, Indira joined India's Congress party and began to forge her own political sensibility. When India gained independence in 1947, her father became prime minister; because he was a widower, he needed Indira to act as his official hostess. During the time of her father's multiple strokes, Indira was tacitly acting as prime minister. Upon his death in 1964, Indira became president of the India National Congress. After her father's successor Lal Bahadur Shastri's brief ministry and death from heart failure, Indira won the election by a landslide and became the leader of the world's largest democracy, a leader of a country where women's rights were not a top priority. Immediately she became a role model for millions of India's women, traditionally subservient to men.

Indira inherited a land where starvation, civil wars, severe inflation, and religious revolts were a daily reality. She constantly endangered her health by working sixteen hour days trying to meet the needs of the second most populated country on earth. Her political fortunes rose and fell; she was booted out of office in 1977, only to be reelected a few years later to her fourth term as prime minister. Her controversial birth-control program is overlooked oftentimes in the criticisms that she traded political favors in order to hang onto the ministry.

Indira was constantly caught in between the warring factions and divisions of India's various provinces and interests, and the history of her ministry reads like a veritable laundry list of riots, uprisings, and revolutions all played out on partisan quicksand. Her assassination demonstrates this fully. In 1919, British troops had massacred thousands of Sikhs, a proud warrior caste, in their sacred place of worship—the Golden Temple of Amritsar. Sixty-five years later, Amritsar again ran red with the blood of Sikh extremists attempting to create a stronghold in which to make their demand for greater autonomy. When the Indian army invaded and seized back the temple, the sparks of anger flamed out of control. Across India, Sikhs were cursing the name of Gandhi, including some of her personal security guards. Four months later, Indira was shot to death by a Sikh in her garden where she was about to be interviewed by Peter Ustinov. Her son, Rajiv, became the next prime minister and met an equally violent end when a Sri Lankan Tamil woman leapt onto him and detonated a bomb she had strapped to herself.

Indira Gandhi's life is difficult to fully comprehend without a grasp of Indian history. Perhaps, the deepest understanding of her comes through consideration of her chosen role model, Joan of Arc, a model for self-sacrifice who places the interests of her country above the value of her own life, and as a woman warrior in a battle of religious politics pitting men against men. Indira Gandhi's own insistence to reporters who wanted to talk about her uniqueness as a woman prime minster speaks volumes as well: "I am not a woman. I am a human being."

Margaret Thatcher: Iron Maiden

Margaret Thatcher may draw fire from critics for her staunch conservatism, but she has the respect of the world for her no-nonsense strength and for her rise from greengrocer's daughter to the first woman prime minster of Great Britain. MT earned all her laurels through sheer hard work, studying diligently to get into Oxford where she studied chemistry and got her first taste for politics. Upon graduation, she got a law degree, married Dennis Thatcher, and had twins in short order. Her passion for conservative politics increased, and she impressed party members with her zeal and talent for debate. She won a seat in the House of Commons in 1959 and her rise in the party ranks was steady and sure, leading to her election in the eighties as Prime Minister, the first woman ever to head a major Western democracy. Vehemently anti-Communist and antiwaste, she curtailed government with a singular fervor, surprising everyone by going to war with Argentina over the Faulkland Islands. Tough as nails, Margaret explains her modus operandi thusly: "I've got a fantastic stamina and great physical strength, and I have a woman's ability to stick to a job and get on with it when everyone else walks off and leaves."

Phoolan Devi:
India's Bandit Queen

While many Indians reviled their own elected Prime Minster Indira Gandhi, they embraced Phoolan Devi, an outlaw believed to have killed sixty people in central India's Chambal Valley. While it is difficult to separate fact from fiction in the story (the male outlaw figure is a common subject of North Indian folklore, and Phoolan's tale has many of the same elements). This version is based on the story reported by Mala Sen, in her fascinating and assiduously researched biography of Devi.

Born in 1956 into a boatman subcaste, Phoolan's (which means "flowerlike" in Hindi, but she's more like a steel magnolia!) first insurrection took place when she and her sister wanted to sit in the mustard field they had worked in all day to "stop and smell the mustard blossoms." When their higher caste landlord beat them up because they wouldn't instantly leave, Phoolan watched her sister and parents nearly bleed to death. When she refused at age ten to put up with an arranged marriage to a man twenty years older, her traditionally minded village couldn't deal with it and Phoolan fell victim to a kidnapping by a group of *dacoits*; bandits to you and me. The kidnapping was just as violent as you might expect a gang of marauders to be, and she was dragged, kicked, slapped, and suffered indignities of guns aimed at her private parts and a threat to cut off her nose. It is a real testament to Phoolan's strength that she wasn't utterly broken by the repeated rapings. Phoolan's family was unable to get any help from authorities who refused to waste their time looking for their rebellious "good-for-nothing" daughter. Meanwhile, the press had a field day with the story, inventing sensational details of their own to make for a good read in the papers. One such tall tale involved Phoolan engineering her own kidnapping because she *wanted* to be with the dacoits.

Whatever happened, one year later, Phoolan took charge of the gang through her own strength of will and personal power. Mala Sen also reports that the gang (thanks to the execution of the rapists by Phoolan's champion, Vikram Mallah) turned into post-Raj Robin Hoods, giving stolen money to elderly and poor Indians. Well-embroidered accounts of Phoolan Devi's exploits were soon making her the second most famous woman in India after Indira Gandhi, who urged peaceful measures in dealing with the headline-grabbing outlaw girl.

Soon, songs about the "Rebel of the Ravines" were being composed, statues of Phoolan Devi were sold in the market next to Krishna and Kali, and millions of Indians begged for her life to be spared in the "manhunt" to bring "The Bandit Queen" in after the alleged massacre of twenty-two Hindu men by Devi's gang. Thanks to the national attention, Phoolan's capture took place safely in front of thousands of witnesses and she kept up good spirits in prison where she gave interviews, prayed, and walked unshackled. (She spent eleven years in prison without ever being charged.) India was even more delighted when they finally saw the Phoolan Devi they'd heard so much about; she is strikingly beautiful, with dark, commanding eyes and a magnificent smile. (Phoolan's fairy tale-like story contains a tragic footnote, exemplifying the place of women in a societal admixture of medieval and modern. In prison, she suffered a ruptured ovarian cyst and the presiding doctor performed a hysterectomy, admittedly to prevent "Phoolan Devi breeding more Phoolan Devis!")

Her legend lives on around the globe and Mala Sen's excellent biography has been made into an acclaimed feature film. In India and England, she has become a folk shero. At her surrender, she is reported to have said, "If I had money, I would build a house with rooms as large as the hall of this prison. But I know this is all a dream. If any woman were to go through my experience, then she too would not be able to think of a normal life. What do I know, except cutting grass and using a rifle?"

Phoolan was freed and all charges against her were dropped in 1994. In 1996, she ran for

▲ *India's national folk shero—"Bandit Queen" Phoolan Devi.*

and was elected to the Samajwadi Party, but the prejudicial odds against a lower caste woman, even an internationally famous one, are against her in the subcontinent. In August of 1997, Phoolan threatened to kill herself when the criminal charges against her were again raised. The saga of India's Bandit Queen looks to be far from over. Phoolan Devi, flowerlike goddess, is still fighting for her life.

"She was walking tall, taunting them all, answering the call . . . with her rifle by her side"—a popular Indian Phoolan Devi street song

Devi Alert

Although the reports that trickle out of India about her aren't always completely reliable, Devi-devotee Penny Arcade has a home page devoted to
the embattled shero on the World Wide Web that is updated regularly.
Stay tuned! http://www.pennyarcade.com/phoolan.html

Corazon Aquino:
Mother in the Limelight

Hot on the heels of anti-shero Imelda Marcos (or should I say hot on the 1,600 heels;
remember the 800 pairs of shoes scandal?) came Corazon Aquino, a political neo-
phyte who quietly and competently took the helm of the volatile islands nation in the
aftermath of the Marcos regime.

Cory didn't set out to run a country. Educated in the Catholic school system in
the United States and the Phillippines, she abandoned higher education to marry
Benigno Aquino, a promising politician, and served as his helpmate and mother of
their five children. Benigno opposed the martial law of Marcos and was jailed in 1972;
when he was released, the family fled to the United States, where they lived until 1983.
By this time Marcos was losing control of the reins of power and Benigno decided to
return to help agitate for his resignation. As the Aquinos stepped off the plane,
Benigno was assassinated. In that moment, Cory had to decide—turn tail or take up
the mantle of her slain husband. She chose the latter, uniting the dissidents against
Marcos. In 1986, she ran for the presidency of the Philippines, abandoning the
speeches that had been prepared for her to talk of the suffering that Marcos had

caused in her life. Although both sides declared victory, Marcos soon fled and Cory assumed power.

After the tabloid dictatorship style of the Marcos family, the widow-turned-stateswoman stunned the world with her no-nonsense manner and absolute fearlessness. Corazon Cojuangco Aquino stood fast amid the corrupt circus of Filipino politics even though coup after coup attempted to remove her from office. She quickly earned the respect of her enemies when they discovered it wasn't so easy to knock the homemaker and mother of five from her post as president of the explosively unstable nation. And she refused to live in the opulent palace the Marcos had built, proclaiming it a symbol of oppression of the poor masses by the wealthy few and chose to live in a modest residence nearby.

However, longtime leadership proved difficult. Although she was credited with drafting a new democratic constitution that was ratified by a landslide popular vote, her support dwindled in the face of chronic poverty, an overstrong military, and governmental corruption. Her presidency ended in 1992.

For her achievements and courage, Cory Aquino has received numerous honorary degrees from as diverse sources as Fordham University and Waseda University in Tokyo. Named *Time* magazine's Woman of the Year, Cory is also the recipient of many awards and distinctions including the Eleanor Roosevelt Human Rights Award, the United Nations Silver Medal, and the Canadian International Prize for Freedom. Acknowledged by the Women's International Center for her "perseverance and dedication," Corazon Aquino was honored with an International Leadership Living Legacy who "faced adversity with courage and directness."

Anita Hill:
We Always Believed You

N obody could have guessed that the televised Senate hearings on the nominations of Clarence Thomas to the U.S Supreme Court would be the top-rated show of 1991. America's collective mouth hung open in amazement at the brouhaha that brewed up around Judge Thomas' worthiness based on the charges of sexual harassment by one Anita Hill. The hearings catapulted the issue of sexual harassment in the workplace into the most hotly debated and analyzed topic of the day, one that still reverberates at the close of the decade. Prior to Anita's brave stand, sexual harassment was mainly swept under the industrial gray carpeting of most offices, but she singlehandedly forced it to the very center of the national agenda.

The nation and, indeed, the world, watched transfixed as the incredibly poised Anita revealed her experiences of Clarence Thomas as a coworker. With great dignity, she testified that Thomas kept after her to go out with him, referred to himself as "an individual who had a very large penis and . . . used a name . . . in pornographic material," asked her to see "this woman (who) has this kind of breasts that measure this size," in a seemingly endless barrage of ludicrous and lugubrious insults to her as a fellow professional. Senate hearings, usually desert dry and devoid of tabloid titillation, suddenly featured long discussions including the terms "penis" and "pubic hair."

The prelude to the media circus took place when the president announced his choice of "black Horatio Alger" Clarence Thomas as the Supreme Court replacement for the retiring Thurgood Marshall. Anita Hill, a law professor at the University of Oklahoma, contacted Harriet Grant, the Judiciary Committee's nominations counsel. She told Grant that Thomas had harassed her in a sexual and inappropriate manner when she had worked as his assistant at the Equal Employment Opportunity Commission. She had, in fact, quit the EEOC because of his behavior and gone into academia. Grant cc'd the senatorial committee on the allegations, but the Senate whipped through the approval process with nary a word about Hill's report and prepared to vote for confirmation of Thomas. Then journalist shero Nina Totenberg of national public radio and New York *Newsday*'s Timothy Phelps broke the story wide open to a shocked public. Seven women from the House of Representatives marched in protest to the Senate building demanding of the sheepish Senate committee to know why the committee had ignored Hill's complaint.

Nothing in Hill's background could have prepared her for the media onslaught. Born in 1956 as the youngest of thirteen children, she was raised in rural Oklahoma in a deeply religious family. An outstanding student, she graduated valedictorian of her integrated high school, got top honors in college, and was one of only eleven black students out of a class of 160 at Yale University Law School.

Even though Anita Hill had been promised immunity and total confidentiality, she appeared before the committee in a special session before the scrutiny of the nation. The Judiciary Committee was dismissive, as only Old Boys can be, of Anita Hill and her testimony, even going so far as to ask her if she was taking her revenge as the "woman scorned," and they suggested that she was a patsy for radical liberals and feminists. While Anita's allegations were ultimately disregarded and Clarence Thomas was voted in, Anita's grace under pressure won many admirers who protested the Thomas appointment. The

▲ *Anita Hill mesmerized the world in the Clarence Thomas senate hearing.*

controversy remained headline news for months; polls of public opinion showed Anita Hill gaining and Bush losing points as I Believe You Anita! bumper stickers appeared on thousands of cars across America. For her outspokenness, she was awarded the Ida B. Wells Award from the National Coalition of 100 Black Women and named one of *Glamour*'s Ten Women of the Year in 1991.

Anita Hill's courage of conviction made her a shero for the nineties. In her words, "I felt I had to tell the truth. I could not keep silent."

> *"You just have to tell the truth and that's the most anyone can expect*
> *from you and if you get that opportunity, you will have*
> *accomplished something."*—Anita Hill

Ten Nobel Women:
Sheroes of Peace

The Nobel Peace Prize is one of highest honors a human being can receive; I like to think of it as the designation for the truly evolved! The lore behind the prize is that Alfred Nobel was always interested in the cause of peace, but he was moved to do something about it by his friend baroness Bertha von Suttner. She became involved in the international movement against war founded in the 1890s and inspired Nobel to back it financially. By January 1893, Alfred wrote the good baroness a letter of his intentions to establish a prize for "him or her who would have brought about the greatest step toward advancing toward the pacification of Europe." Clearly this prestigious endowment has spread to include the whole world and includes women and men from many different ethnicities and backgrounds. Since 1901, ninety-six Peace Prizes have been awarded. So far, only ten women have received the laurel for a 10 percent average, but as of the last decade, women are catching up! Here are the ten priestesses of pacifism:

Baroness Bertha von Suttner was sheroic from the start when she went against her family's aristocratic ways and worked as a governess and nanny (Does that remind you of any other titled nanny turned peace activist sheroes?!) going on to write an antiwar novel *Die Waffen Nieder* (Lay Down Your Arms) and receiving the prize on the designated day of December 10, 1905.

Jane Addams received the Nobel Peace Prize in 1931 when she was near death. She had been a strong opponent of World War I and was a controversial choice for that reason; in fact, in an extremely strange pairing, her corecipient Nicholas Murray Butler had been her greatest critic. Her commitment to activism was so great she requested that the organizations she founded, Hull House and the Women's International League for Peace and Freedom (WILPF), be listed on her gravestone!

One of Jane Addams' partners in pacifism was **Emily Greene Balch** who worked with her in WILPF and took over leadership of the league upon Addams' death in 1935. In 1946, Balch received the illustrious honor wherein she was acknowledged for her practical, solution-oriented approach to peace in her special work with Slav immigrants, her staunchness in the face of being fired from Wellesley for her war protests, and her key role in obtaining the withdrawal of U.S. troops from Haiti in 1926 after a decade-long occupation.

After a gap of *thirty years* in which no women won, two sheroes took the prize for peace in 1976—**Betty Williams and Mairead Corrigan**. Williams, a Belfast housewife, and Corrigan, who had lost two children in her family to the war between the Irish Republican Army and the British soldiers, were leaders in the movement to stop the senseless violence in Northern Ireland. They were cited as having demonstrated "what ordinary people can do to promote peace."

In 1979, **Mother Teresa** was awarded the highest honor for her incredible contribution to social justice. By the age of twelve, the devout Catholic girl from Albania knew she wanted to devote her life to the poor and went to India soon after, teaching and working in the Calcutta slums. She founded a new order, The Missionaries of Charity, and continued the work that crossed all boundaries of race and religion. Her image came to symbolize kindness and spirit in action. Her tragic death one week after Princess Diana's in September of 1997 saw the loss of two great advocates for the poor, the sick, and the disenfranchised.

1982's Nobel Peace Prize went to **Alvar Myrdal** of Mexico who shared it with her countryman Alfonso Garcia Robles, both of whose work in the disarmament movement has gone far to lessen the treat of global destruction. Myrdal has worked with peace and social justice since the thirties, and she has written one of the most important books on the subject. She had been passed over (along with many other peaceful sheroes) by the Nobel Committee for mostly male choices until such a hue and cry arose that the prize pickers listened! Alva described her Nobel moment as her "peak" but said the "Norwegian People's Prize" was "dear to her heart."

Aside from Mother Teresa, the Nobel shero receiving the most publicity has to be Burmese Buddhist and political prisoner **Aung San Suu Kyi** who won in 1991. Deeply inspired by the work of Mahatma Gandhi, Aung San based her life and actions on what she calls "a profound simplicity," delineated beautifully in her book *Freedom From Fear*. Her dedication to freeing the people of Burma from their government under a brutally oppressive dictatorship has gained the respect of the world. Aung San was jailed after winning an election that opposed the military government of Myanmar (Burma). She is not only the national shero of her country but of the world, for her unswerving courage in the face of a cruel and corrupt power.

Rigoberta Menchu Tum was a controversial choice the Nobel committee made in 1992. A Mayan Indian and Guatemalan native, Tum was criticized by many conservative pundits for her involvement in the guerilla rebel group of her country; they saw it as being in conflict with the Nobel ethics of commitment to nonviolence. The truth is, however, that even though her father and many friends and fellow *campesinos* were burned alive in a peaceful protest at the Mexican embassy, she never participated in violence and has always worked toward peace and justice for her country within the social political arenas, explaining "we understood revolutionary in the real meaning of the word 'transformation.' If I had chosen the armed struggle, I would be in the mountains now."

Jody Williams received the Nobel Peace Prize for her work with the International Campaign to Ban Landmines (ICBL) on October 10, 1997, the day after her forty-seventh birthday. Jody, a frank, down-to-earth New Englander has pulled off the impossible—getting governments around the world to agree to help in the clean up of landmine fields across the globe. Unlike many other eco-political issues, this one has a very human face to it—hundreds of people, many children, are maimed and crippled for life with limbs simply blown off when they step on a landmine as they play or do farm work. It is thanks to Jody's work with ICBL that the landmine crisis received international publicity that helped catapult it to resolution. Jody received some very important assistance in drawing the problem to the world's attention from another shero, Princess Diana, whose disastrous death in Paris three months before the Nobel award prevented her from seeing the fruition of her landmine work in Jody's triumph.

Musical Sheroes:
Taking Center Stage

The recent hype about women breaking onto the music scene in the mid-nineties is pretty tiresome. Women have been making music since hominid Lucy rattled the skulls and drummed with the bones of her ancestors in the grasslands of ancient Africa. The truth of the matter is more likely to be a scared and sagging music industry, running on the empty recyclings of male-dominated rock, finally realizing that record-buying audiences want more. The breakaway successes of Alanis Morissette, k.d. lang, Jewel, Melissa Etheridge, and legions of other enormously talented women proved the point. A definite paradigm shift is taking place, but the women on center stage today are standing on foundations built by women who fought to get the opportunity to perform, get recorded, get air play, and just get a chance. For example, Billie Holiday, an enormous talent, struggled throughout her career and paid the price for the ill-treatment she received as a black woman insisting on being taken seriously for her music. Janis Joplin, similarly tragic and equally awe-inspiring, also met a tragic end with drugs and booze. She was another light who burned too brightly, surrounded by parasitic moths and living with the crushing pressure of maintaining authenticity as a superstar commodity.

Thankfully, things have changed. Women now keep the copyrights to their music, run their own record companies, call the shots, direct the videos, and manage their money with the strategic elan of MBAs. Madonna has gone from eating garbage and squatting in New York City to become an icon and mogul. Tina Turner turned the tables on an abusive Svengali Ike, started meditating, and came back with a vengeance for an amazing career as a seemingly ageless R & B goddess. Ani DiFranco took the "DIY" (do it yourself) credo all the way with Righteous Babe Records, her own label, which she started at age fifteen. The Lilith Fair, an all-woman traveling rock show, stunned the world with sold out shows in every city and a media firestorm that blew the other, mostly male festivals like, Lollapolooza, Horde, out of the water.

Offstage, the business of music has seen a power shift, as well. Sylvia Rhone was the first woman ever to run a record company, Elektra, by pushing up through the ranks of an industry she describes as having a "pimp mentality." Today, several women are at the top of the ranks of Sony, MTV, and Epic Records. However, these women's success stories are cautionary tales of working with the constraints of boy's club corporations where women are mere window dressing or products sold with an emphasis on sex. Pope-bashing radical feminist singer and proud mother Sinead O'Connor (whose record company tried to tell her she couldn't have children because it would interfere with record promotion and who withdrew from the Grammys when she discovered that misogynist comedian Andrew Dice Clay was a presenter) offers this advice to women: "Learn to say no straight off. You don't have to look like the makeup artist wants. Trust your instincts. One can't make an omelet without breaking eggs . . ." Rapper shero Mary J. Blige, puts it most succinctly, with her cut-to-the-chase wisdom for women: "Don't let anybody stomp you out!"

Big Mama Thornton:
Lady Sang the Blues

Willie Mae "Big Mama" Thornton checked out for good when the New Wave washed onto the music scene, dying of heart and liver failure in 1984. After fifty-seven years of hard living and a good deal of hard drinking, she was a mere shadow of herself in her last year, weighing only ninety-seven pounds. At the height of her career, Thornton held center stage singing, drumming, and blowing harmonica with rhythm 'n blues luminaries Muddy Waters, B. B. King, Eddie Vinson, and Janis Joplin.

Her most remembered contribution to music history will always be the song "Hound Dog," a number one hit in 1953 written especially for her by Jerry Leiber and Mike Stoller. It was as much her appearance as her blues style that influenced the writing of "Hound Dog." "We wanted her to growl it," Stoller later told *Rolling Stone*. Three years later, Elvis Presley covered Big Mama's tune and took her signature song for his own. Like so many other black blues stars, she wasn't mainstream enough; by 1957 her star had fallen so low she was dropped by her record label. And, like many other blues stars of the day, she was inadequately compensated for her work; although, her incredible, soul-ripping rendition of "Hound Dog" sold two million copies, Big Mama received only one royalty check for $500!

Unstoppable, however, she hit the road, jamming with fellow blues masters, amazing audiences across

▲ *Big Mama Thornton: this raging talent never earned any royalties!*

America. Big Mama's success came from her powerful presence on stage. She had begun performing publicly in the forties as an Atlanta teen where she danced in variety shows and in Sammy Green's Hot Harlem Review. Thornton's own musical heroes were Bessie Smith and Memphis Minnie, whom she always held as great inspirations for her decision to pursue music as a career. Thornton was a completely self-taught musician, learning through watching, "I never had no one teach me nothing. I taught myself to sing and to blow the harmonica and even to play drums, by watching other people."

James Brown, Otis Redding, The Rolling Stones, and Janis Joplin helped create a resurgence of interest in the blues in the sixties. Janis covered "Ball and Chain," making that a huge hit to millions of fans who never knew Thornton's version. In a sad repetition of history, the royalties to Big Mama's "Ball and Chain" were contracted to her record company, meaning she didn't get a dime from the sales of Joplin's cover of the tune. However, because of the popularization, artists like Big Mama began to enjoy a crossover audience and the spotlight they had previously been denied by a record-buying public producers believed preferred black music sanitized by singers such as Presley.

With a new interest in the real thing, Big Mama started performing at blues festivals around the world, resulting in classic recordings such as "Big Mama in Europe," "Big Mama Thornton with the Chicago Blues Band Including Guitarist Buddy Guy" and "Stronger than Dirt," where she was backed by Muddy Waters, James Cotton, and Otis Spann. "Stronger than Dirt" featured Thornton's interpretations of Wilson Pickett's "Funky Broadway" and Bob Dylan's "I Shall Be Released." Big Mama's final albums were "Sassy Mama!" and "Jail," a live album recorded in prisons. In 1980, Thornton, Sippie Wallace, and Koko Taylor headlined at the unforgettable "Blues Is a Woman" show at the Newport Jazz Festival. Although Big Mama barely made enough money to live on through her music, her contribution to blues was enormous. She died penniless and alone in a Los Angeles boardinghouse, decimated by drink and disappointed by her ill-treatment from the music industry. But she received tremendous respect from her peers and influenced dozens of musicians, even to this day.

"At what point did rhythm 'n blues start becoming rock and roll? When the white kids started to dance to it."—Ruth Brown

Peggy Jones:
Lady Bo

A woman who followed her own star and in so doing shattered several musical stereotypes, Peggy Jones had music in her soul from the beginning; a dancer in her toddler years, she had performed in Carnegie Hall by the age of nine. As a youngster, the New Yorker was intrigued by the ukelele and discovered she had a talent for playing it; later she switched to guitar when she felt the ukelele might seem silly. It never occurred to her that it would seem unusual for a woman to play guitar in the forties. "Little did I know that a female playing any instrument was like a new thing. I was breaking a lot of barriers."

By the age of seventeen, she was producing and cutting singles such as "Honey Bunny Baby/Why Do I Love You?" and "Everybody's Talking/I'm Gonna Love My Way." In the late fifties, she and her friends and future husband Bobby Bakersfield formed The Jewels, a band made up of men and women, very unusual for the time; even more unique, the band included both black and white members. The Jewels got a lot of flack for their disregard for gender and racial boundaries, but they persisted in performing to enthusiastic audiences. Jones recalls fighting past the objections, "I just hung in there because this is what I wanted to do, and I had a real strong constitution as to the way I thought I should go about it."

Peggy's singular instrumentation is one of the components of Bo Diddley's successful albums and national tours throughout the fifties and sixties. Diddley, famous for his signature rhythm, saw Jones walking down the street with her guitar one day, and, ever the savvy showman, recognized that having a pretty girl playing guitar in his band would be a very good thing for ticket and record sales. Peggy was ushered into the world of professional musicianship full-time with Diddley's touring band. She learned a great deal, perfecting her guitar playing to the point where Diddley himself was a bit threatened by her hot licks. She also saw the hardships of the road and experienced firsthand the color line that existed even for music stars. When they hit the South in the hearse they toured in, the band often had to stay in nonwhite hotels and had to use separate bathrooms for "coloreds." They even figured out a way to cook in the car when they couldn't find a restaurant that would service black people.

However, Jones wasn't content with just backup and line note credits and took a hiatus from the nonstop Bo Diddley road show. She again wrote her own material and performed with The Jewels again. In the late sixties, she formed her own band, "The Family Jewel," after divorcing her husband when he became abusive. The group still performs on its own and occasionally backs Bo Diddley.

Peggy Jones was a true pioneer for women in music. Because of her, the idea of a woman playing guitar—or any instrument in a band—became much more acceptable.

"I don't think I went in with any attitude that 'Oh, oh, I'm a girl, they're not going to like my playing.' So probably that might have been my savior, because I just went in as a musician and expected to be accepted as a musician." —Peggy Jones

Joan Baez: Not Just Blowin' in the Wind

Folk shero and guitarist Joan Baez was one of the women musicians who benefitted from Peggy Jones' career. Joan tapped her muse young—as a college student at Boston University. In 1960, at age nineteen, she became a household name overnight with her album *Joan Baez*. Fiercely political, her recordings such as "We Shall Overcome" point to her alignment with civil rights, and she was one of the best known Vietnam War protesters and worked for the No Nukes campaign, as well. Oddly enough, one of the causes Joan never aligned herself with was feminism. "I don't relate with

▲ *Joan Baez: her songs were anthems of the Civil Rights movement.*

feminism. I see the whole human race as being broken and terribly in need, not just women." With her inspirational voice and her long dark hair, she gave a generation of women a model of activism, personal freedom, and self-determination. Baez lives by her own light—and in so doing, encourages us all to follow our consciences.

Yoko Ono:
Avant Savant

One of the most controversial figures in rock history, Yoko Ono was an acquired taste for those willing to go with her past the edge of musical experimentalism. Unfairly maligned as the woman who broke up the Beatles, she is a classically trained musician and was one of New York's most cutting edge artists before the Fab Four even cut a record. Born in Tokyo in 1933, she moved to New York in 1953 and attended Sarah Lawrence, but even then had trouble finding a form to fit into; her poetry was criticized for being too long, her short stories too short. Then she was befriended by avant-garde composers such as Arnold Schoenberg and John Cage.

Soon, Yoko was making a splash with her originality in post-Beatnik Greenwich Village, going places even Andy Warhol hadn't dared with her films of 365 nude derrieres, her performance art (inviting people to cut her clothes off her), and her bizarre collages and constructions. Called the "High Priestess of the Happening," she enthralled visitors to her loft with such art installations as tossing dried peas at the audience while whirling her long hair. Yoko Ono had an ability to shock, endless imagination, and a way of attracting publicity that P. T. Barnum himself would've envied!

When John Lennon climbed the ladder on that fateful day to peer at the artful affirmation Yoko created in her piece "Yes," rock history was made. Their collaborations—The Plastic Ono Band, Bed-Ins, Love-Ins, Peace-Ins, and son Sean Lennon—have created a legacy that continues to fascinate a world that has finally grudgingly accepted and respected this bona fide original. Yoko's singing style—howling and shrieking in a dissonant barrage—has been a major influence on The B52s and the recent spate of gr-r-r-r-l bands.

Now Yoko Ono and her talented son, Sean, tour together and work on behalf of the cases they are committed to—the environment, peace, and Tibet. Ono, whose sweet speaking voice belies the steely strength underneath that has enabled her to endure for so long, explains her sheroic journey in the preface she contributed to Gillian G. Gaar's excellent book on women in music, *She's a Rebel.* In it, she relates her pain at her father's discouragement of her dream of becoming a composer, doubting her "aptitude" because of her gender. " 'Women may not be good creators of music, but they're good at interpreting music' was what he said." Happy that times have changed, she points to the valiant efforts made by "women artists who kept making music despite overwhelming odds till finally the music industry had to realize that women were there to stay."

In retrospect, Yoko Ono was breaking real musical ground when others were cranking out bubble gum pop and imitating—who else—The Beatles. Yoko's feminism gets lost in the shuffle of the attention to her as an iconoclast. She was an enormous influence on awakening John's interest in the women's movement and together they attended the international feminist conference in June of 1973 and together wrote songs inspired by the woman's movement, including "Woman is the Nigger of the World." Much of Yoko's musical output in the seventies was on the theme of feminism; her song "Sisters O Sisters" is one of her finest works, a reggae-rhythmed number. Yoko's sheroism lies in her intense idealism and her commitment to making this a better world.

"I'm a Witch. I'm a Bitch. I don't care what you say."
—Yoko Ono in 1973

Aretha Franklin:
Earning Our Respect

A preacher's daughter, Aretha Franklin started her musical career early, appearing with her famous dad, Reverend Clarence LaVaugh Franklin, at Detroit's New Baptist Church. She is a talented musician who eschewed piano lessons so she could experiment with her own style of playing. By the age of eight, in 1950, Aretha electrified her father's congregation with her first gospel solo; by fourteen, she'd cut her first gospel record, "Songs of Faith." Encouraged by her father and his circle of friends and acquaintances, which included Dinah Washington, Reverend James Cleveland, Mahalia Jackson, Clara Ward, Sam Cooke, and Art Tatum, the budding gospel great had her eyes on the glittery prize of pop stardom. She decided to move to New York and pursue her dream in 1960.

The following year she had an album, *Aretha,* on Columbia, which positioned her as a jazz artist, covering classics like "God Bless the Child," "Ol' Man River," and "Over the Rainbow." Franklin went on to record ten albums with Columbia, while record execs waffled about how to package her. Jerry Wexler of Atlantic Records was a fan of Aretha and signed her immediately when her contract with Columbia ran out. Wexler, rightly, saw Aretha as an R & B singer. She agreed. Her debut album on Atlantic, *I Never Loved a Man,* contained the hit "Respect," which catapulted Franklin to number one on both the pop and the R & B charts. "Respect" became an anthem in 1967 for both feminists and black activists.

"Respect" was just the beginning of a chain of hits for the singer: "Baby, I Love You," "Natural Woman," and "Chain of Fools" came hot on the heels of the international smash hit, and soon Aretha was dubbed the "Queen of Soul" and reigned over the music world with the power and authority of her god-given gift.

Aretha was inspired to sing, rather than be a church pianist when she heard Clara

Ward. "From then on I knew what I wanted to do—sing! I liked all of Miss Ward's records." She also idolized Dinah Washington and recorded a tribute album in 1964 after Washington's tragic death at the peak of her prime. Much like Washington did for Bessie Smith, Aretha did an amazing and moving set of covers to honor the brilliance and glory of the Detroit diva entitled "Unforgettable." And it is—as is her 1985 duet with Annie Lennox, summing up the sherodom of legends of women: "Sisters Are Doin' It for Themselves." Amen, Sisters!

Dinah Washington: Legendary Voice

Rolling Stone journalist Gerry Hershey makes the claim, "If there is a paramount body for evidence to support the feminist poster 'Sisterhood is powerful,' it is Dinah Washington's 1958 LP tribute to the Empress, *The Bessie Smith Songbook*." Dinah Washington is one of the all-time great vocalists who immediately took ownership of any song she sang. In addition to a great set of pipes, she had a good head for business, running a restaurant in Detroit and a booking agency, Queen Attractions, where she signed talent like Muhammad Ali and Sammy Davis, Jr. Able to juggle many different gambits, Washington also dominated the stage of the Flame Show Bar and Detroit's Twenty Grand Club where future superstars Marvin Gaye, Diane Ross, and Aretha Franklin sat enthralled, watching a master at work. Motown was just gearing up when Dinah Washington died accidentally of an unfortunate combination of pills and alcohol. A legend in her own time, she is rumored to have married as many as nine times before her untimely demise at age thirty-nine. Dinah Washington, one of the most gifted singers to have ever held a microphone, lived large, predated the excess of rock stars with peroxide wigs, and a home filled with gorgeous cut crystal chandeliers, and toilet-seat covers made from mink!

Joni Mitchell:
The Lady of the Canyon

Nearly every significant contemporary musician, male or female, cites Joni Mitchell as a major influence. Born in Alberta to a Royal Canadian officer and a school teacher in 1943, Roberta Joan Anderson contracted polio at nine and spent much time inside her own head during her lonely convalescence. She remained introspective throughout her life and developed a love of the arts that informs her sensibility still. Like other fifties teens, Joni danced to Elvis, Chuck Berry, and the Kingston Trio, buying a guitar to sing at Wednesday dance parties. She lost her taste for art school when the classes appeared to be assembly-line training for commercial artists. Instead she started singing in Toronto cafes where she met and married fellow singer Chuck Mitchell, a liaison that lasted for two years. Upon the breakup of their marriage, she rebounded to New York where she tried her hand at professional songwriting. She was soon successful; her material was selected by Tom Rush, Judy Collins, and Buffy Saint-Marie.

Like sister-shero Carol King in her opus *Tapestry,* the songwriter recorded some tracks of her own with great success. Joni Mitchell's late sixties album *Ladies of the Canyon* was a moody sensation, followed immediately by *Blue, Court and Spark* and a subsequent catalog of impressive diversity and size. She branched out from her folk

origins into jazz, blues, and electronic music, composing, singing, and recording, among other eclectic
works, a vocal tribute to Charles Mingus. Joni Mitchell
became a musician's and critic's darling (though some
dismissed her more avant-garde work as self-indul-
gent noise) and a favorite with progressive radio listeners.

Cool and ethereally beautiful, Joni's personal life
drew much attention from the press, embarrassing her
and her lovers with exposés tracking her numerous
liaisons, including those with rockers Graham Nash,
Jackson Browne, and horn player Tom Scott. This was
echoed recently in extensive coverage of her reunion
with the daughter she gave up for adoption in infancy.

Joni Mitchell, who thinks of herself as a poet of
the prairies, has left an indelible mark on twentieth-
century music herstory. Her smart, ironic, saturnine
music is played by the serious listeners and musicians
of each generation that comes along. For her part, Joni
prefers simplicity, clarity, truth. "For a while it was
assumed that I was writing women's music. Then men began to notice that they saw
themselves in the songs, too. A good piece of art should be androgynous."

▲ *Joni Mitchell: musician and
inspiration to a generation.*

> *"A man in the promotion department criticized my music for its
> lack of masculinity. They said I didn't have any balls. Since when do
> women have balls anyway? Why do I have to be like that?"*—Joni Mitchell

Alison Steele:
Song of the Nightbird

Alison broke important ground for women in radio when she took "wing" on the airwaves in the 1960s as the first female disc jockey at a major radio station."I listened to her faithfully," says author Joan Steinau Lester. "She was absolutely fantastic. At the time, I only knew I liked her and the show. It was only years later that I realized she'd broken ground for women in a male-dominated industry."

Progressive rock radio was becoming the hottest sound across the nation and WNEW was one of the top stations in the nation. Alison was well on her way to a very Mary Tyler Moore-type career in TV, starting by leading a morning exercise program on TV and climbing her way up the ladder to "weather girl." When AM and FM radios split apart instead of simulcasting, competitive radio stations were forced to hire another staff to man the FM stations, putting many in a bind for salaries. Alison recalls that the standard rate for AM jocks at the time was $150,000 a year while the FM scale was a mere $125.00 a week. Management at WNEW figured they could hire an all-woman FM crew and stay within the standard FM pay scale!

Alison and her companion women disc jockeys, mostly actresses and models, made their debut on July 4, 1966. Alison was nearly the only one with any previous experience in any realm of broadcasting. By September 1967, the all-woman stable of jocks was out of a job for a reason that Alison herself puts most succinctly, "America, New York, was not ready for lady DJs!" Thanks to creativity and experience in the world of entertainment, Alison wasn't let go—the only woman to have survived. She had been experimenting within her on-air time trying angles that kept the listeners interest high—theater reviews, celebrity interviews, and lots of high energy personality. When management found in a pre-purge survey that 90 percent of the listeners knew her name and enjoyed her show they made the smart decision to keep her on board.

Along with drastic personnel changes, the station management also made a format change to progressive rock. Alison was out of familiar terrain with rock music, as was the remaining all-male staff and the all-male management. When Alison asked for guidance, she was given the precise and, as it turned out, appropriate advice to simply "do her thing." They gave her the graveyard shift, too—midnight to 6:00 A.M. The ever-intrepid Alison figured her nighttime listeners were a special breed of insomniacs, lonely people, and assorted other nocturnal types. "I felt that night was a very special time." She knew from personal experience that emotions intensify at night—loneliness, depression, and illness. Alison's sensitivity to people paid in spades, she reached out and connected to her listeners by creating this special persona, The Nightbird, and the listeners responded overwhelmingly. "I felt that if I could make this bond visible between people who are feeling things at night, then I'd have something going." She put all of her creativity into her alter ego with high drama, fantasy, and many completely unique elements the likes of which nighttime radio had never heard Listeners were hooked after her jazzy intro with the sound of softly fluttering wings and the poetic intro Alison had written ending with "as the Nightbird lifts her wings and soars above the earth into another level of comprehension, where we exist only to feel. Come fly with me, Alison Steele, The Nightbird at WNEW-FM until dawn."

The phones at the station rang off the hook that first night. Station management told her she had a "little hit" and then her male boss told her he would tell her how to do it. Instead of being congratulated for originality and the instant popularity of her new show, Alison was treated like a loose cannon and they tried really hard to mold her and her show into something less unique and more like the shows all the other DJs, all men at this point, were doing. Alison stuck to her guns and refused to change the Nightbird only to be buried even further into the night, beginning at 2:00 A.M.! Alison's stories include the station's refusal to buy a step stool so she could reach the records on the top shelf. The response to the most popular DJ at the station was a threat to hire "a taller person."

Alison went on the win Billboard's "FM Personality of the Year" in 1978, the first woman to receive this honor. Although she was enormously popular, she was regarded with resentment by many of her fellow jocks. In fact, the station made very little effort to clue Alison in to just how important she was to the station. WNEW was the top station in the country in the hot new category of progressive rock. They were also beloved in their own backyard of New York and began doing public appearances including one at a concert in Madison Square Garden. This was really the eye-opener. Alison loves to tell this story, "I was the last person to be introduced. So they were all on stage when they were introduced, Alison Steele, 'the Nightbird,'" The six male DJs who had been introduced before her had to stand there and eat crow while the entire crowd stood and cheered and screamed and clapped for their favorite DJ, Alison, The Nightbird.

Sheroes don't always get to reap the rewards of their actions during their lifetimes. For Alison, this standing ovation from 20,000 fans who adored her courage and creativity was music to her ears. For proof of Alison Steele's popularity, look no further than the 70's TV show, "B. J. and the Bear," which boasted a female trucker character named Angie who worked as a radio DJ at night with the air name of "The Nightingale."

> *"It was my moment of glory, I worked hard for it. I took a lot of s****
> *over it. And I enjoyed every minute of it."* —Alison Steele

Helen Reddy: "I Am Strong. I Am Invincible."

Along with Led Zeppelin, art rockers Yes and Fairport Convention, one of the artists Alison Steele played on her nationally popular radio show was Helen Reddy. Both of these women struggled for years to make it. Reddy's songs were embraced as anthems for a nation of women collectively committed to shattering the glass ceiling. For the time, Helen Reddy's achievement was stunning. She wrote a hard-core feminist song and took it to the top of the charts; "I Am Woman" was the number one hit on the charts in 1972. In clear ringing tones, Helen declared a message that empowered and encouraged women around the world, "I am woman, hear me roar. I am too strong to ignore . . . if I have to, I can do anything. I am strong. I am invincible!"

Sing it, Sister!

Bonnie Raitt:
Born to Sing the Blues

Born in 1949 in Burbank to a show biz family, Bonnie Raitt plays the slide guitar like she was born in the Blue Ridge Mountains. Her first exposure to the music scene was classical piano (her mother's forte), her father's Broadway show tunes, and the Beach Boy harmonies she grew up with. A Christmas gift changed Bonnie's life—at age eight, she received a guitar and worked diligently at getting good at playing it. The first time she heard Joan Baez, Bonnie went the way of folk and moved to Cambridge, Massachusetts, to be a part of the folkie coffeehouse scene. Unfortunately for her, folk music was on its

▲ *Bonnie Raitt: after years of performing on the road, her sucess came in the "nick of time."*

last legs. Instead she hooked up with Dick Waterman, a beau who just happened to manage the careers of Bonnie's musical icons: Son House, Fred McDowell, Sippie Wallace, and Muddy Waters. By the age of twenty, she was playing with Buddy Guy and Junior Wells—opening for the Rolling Stones with the two blues greats.

Bonnie's road to fame, however, was very long and winding. It had to come on her terms. Always more interested in artistic integrity than commercial success, she had exacting standards and tastes. She demanded authenticity in playing the blues she loved and reinterpreting those riffs through the influences of country and rock. She didn't play the game and, a musician's musician, she rarely got radio air play. Thus she made her living traveling the country, performing in small clubs. Bonnie was also very outspoken on political causes. Raised as a Quaker, she has always been involved in political causes, doing many benefit concerts; in 1979, she cofounded Musicians United for Safe Energy.

The stress of the road, and of being a novelty in the music industry—a female blues guitarist—eventually took its toll and Bonnie drowned her sorrows for a time in drugs and booze. In the mid-eighties, when her record label dumped her, she bottomed out, became clean and sober, and made the climb back up. In 1989, her smash album "Nick of Time" won her a Grammy and garnered sales in excess of four million.

Since then, she hasn't stopped making her great earthy blend of blues, folk, pop, and R & B, or working on behalf of the causes that are meaningful to her. Happily married since 1991 to actor Michael O'Keefe, Bonnie Raitt is a consummate musician who loves to perform live, loves to pay homage to the blues greats, and continues to speak her mind. In an interview in *Rolling Stone,* she laid it on the line about the current looks-dominated music industry: "In the 70s, all these earthy women were getting record deals—you didn't have to be some gorgeous babe. There's been some backsliding since."

> *"Any guy who has a problem with feminists is signaling*
> *a shortage in his pants. If I had to be a woman before men*
> *and women were more equal, I would've shot somebody*
> *and been in jail."*—Bonnie Raitt

Melissa Etheridge:
The Mouth that Roared

Melissa is beloved for the great music she makes, but she achieved eternal sheroism with her album "Yes, I Am," a public coming-out and celebration of her lesbianism. An ebullient spirt who can sing, play killer guitar, and write hit songs by the droves, Melissa Etheridge hails from Kansas and at thirty-six, embraced the shared motherhood her child with her partner of ten years, film maker Julie Cypher. Melissa's personal shero is Janis Joplin, and she's developing a film project in which she hopes to portray the Texas rock legend. Etheridge, who has enjoyed the changing tide for women in the music industry, delights in the success of musicians she respects: Edie Brickell, Tracy Chapman, Toni Childs, Natalie Merchant, Michelle Shocked, and the

Indigo Girls, all who sell records by the millions. Even a few years ago, Etheridge remembers that rock radio jocks claimed they could only play one woman a day or risk losing their male listeners. "All of a sudden the whole lid was blown off . . . people were coming to our concerts, and they were requesting our songs on the radio, and radio changed. That's the way America works. The public ultimately says 'This is what we want.' The world was ready for strong women's inspired music." And Melissa Etheridge was at the forefront of the revolution!

▶ *Melissa Ethridge: brilliant rock musician and symbol of lesbian pride.*

Madonna:
The Cultural Chameleon

Has there been anyone in American culture who has remade herself as often—or as well—as Madonna? Truly an artist of her own physical form and image, Madonna has been vamp, tramp, scamp; been a Brooke Shields look-alike, a Marilyn Monroe look-alike, an Evita look-alike and a Madonna (the original) look-alike. Her well publicized romances with Sean Penn, Warren Beatty, and her trainer Carlos Leon; the Material Girl; Girlie Show; and Sex Kitten—these incarnations almost seem like different women's lives. And in each of them, Madonna has evoked controversy.

She's been a target for her open approach to sex and the presence of eroticism in her work. Her sheroism as a gay rights and AIDS activist received much less press than her pointy bras did. Madonna was threatened with jail on several occasions for her progay stance; she took the challenge and remained steadfast in her solidarity with the gay community.

Madonna Louise Veronica Ciccone was born into a staunchly Catholic home in Michigan in 1958. Her mother was extremely Puritanical; before she died when Madonna was six, she taught her that pants that zip up the front were sinful. By the time Madonna was a teen, she had fame on the brain and escaped to New York City as soon as possible to make it happen. Struggling as a dancer, she lived as a squatter until she hit the big time with "Lucky Star" in 1984. Since then, she has sold more than 100 million records, has appeared in fifteen films, had twenty-nine top ten hits, and penned a very controversial book, *Sex*.

Now on the right side of forty, Madonna has matured into her full glory. Beautiful, powerful, and unflinchingly honest, Madonna has come into her own, removed the many masks, and dared to reveal her heart. Motherhood suits her well, and she has flourished as a businesswoman with her successful Maverick Records. After her highly praised performance as Evita in the musical drama, Madonna no longer has to prove herself in any arena and is relaxed, confident, and grounded. She is also more vibrant than ever, looking back over her Manhattan days as a starving squatter, her hard-earned stardom and musing at the changes daughter Lourdes Maria Ciccone Leon brought to her life. "Becoming a mother, I just have a whole new outlook on life. I see the world as a much more hopeful place." What is next in store for the former Material Girl? Stay tuned.

"I knew every word to Court and Spark; *I worshiped her when I was in high school.* Blue *is amazing. I would have to say of all the women I've heard, she had the most profound effect on me from a lyrical point of view."*
—Madonna on pensive poetess and musical shero Joni Mitchell.

Queen Latifah: Playing with the Big Boys

When Jersey girl Dana Owens renamed herself Queen Latifah and started rapping, she broke the barriers in the very male world of hip-hop. Taking up the mantle of an African Queen, her music efforts—*Ladies First, All Hail the Queen, Nature of Sistah*, and *Black Reign*—proved to everyone that women could rap, rap well, and find a huge audience across gender lines. Queen Latifah crossed over mediums, as well, starring in the popular television series *Living Single* and in feature films *Set if Off, Jungle Fever,* and *Juice* for starters. She paved the way for a new wave of female rappers such as breakout hip-hop stars Foxy Brown and Lil' Kim, with the intention of establishing a woman-positive place within the musical style she claims is to the eighties and nineties what rock and roll was to the fifties and sixties. "My thing was to start with the ladies and get the self-esteem up."

Courtney Love:
The Girl with the Most Cake

Compared to Madonna and Yoko Ono and vilified by none other than Camille Paglia, Courtney Love is another chameleon—punk turned glamour grrrrl who set the world on its ear with her amazing portrayal of Althea Flynt in *The People vs Larry Flynt*.

Love had lived a lot of life in a short amount of time. Born to San Francisco hippies in 1964, Love renamed herself and traveled in the mid-80s international punk circuit, playing bit parts in the filmmaker Alex Cox's prophetic *Sid and Nancy* and *Straight to Hell* before settling in Los Angles and stripping for a living. In 1989 she formed the band, Hole. Ironically, Hole's album "Pretty on the Inside" was selling twice as well as husband Kurt Cobain's band Nirvana's debut "Bleach," although Nirvana got all the press.

With "Smells Like Teen Spirit" from Nirvana's second effort *Nevermind*, Courtney and Kurt became the gods of grunge and grappled with fame, authenticity, and drugs. Upon Cobain's Seattle suicide by gunshot in 1994, Courtney acted out her pain publicly. When Hole lost their excellent bassist Kirsten Pfaff to a heroin overdose, Love hired Melissa Auf der Maur to play bass guitar. The world watched Courtney Love's cartharsis in the tour for Hole's second album, the appropriately titled *Live Through This*. The world started to listen, too, in a big way. Hole started selling records and getting the long overdue respect for Love's songwriting, raw and powerful singing, and fearless stage diving.

▲ *Courtney Love: controversial chameleon and "third wave feminist" punk.*

Love, whose post-modern "*Whatever Happened to Baby Jane*" tatters had been her trademark, surprised everyone recently with a 180-degree style-switch and much-hyped "makeover." Courtney responded by saying, "Somebody wrote, 'How can she rock in a Versace gown?' Well, easy, let me show you." No one should really have been surprised, though. Courtney Love is the best at throwing the unexpected left-curve. A bundle of contradictions, she is a searcher, a doer, a thinker, a self-described "militant feminist," who can quote Dickens or Dickenson, deconstruct Camille Paglia's occasionally obtuse critical theory, and can hold forth on any subject from her daughter Frances Bean Cobain (whom she dotes on) to Buddhism (which she practices) to Jungian archetypes (which fascinates her) rather eloquently, punctuated of course with a healthy dose of expletives. Courtney Love has courted controversy all her life in her quest to express herself and her creativity with complete, unvarnished honesty. Her phoenix-like rise from the ashes of a traumatic and abusive childhood, as well as a tragic superstar marriage to become the leader of a successful "third-wave" feminist band and a critically acclaimed actress has been awesome. Clearly, she is one to watch!

Wild Words from a Wild Thing

"I've sought the feminine all my life. I looked for female protagonists in everything. My first record was a Joan Baez record my parents gave me. [And there were] Julie London and Patsy Cline and Loretta Lynn and Tammy Wynette and Joni Mitchell—the seminal."

"When I heard my first Patti Smith record, *Horses*, it was like, the ticket's right here in my hand; I can write it. It's a free zone."

"Are you in a Bette Davis mood? Are you in a Stevie Nicks mood? They're like goddesses."

"In the pinnacle of my rock stardom, I was probably part of this archetype . . . almost like Artemis: that very free androgynous archetype. Amazonian."

"There have always been female gladiators of some sort."

Patti Smith: Hard Rocking Woman

A poet who also makes music, Patti Smith has more in common with Jim Morrison than she does with Courtney Love. Like Morrison, Patti Smith was a Romantic, steeped in Byronic passion, Baudelaire's dark beauty, and Rilke's angel-haunted obsessions who lived in a world of grand imaginings far from her working-class Jersey. Self-schooled and self-styled, the former factory worker found New York in the late '60s to be the perfect canvas for her artistic ambitions. She also found a soulmate in photographer Robert Mapplethorpe who turned their friendship into art with his now-famous monotints. Patti read poetry at Max's Kansas City to audiences of glittery night creatures like Andy Warhol, Edie Sedgewick and her boyfriend Sam Shepard, and hosts of trannie hookers and actresses, in a coked-up atmosphere somewhere between William Blake's Hell and an über-noir Berlin nightclub. She started by accompanying her ripping poems on a toy piano and graduated to a full band where she astonished everyone with her singing. Her song "Because the Night" became a Top 40 hit and made her a rock star. Then in 1978, she fell off stage one night, shattering her neck.

Soon after, she pulled one of the great disappearing acts of music history when she moved to Detroit, to raise two children and run a household with her husband, Fred "Sonic" Smith, the guitarist for MC5. The deaths of both Robert Mapplethorpe and Fred Smith moved Patti to music again. Her album *Gone Again* and sold-out tour established Patti as a survivor. She still reads poetry at her shows, to rapt audiences who understand her as she screams out, "Jesus died for somebody's sins, but not mine!"

Jewel:
Free to Be

Singing sensation Jewel Kilcher will turn twenty-five in the year 2000 and, in many ways, represents the new breed of women artists, born in a feminized world where women are free to pursue success, creativity, and individuality more so than ever before. Her life's story isn't typical of a pop-superstar except that she has the drive and talent. Jewel certainly hasn't been groomed or shaped and packaged by any Pygmalion-type producer. If anything, she might seem destined for remainder record bins with her neo-folk yodeling and emotionality. But she is utterly her own person, completely comfortable in that, and she clearly loves to sing.

Contrary to general opinion, Jewel was not an overnight sensation. She has played music all her life and struggled to do what she loves. Her Alaskan childhood was rough, in keeping with the "last of the frontier" lifestyle her folk-singing parents Atz and Nedra sought. Raised with her two brothers in a log cabin with no indoor plumbing, Jewel displayed a powerful voice and vocal range, yodeling under her father's tutelage and performing with him, singing for their supper since she was six. When her parents divorced after Jewel's eighth birthday, her father got custody of her. In her late teens, she moved around a lot, living in Hawaii, art school in Michigan, and finally landing in San Diego where she sang for her supper again in the coffeehouse revival, most notably in Innerchange where some record execs noticed both her ability and the devotion of her fans.

Her first record, the 1994 *Pieces of You* started slowly and built through word of mouth and a schedule of live performances that had the twenty-year-old playing every day. *Pieces of You* has since gone quintuple platinum with the breakthrough of her songs "Who Will Save Your Soul" and "You Were Meant for Me." Before getting tapped by Atlantic records, Jewel had lived in her car (her mother lived in a car, too) and ate coffeehouse freebies and, like Madonna, tells stories of looking for food in garbage cans. She has had health problems, as well, playing sometimes when she could barely stand up. Her success means that her monetary struggles are over. As she told *Rolling Stone*, "When I sold 8,000 records in one week, I remember crying on my kitchen floor, thanking God that I might not ever have to waitress or live in my car again." Though Jewel's dedication to her craft has paid in spades, she does not take her success for granted and still feels she has a long way to go to prove herself as more than a three-hit wonder.

A poet, Jewel's lyrics are carefully crafted stories, unabashedly passionate and as she says, "emotive." Jewel is not jaded, speaking and behaving with a refreshing candor that draws fire from critics unused to a star who isn't polished to a generic sheen, uttering prespun sound bites scripted by agents and managers. She chafes at the compulsion of the industry and the media to "have something that was very pure which is music, torn apart and dissected and labeled as though it weren't music." She also resists the publicity machine that wants her to lose weight and achieve a more sophisticated look in reaction to the firestorm of attention her Grammy gown garnered when Jewel, unused to the unforgiving eye of the camera, tromped on stage in a gown rendered virtually see-through by the glaring lights. (Remember Shy Di's deer-in-the-headlights photograph of a similarly gauzy school marm skirt after the announcement of her engagement to Charles? Vestal virgins on the slab before being devoured by tabloid publicity hounds, perhaps?)

Jewel's reaction to the criticism? "Who really cares, anyway? It's just a person trying to figure out her life."

Jewel's Gems

In an interview with sheroic grrrrl comic, Janeane Garofalo, Jewel talks about her musical role models:

Ella Fitzgerald: "[She] really got me into perfecting my voice and stuff . . . made me feel better to listen to her."

Patti Smith and Janis Joplin: "The REAL women in rock!"

Madonna: "My favorite quote is Liz Phair's. She said 'Madonna is the speedboat, and the rest of us are just the Go-Go's on water skis. Madonna paved the way in just so many ways. She was never afraid to break down taboos.'"

Lilith:
Women Rocking the World

Nova Scotian Sarah McLachlan had the best idea of her generation in 1997 with the Lilith Fair, a gynocentric road show that sold-out all across the country and show-cased the best minds and biggest talents of the nineties. Classical guitarist turned rocker-mystic-youth-entrepreneurial-producer, Sarah McLachlan was known for her sensitive, sensual, and poetic autobiographical songs before she put together her response to the male-dominated Lollapalooza and Horde festivals. Now she's headed for the stratosphere of pop fame. Here's a sampling of the eclectic collection of female talent she assembled:

Fiona Apple: Medusa-haired angry girl whose debut record at nineteen years old stunned audiences with its sophistication, musicality, and originality.

Jewel: Being on the same stage with one of her personal sheroes, Tracy Chapman, was thrilling, inspiring, and nervous-making, stated the modest star!

Tracy Chapman: The quietly charismatic Chapman brought every crowd to their feet. She's the epitome of women's music in spirit, heart, and soul.

Paula Cole: The answer to her hit song, "Where Have All the Cowboys Gone?" is doubtless, to the record store to buy her CD!

Ani DiFranco:
Righteous Babe

Ani DiFranco has achieved incredible success entirely on her terms without the benefit of a record label by touring, working hard at her distinctive music. A folk punk phenom, DiFranco writes about her own life, offering strength, honesty, and courage to other women—who have responded in droves. Adored by thousands of devoted fans, DiFranco is slightly uncomfortable with being idolized as a role model of female empowerment, writing about it in her "I'm No Hero." Living on her own by the age of fifteen, the guitarist-songwriter who, in her own words has "indie cred" as a "stompy-booted, butch, folk-singer chick," remembers the irritation of walking into music stores and having the clerk assume she was there to pick something up for her boyfriend. She's gladdened to see these same music stores now packed with teenage girls inspired by the success and long-overdue acceptance of women in rock. "I don't feel like the superhero that sometimes I'm made out to be, but I guess I do feel responsible to other young women, and I do feel fortunate."

Pen, Brush, and
Camera-wielding Sheroes:
Unchaining the Muses

Creative women have the advantage, no doubt about it. Before penning a poem or mustering a masterpiece, women have no need to invoke any semidivine beings to give them a good idea. Women embody their own muse. Tapping this inner resource has unleashed an artistry that has changed the world many times over. The impulse to make art, immortalize a moment in time with a photograph, or express the ineffable with poetry and fiction has led many women to make forceful statements. Some powerful truths that couldn't have been expressed in any other way have come through the artistic enterprise, say, of Diane Arbus shooting pictures of the mundane, the bizarre, and the unutterably human. Russian-born Louise Nevelson began sculpting and, in so doing, reshaped the art world, while Harriet Beecher Stowe is credited by none other than Honest Abe Lincoln himself with having picked up her pen and starting the Civil War!

Throughout herstory, room of her own or not, women have written, painted, danced, composed, and shot (as in a shutter), expressing both inner feelings and artistic vision. Eighteenth-century British novelist Jane

Austen, thanks to some sumptuously produced and well acted films, is being read more widely than ever with *Emma, Sense and Sensibility*, and *Persuasion* hitting best-seller lists nearly two hundred years after their publication! Renaissance woman Ethel Smyth lived in nineteenth-century London where she wrote philosophy including *What Matters Most in Life*, golfed pretty seriously, and composed the anthem for the suffrage movement, "March of the Women." Katherine Dunham, an anthropologist and choreographer lived among the Jamaican Accompong people in 1935, researching the African roots of their diasporic culture and incorporating their traditions into interpretive and preservationist dance. The impact of these and countless other artistic women on our culture has been incredible. Their sphere of influence is the globe we inhabit! Fearless creativity and relentless pursuit of artistic truth on the part of these sheroes have freed the imagination to its limitless bounds. They have produced art that shocks, and poetry that pierces, created new ritual dances, designed fantastic fashions, and looked into the very heart of the darkness that is the feminine. The lives of these women suggest that real inspiration can come only from being true to yourself at any cost. Here are a few of the bravest, those who took tremendous risk, often physical, in the pursuit of art.

Sappho:
The Literati of Lesbos

Lyric poet Sappho is universally regarded as the greatest ancient poet. She came to be known as the "tenth muse." Although scholars can't agree whether Homer even existed or not, Sappho's work was recorded and preserved by other writers. An unfortunate destruction of a volume of all her work—nine books of lyric poetry and one of elegiac verse—occurred in the early Middle Ages engendering a search for her writing that continues even now. The Catholic Church deemed her work to be far too erotic and obscene, so they burned the volume containing her complete body of work, thus erasing what could only be some of the finest poetry in all of herstory. Known for her powerful phrasing and the intensity of feeling, erotic and otherwise, Sappho's poetry is immediate and accessible to the reader. Upon reading Sappho, you can feel that you know her, her ecstatic highs as well as the depth of her pain and longings.

Sappho is believed to have been married to a wealthy man from the island of Andros, and she had one daughter. She taught at a small college for women and was also an athlete. One haiku-like fragment reports that she "taught poetry to Hero, a girl athlete from the island of Gyra." She was banished to Sicily for some time, but the majority of her life was lived on the island of Lesbos. Much of her work, her most lustful in fact, is written to other women, whom she exalts for their beauty, often achieving a poetic frenzy of desire. She also writes for her brother Charaxus and makes the occasional reference to the political arena of the ancient world she inhabited. Although Sappho is one of the earliest and best known poets of either gender, she is actually regarded, stylistically, to be the first modern poet!

To Atthis
Though in sardis now,
she thinks of us constantly

215

and of the life we shared.
She saw you as a goddess
and above all your dancing gave deep joy.

Now she shines among Lydian women like
the rose fingered moon
rising after sundown, erasing all

stars around her, and pouring light equally
across the salt sea
and over densely flowered fields

lucent under dew. Her light spreads
on roses and tender thyme
and the blooming honey-lotus

Often while she wanders she remembers you,
gentle Atthis,
and desire eats away at her heart
for us to come.

Women Nobel Prize Winners in Literature

Selma Ottilia Lovisa Lagerlöf, 1909, "in appreciation of the lofty idealism, vivid imagination, and spiritual perception that characterize her writings."

Deledda Grazia, 1926, "for her idealistically inspired writings which with plastic clarity picture the life on her native island and with depth and sympathy deal with human problems in general."

Sigrid Undset, 1928, "principally for her powerful descriptions of Northern life during the Middle Ages."

Pearl Buck, 1938, "for her rich and truly epic descriptions of peasant life in China and for her biographical masterpieces."

Gabriela Mistral, 1945, "for her lyric poetry which, inspired by powerful emotions, has made her name a symbol of the idealistic aspirations of the entire Latin American world."

Nelly Sachs, 1966 (shared), "for her outstanding lyrical and dramatic writing, which interprets Israel's destiny with touching strength."

Nadine Gordimer, 1991, "who through her magnificent epic writing has—in the words of Alfred Nobel— been of very great benefit to humanity."

Toni Morrison, 1993, "who in novels characterized by visionary force and poetic import, gives life to an essential aspect of American reality."

Wislawa Szymborska, 1996, "for poetry that with ironic precision allows the historical and biological context to come to light in fragments of human reality."

Harriet Beecher Stowe:
Civil Warrior

Most schoolchildren are taught that Harriet Beecher Stowe was an extremely creative young woman who, almost accidentally, wrote a book that tore America apart. In this insidiously watered down and sugarcoated version of history we were spoon-fed as children, the most important aspects of Stowe's story are completely omitted. The truth is, and let us please let it be known far and wide, Harriet's opus,

Uncle Tom's Cabin, was written with precisely the intent to publicize the cruelty of slavery and give it a human name and face so people could relate, sympathize, and, most importantly, ACT!

Extremely bright, Harriet was keenly interested in improving humanity even as a child. She lived in a large family of nine children; her father was a Calvinist minister and her mother died when she was five. She was very attached to her older sister, Catherine, who founded the Hartford Female Seminary. The year 1832 found the Beecher family leaving their longtime home of Litchfield, Connecticut, and moving to Cincinnati, right across the Ohio River from Kentucky. From this vantage point so much closer to the south, Harriet had much greater exposure to slavery. A young, idealistic, student of theology, Harriet did not like what she was seeing at all. Her father, Lyman Beecher, was the president of Lane Theological Seminary. Her brothers became involved in the antislavery movement and were extremely vocal about their feelings. Harriet, for her part, aided a runaway slave.

In 1836, Harriet met one of the professors of religion at her father's seminary, Calvin Stowe, married him, and bore six children. Around this time, she discovered her love of writing, contributing articles to numerous religious magazines and papers. She also began working on her first novel, *The Mayflower: Sketches and Scenes and Characters Among the Descendants of the Puritans*. After too many years across the river from the slave state of Kentucky, Harriet Beecher Stowe finally returned to the Northeast with her husband and children.

In 1850, the Fugitive Slave Acts passed Congress. It was this event that moved Harriet to write *Uncle Tom's Cabin*. She couldn't abide the inhumanity of slaves being hunted down and forcibly returned to their former owners after struggling so hard for the freedom that was their birthright. Horror stories of the torture of runaway slaves galvanized the sensitive Harriet to action, and she wrote the book with the full intention of sending out a cry against the whippings, maimings, and hangings of slaves.

Uncle Tom's Cabin or Life Among the Lonely was first run as a series of installments in the national *Era,* an abolitionist newspaper. Upon publication in book form in 1852, Stowe's work was very well received. Harriet had expected her novel to be a nonevent outside the circle of abolitionists, but she was very surprised. The entire printing of 5,000 sold out in two days and sold three million copies around the world before the Civil War! Harriet had outstripped her wildest dreams and had truly fired the shot in what was to become the War Between the States. She also received critical acclaim from such literary luminaries as MacCauley, Longfellow, and Leo Tolstoy who declared *Uncle Tom's Cabin* the "highest moral art." Abraham Lincoln himself called Harriet "the little lady who made this big war."

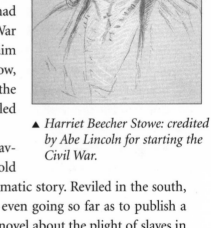

▲ *Harriet Beecher Stowe: credited by Abe Lincoln for starting the Civil War.*

Harriet's strategy was to show the extremes of slavery, culminating in the savage beating of the gentle old slave, Tom. The world was captivated by Stowe's dramatic story. Reviled in the south, Stowe met all her pro-slave detractors with dignity, even going so far as to publish a critical *Key to Uncle Tom's Cabin* and write a second novel about the plight of slaves in *Dred: A Tale of the Great Dismal Swamp.* Harriet Beecher Stowe is a shining example of courage and conviction; her life is proof of how passion and purpose can change the world.

"I won't be any properer than I have a mind to be."
—Harriet Beecher Stowe

Charlotte Perkins Gilman:
Her Land is Your Land

N iece of Catherine Beecher and Harriet Beecher Stowe, Charlotte Perkins Gilman also felt, in her own words, "the Beecher urge to social service, the Beecher wit and gift of words." Born in 1860, Charlotte attended the Rhode Island School of Design and worked after graduation as a commercial artist. Exposed to the "domestic feminism" of the Beechers, the extremely sensitive and imaginative young woman had resolved to avoid her mother's fate of penniless desertion by her father and assiduously avoided marriage, but after two years of relentless wooing, Charlotte reluctantly agreed to marry artist Walter Stetson. After she bore her daughter Katherine, she had the nervous breakdown that inspired her famous story, *The Yellow Wallpaper* and subsequent nonfiction accounts of her struggle with manic-depressive episodes. She wrote *The Yellow Wallpaper* for humanistic reasons: "It was not intended to drive people crazy," she said, "but to save people from being driven crazy, and it worked." Attributing her emotional problems in part to women's status in marriage, she divorced her husband and moved to California with her daughter (later, when Walter remarried, she sent Katherine to live with her father and stepmother, a move that was considered incredibly scandalous).

Although she suffered weakness and "extreme distress, shame, discouragement, and misery," her whole life, Charlotte's accomplishments are more than that of most healthy folks. A social reformer who wrote in order to push for equality for women, she lectured, founded the Women's Peace Part with Jane Addams in World War I, and wrote her best-known book, *Women and Economics* in only seventeen days. At one point, she undertook a well-publicized debate in the *New York Times* with Anna Howard Shaw, defending her contention that women are not "rewarded in proportion to their work" as "unpaid servant(s) merely a comfort and a luxury agreeable to have if a man can afford it." Gilman was unbelievably forward thinking for her time, even going so far as to devise architectural plans for houses without kitchens to end women's slavery to the stove so they could take up professional occupations.

Perkins Gilman wrote five more books pushing for economic change for women, a critically acclaimed autobiography, three utopian novels, and countless articles, stories, and poetry before her death by suicide after a long struggle with cancer in 1935. With the passing of time, Charlotte Perkins Gilman is usually remembered only for *The Yellow Wallpaper* and for her feminist utopian novel *Herland* in which three American men enter Herland, an all-female society that reproduces through parthenogenesis, the development of an unfertilized egg. Less known is her impact as a nationally recognized speaker, political theorist, and tireless champion of women's causes at the turn of the century. She lived an unconventional life and suffered for it, revealing through her writing the often grim realities behind the Victorian ideals of womanhood and how it was possible to change the way men and women related to one another.

> *"I knew it was normal and right in general, and held that a woman should be able to have marriage and motherhood, and do her work in the world, also."*—Charlotte Perkins Gilman

Charlotte Gilman Perkin on Sheroism

- In 1870, as a ten-year old girl, Charlotte wrote a feminist tale of the sheroism of Princess Araphenia, only heir to the good King Ezephon. When the kingdom fell under attack from a wicked enemy, Princess Araphenia disguised herself as a warrior-prince with a magical sword supplied by an interplanetary visitor, Elmondine. Brave Princess Araphenia saved her father's kingdom and revealed herself after vanquishing the evil foes to the amazement and delight of her royal father.

- In 1911 on the subject of heroes: "strong, square, determined jaw. He may be cross-eyed, wide-eared, thick-necked, bandy-legged—what you please; but he must have a more or less (protruding) jaw."

- On society run by women as depicted in Herland, written in 1915: "like a pleasant family—an old, established, perfectly-run country place." Herland's society is made up entirely of women; therefore they have no enemies thanks to policies of "sister love" and "mother love."

Mary Stevenson Cassatt:
Making an Impression

Mary Cassatt was the one American artist to be acknowledged and accepted by the French Impressionists. Born to privilege in Pennsylvania in 1844, Mary was lucky to have the opportunity to live abroad. Her father was president of the Pennsylvania Railroad; he relocated his family and lived in Germany so Mary's brother Alexander could study engineering. Later, they stayed in France. Mary was especially struck by Paris and although she was self-identified as an American, she really did most of her work in the French capital. Her family wasn't supportive of her decision to be an artist. They tried to talk her out of studying at the Pennsylvania Academy of the Fine Arts; her father's reaction to her stated desire to pursue a career as an artist was, "I'd rather have you dead!" (Although Father Cassatt's comment was extreme, it's important to remember that women simply weren't going off to foreign countries in 1865. Shero

Mary did just that, helping knock down one more barrier for womankind.)

Cassatt was nothing if not persistent and managed to talk her difficult father into allowing her to study the Old Masters abroad. She made tracks for Spain, Italy, and then alighted in Paris for serious application of her training. By 1868, Mary had a painting accepted at the Paris Salon to whom she submitted work until 1877 when Degas took a personal interest in her painting, asked her to join the Impressionist School and encouraged the young woman to take up photography and Japanese print-making. Although Cassatt has her own distinctive style, she credits Degas as having been a wonderful encouragement, inspiration, and influence on her art. As a counterpoint and reality check, Degas' remark upon seeing Cassatt's work for the first time should be kept in mind: "I am not willing to admit that a woman can draw that well."

▼ *Mary Cassatt: preeminent painter and the lone female in the impressionist school.*

As if being the only woman Impressionist and the only American Impressionist weren't enough, Cassatt's contribution to art herstory is even more sheroic in her choice of subject matter—young women and girls, mother and their children. She approached her subjects with simplicity and directness, going about painting her models with no intent to glorify or sentimentalize. Unlike some of her fellow Impressionists, Mary drew her subjects prior to the application of pastels or oils. Her work has, to a certain degree, a great clarity because of this.

Mary Cassatt had a series of one-woman shows in Paris, establishing her reputation outside her immediate circle. She was also a discerning businesswoman, selling her own work and that of her artist friends, and advancing the cause of art a great deal when she convinced museums such as the Met and the Mavermeyer to exhibit contemporary art. She also very successfully advocated American tourists to collect the bold new art; she was quite right when she told the visiting buyers it would be immensely valuable soon enough. She persuaded her wealthy brother Alexander to purchase paintings by Renoir, Degas, Monet, Pissarro, and Manet, making him the first real collector of this important school of art.

Eventually her reputation as an important artist crossed the Atlantic. In 1891, she accepted a commission from the Chicago World's Fair to paint a mural on "modern women." In 1904, she was given France's Highest distinction when she was made Chevalier of the French Legion of Honor in 1904. As time went on, Mary had to take care of her sick sister and mother, cutting severely into her time to paint, and by 1913, she was so blinded by cataracts that she couldn't paint any longer.

Although some historians speculate that the relationship between Cassatt and Degas might have gone beyond platonic, Mary lived a very discreet private life, dedicated to her art, her family, and her independence. Toward the end of her life, she enjoyed hosting young would-be artists from America at her chateau with whom she passionately discussed art. She lived in France until her death in 1926, having accomplished more than she (or her doubting Thomas father) ever envisioned.

"Now I could work with absolute independence without considering
the opinion of a jury. I had already recognized who were my true masters.
I admired Manet, Courbet, and Degas. I took leave of
conventional art. I began to live."—Mary Cassatt

Camille Claudel:
The Feeler

Camille Claudel, born in France in 1864, is beginning to be accorded more respect for her sculpture, after being hidden in the looming shadow of August Rodin, best known for "The Thinker." Part of a creative clique in France that included Camille's brother Paul who was a Catholic poet and playwright of note in the late nineteenth century, Camille was an artist of considerable talent. She studied with Rodin, becoming his model and mistress. Their relationship was stormy; the two artists' tempers would burn brightly and they were constantly breaking up and making up, but the relationship endured until 1898. When her brother Paul abandoned her, she committed an auto-de-fé. As was typical in that era, Camille was institutionalized for depression and hysteria starting in 1913, eroding her ability to continue her forceful sculpting until her death in 1943. Anne Delbee's 1982 play "Une Femme: Camille Claudel" was the beginning of a revival of interest in Claudel. Controversial, the play posits the theory that Camille was more than a muse; indeed, she was the true artist of the two, infusing Rodin with creativity and ideas. In 1989, Isabella Adjani and Gerard Depardieu did a wonderful job of bringing the creative couple to the big screen. Despite the difficulty of her last years, Camille Claudel has become a French national sheroine and cause celebre.

Käthe Kollwitz:
Torn from Her Soul

German lithographer Käthe Kollwitz's art became the vehicle for her protest of the senselessness of war. She couldn't have found a more effective way to express her sentiments. The body of work she produced moved art historians the world over to classify Kollwitz as one of the four most important graphic artists of the twentieth century. Tragically, a great deal of her work was destroyed by the Nazis and by bombings in World War II, but what has survived is a record of her power. It is not only her powerful graphic technique that has provided lasting fame, but her subject matter—almost always a peasant woman with a strong body, often surrounded by children, very different from the typical passive, sexualized women found in male-dominated art.

Born in 1867, Kollwitz became the first woman to be elected to Berlin's prestigious Academy of Art and became director there in 1928. She was also the only female of the *fin de siècle* group of left-wing liberal artists who founded To the Secession, an organization dedicated to opposing artists affiliated with the German establishment. When her son died in World War I, the focus of her art became to graphically depict the effects on women and children of the social and political events of her lifetime. Her piece entitled "To the Weaver's Rebellion" portrayed the nightmarish conditions of the poor along with the sequel of lithographs in "To the Peasant War" about the harsh lives of the working class in Germany. In her print "Outbreak" from this series, she created a portrait of a woman, "Black Anna," who singlehandedly started a revolution. "Raped" is one of the first pictures in Western art that dared to show the war of violence waged on women.

She was kicked out of the Academy of Art by the Nazis in 1933 who regarded her as a pariah—a political artist depicting poverty, reality, and less-than-über-ideal peasant folk! She died penniless and homeless in 1945, having been stripped of her rightful position in the art world and having witnessed the destruction of her sheroic lithographic art.

Amazingly, her surviving son discovered a diary she kept, describing her inner emotional life and her struggle to make art at the turn of the century, as a woman, a wife, and mother. Her entries, published as *To the Diary and Letters of Käthe Kollwitz* are a fascinating delineation of the emotional price women often have to pay to be creative, to be political, and to break new ground.

Her surviving art continues to affect people worldwide. In the cemetery in which she is buried there is a note in the visitors' book dated September 22, 1996: "God bless you Käthe. And all your children. We carry on what you have wished. Signed, A former enemy."

"It always comes back to this, that only one's inner feelings represent the truth. I have never done any work cold; I have always worked with my blood, so to speak." —Käthe Kollwitz

Isadora Duncan:
Dancing for Her Life

]sadora neé Angela Duncan was born in San Francisco on a summer's day in 1877. Brought up in the manner of fallen aristocracy by her poor mother, a music teacher, young Angela studied classical ballet, but soon discarded the rules in favor of her own, freer, interpretive dance. Her public debut of this new style of dance was a total flop in New York City and Chicago so she scraped together some savings and headed for Europe on board a cattle boat.

In London, she studied the sculptures of pagan Greece and integrated the sense of movement from these classical remnants into her dance practice. A

▲ *Isadora Duncan: this native San Franciscan became a global dance sensation.*

grande dame of the British stage, Mrs. Patrick Campbell, became the young American's patron and set up private dance salons for Isadora at the homes of the most cultured creme de la creme. Soon, snooty Brits couldn't get enough of the barefoot and beautiful young nymph, dancing her heart out in a dryad costume that left very little guesswork as to Duncan's anatomy. Soon she was packing theaters and concert halls all over the continent. In 1905, she toured Russia as well.

Isadora Duncan was not only the dance diva of her day, but a woman who dared to flaunt social convention, bearing children out of wedlock (wedlock was a notion utterly repugnant to Duncan and her pack) to stage designer Gordon Craig and Paris Singer, of the sewing machine dynasty. But her life was not all roses—Duncan lost her two babies and their nurse when their car rolled into the Seine and all three drowned. Duncan tried to sublimate her grief with work, opening dance schools around Europe and touring South America, Germany, and France.

In 1920, she received an invitation to establish a school in the Soviet Union where she fell in undying love with Sergey Aleksandrovish Yesenin, a respected poet half her age. The two married, despite Duncan's abhorrence of the institution, and were taken for Bolshevik spies as they traveled the globe. Upon being heckled mercilessly at a performance in Boston's Symphony Hall, Isadora Duncan bid her homeland adieu forever: "Good-bye America, I shall never see you again!" She was as good as her word; the honeymooners scuttled back to Europe where their relationship crashed against the rocks of Yesenin's insanity. He committed suicide in 1925 and Duncan lived the remainder of her live on the French Riviera where another auto accident ended her life. One of her dramatic Greek inspired scarves got tangled in the wheel of her car and she was strangled.

Though her life was sad and messy, Isadora Duncan's real triumph was her art. She changed the dance world forever, freeing the form from Victorian constriction to allow more natural movement. Duncan believed in celebrating the sculptural beauty of the female body and that dance, at its zenith, was "divine expression." Duncan is regarded by many to have been the chief pioneer of modern dance. She was a free spirit for whom "to dance is to live."

"If my art is symbolic of any one thing, it is symbolic of the freedom of woman and her emancipation." —Isadora Duncan

Gabrielle "Coco" Chanel:
Fashion Shero

Considered by many to be the mother of modern fashion, Gabrielle "Coco" Chanel was the first fashion designer to create clothes that matched the emerging attitudes of women for greater freedom and independence. Born in France around 1883, Coco's first step toward a life in the fashion industry was a job in a hatmaker's shop in Deauville, France, where she worked until 1912. At thirty-one years old, she struck out on her own, opening her very own shop featuring streamlined and unfussy wool jersey dresses. Strikingly new, her simple style caught on quickly. Chanel's success with the dresses and the celebratory atmosphere following World War I encouraged her to really

▲ *Coco Chanel: founded a fashion empire and freed the female form.*

go to town with smartly cut suits, sophisticated short skirts, and bold, chunky jewelry designed at her very own coutour house in Paris!

In 1922, she created Chanel #5, the perfume every woman wanted, named for her lucky number; to this day, it remains one of the all-time favorite perfumes. Chanel's innovations are legendary—costume jewelry, evening scarves, short skirts, and the little black dress all came from the steel-trap mind of Coco Chanel. She retired in 1938, but got bored and staged a remarkably successful comeback in the mid-fifties.

Coco, the ultimate Frenchwoman, never married, but seemed to be utterly happy with her career as an independent businesswoman, in charge of her own time and her own life. She makes America's Horatio Alger look shabby—the daughter of a vagabond street pedlar, she was raised in orphanages and went on to found an empire, live a busy glamourous life, and leave behind a legacy that will last forever. The idol of practically everyone in the industry, Coco Chanel was the epitome of the modern woman. Yves St. Laurent once called her "The Godmother of us all," and French surrealist Jean Cocteau remarked, "(Coco Chanel) has, by a kind of miracle, worked in fashion according to rules that would seem to have value for painters, musicians, poets."

"There have been many Duchesses of Westminster, but there is only one Coco Chanel."—Coco Chanel on why she rejected a famous suitor

Supermodels Take on Issues

- Coco Chanel, famous for her quote that "A woman doesn't become interesting until she reaches forty" would probably be amused with cartoon shero Sandee, the "SuperHero SuperModel" the creation of designer Isaac Mizrahi. Sandee is a fun, enchanting, and good-hearted high-fashion model who has a mission. She's advocating for the acceptance of aging; to be specific, she wants it made perfectly clear that it is okay to be over thirty!

- Sandee's polar opposite in every way is real life supershero supermodel Waris Dirie, a resplendent Somali native who has come out of the closet about a horrific secret from her childhood—a female circumcision performed on her at the age of six. Waris saw her sister die from the same mutilation, and Waris has suffered tremendous health problems as a result. This only makes her all the more sheroic in stepping up to take on the role of spokesperson against this heinous crime against women that still happens all across the world. Waris is providing a human face to this twentieth-century atrocity. Since she took on the role, cliterectomies have already been outlawed in one African nation! "It was entirely my idea to reveal it publicly," says Waris, "No one knew before. With my modeling exposure, I thought maybe now I've got the power to do something about it. To let people know about this terrible thing that happens to girls around the world."

- Sample these Dishes! The DISHES Project is the modeling industry's first nonprofit foundation rasing both awareness and badly needed funds for pediatric AIDS patients. The brainchild of former model Bonnie Pfeifer, DISHES is an acronym for Determined Involved Supermodels Helping to End Suffering. You can contact them via email at info@DISHES.org or write to Box 3939, New York, NY 10185.

Georgia O'Keeffe:
An American Icon

Georgia O'Keeffe was born on a Wisconsin farm in 1887. The closest town was called Sun Prairie. O'Keeffe knew at a fairly early age that she wanted to be an artist and enrolled in the Art Institute of Chicago in 1904 until a bout of typhoid caused her to drop out. Upon her recovery, rather than returning to Chicago, she moved to New York, where she enrolled in the Art Students League. Feeling she didn't have what it takes to be a painter, she moved to the South and made a living, first as a commercial artist and later as an art teacher. Rededicating herself to art in 1914, she took a teaching position at Columbia College in South Carolina, where, she felt, the easy teaching load would give her time to devote to drawing.

In 1916, Alfred Stieglitz came across her drawings and arranged for a show, exclaiming "At last a woman on paper!" They married in 1924, and had a lifelong companionship documented by the hundreds of photographs Stieglitz took of O'Keeffe. The relationship had many ups and downs, but through it all, Georgia painted, taking trips to the Southwest to give herself and her husband the emotional space they each needed. The terrain would increasingly come to dominate her work.

Upon Stieglitz's death in 1946, O'Keeffe moved to Santa Fe, where she purchased Ghost Ranch and opened her own gallery, An America. O'Keeffe loved the light and lines of her ranch, living there in her treasured privacy, painting up to her death at age ninety-nine. She won many awards, including the Medal of Freedom in 1977, and was elected to the American Academy of Arts and Letters, and her works grace many of the most prestigious museums around the world.

Georgia O'Keeffe's style is unique; her paintings are at once both stark and rich. Her precise brush strokes applied to organic forms, flowers, skulls, and rocks overlaid with luminous color washes command the eye. Ever an iconoclast, Georgia O'Keeffe lived, and painted, by her own rules.

Regarded as one of the most important women artists of the twentieth century, she laid important groundwork for the ambitions of women artists simply by pursuing her singular vision. In 1930, O'Keeffe shared her thoughts on feminism, forty years before the second wave of activism. "I am interested in the oppression of women of all classes ... though not nearly so definitely and so consistently as I am in the abstractions of paintings. But one has affected the other ... I have had to go to men as sources in my painting because the past has left us so small an inheritance of women's painting that has widened life ... Before I put a brush to canvas I question, 'Is this mine? Is it all intrinsically of myself? Is it influenced by some idea or some photograph of an idea which I have acquired from some man?' That too implied a social consciousness, a social struggle. I am trying with all my skill to do painting that is all of a woman, as well as all of me."

> *"I am going to be an artist!"*—Georgia O'Keeffe at age eight, when asked what she was going to be when she grew up

Gabriela Mistral:
Voice of the People

The first Latin American woman to win a Nobel Prize in Literature, Gabriella Mistral was born in the Chilean village of Montegrande in 1889. Her mother, Basque Petronila Alcayaga, was a teacher and her father was Jeronimo Villanueva, also a teacher and a gypsy poet of Indian and Jewish birth. Jeronimo was overfond of wine and not quite so attached to his duties as a breadwinner and father; he deserted the family when Gabriela was three. As a schoolgirl, Gabriela discovered her call to poetry and also tapped her own stubborn independence, switching her birth name, Lucila, for her choice, Gabriela. Several years later, as an adult, she chose a fitting surname, Mistral, hinting of a fragrant Mediterranean wind.

Her first love was a hopelessly romantic railroad worker who killed himself when the relationship faltered after two years. Her first book of poetry, *Sonetas de la Muerta* [Sonnets of Death] was written as result of her sadness, guilt, and pain over the death of her ex–lover. When Gabriela published three of the Sonetas in 1914, she received Chile's top prize for poetry.

In the twenties and thirties, she wrote many volumes of poetry including *Desolacion* (Desolation), *Tenura* (Tenderness), *Questions, Tala,* and a mixed media anthology, *Readings for Women.* Mistral felt a special interest and sympathy for women and children, and worked to help the victims of World Wars I and II. Gabriela made real strides as an educator, as well. She initiated programs of schooling the poor, founded a mobile library system, and traveled the world, gleaning whatever she could to bring back and improve Chile's education system. In 1923, she was named "Teacher of the Nation." She became an international envoy and ambassador off and on for her country for twenty years, eventually serving in the League of Nations and the United Nations.

In the late 1920s, a military government seized power in Chile and offered Mistral an ambassadorship to all the nations of Central America. Mistral refused to work for the military state and made a scathing public denouncement of the government machine. Her pension was revoked and, sheroically, Mistral had to support herself, her mother, and her sister through her writing. She lived in exile in France, eventually moving to the United States where she taught at Middlebury, Barnard, and the University of Puerto Rico.

She received the prestigious Nobel Prize in 1945. Upon accepting the revered award, Gabriela Mistral made a sharp contrast with dashing Sweden's King Gustav in her plain black velvet. Pointedly, she didn't accept the prize for herself, but on behalf of the "poets of my race." Mistral died in 1957, mourned by her native Chile where she was revered as a national treasure. A poor, rural schoolteacher of mixed race, Gabriela Mistral achieved the top posts and honors in her mountainous country. She was the "people's poet," giving voice to the humble people to whom she belonged, the Indians, mestizos, and Campesanos, and scorning the rampant elitism and attempts at creating a racial hierarchy in Europe and in her beloved Chile.

> *"I consider myself to be among the children of that twisted thing that is called a racial experience, or better, a racial violence."* —Gabriela Mistral

Gwendolyn Brooks: Poet of the Beat

Gwendolyn Brooks is one of the most innovative poets in the literary landscape of America. Born in 1917 in Topeka, Kansas, Gwendolyn's family moved when she was young to the far more urban city of Chicago, a street-smart influence that still informs her work. Brooks wanted to bring poetry to the poor black kids of the inner city. She did—rapid fire, tightly wound iambic pentameter that predated rap and won her the distinction of being the first black person to receive the Pulitzer Prize (for *Annie Allen* in 1950.) In later life, she took a more radical bent, hooking up with revolutionary black Beat LeRoi Jones (now Amiri Baraka) and Don L. Lee, and jumping into the causes of African Americans with both feet. She became a tough and angry Black Power poet penning verses grounded in classical style deconstructed through the lens of her newfound racial awareness and commitment to cause. Forty years after her prize-winning feat, her poetry is still raw, fresh, and commanding. "I want to clarify my language. I want these poems to be free. I want them to be direct without sacrificing the kind of music, the picture-making I've always been interested in." —Gwendolyn Brooks

Zora Neale Hurston:
Seraph of the Sun

Zora Neale Hurston's readership is much larger now than at the height of her career. Almost forty years after her death in 1960, her body of work has been reprinted hundred of times, ensuring her legacy in our literary heritage. A writer of the Harlem Renaissance, Hurston spoke for the silenced—black women. Her work—five novels, more than fifty short stories and essays, a collection of short stories, and her autobiography—demonstrates her commitment to the culture of her people and her anthropological scholarship of black language and history.

Born in rural Florida in 1891, Zora was very outspoken, insisting upon equality and eschewing traditional roles for a black woman of her day. For this, she credits her precious mother, Lucy, who urged her to "jump at de sun!" when she was nine. Despite a bumpy childhood with a stepmother she didn't care for, Hurston thrived in the all-black town of Eatonville, where she saw the example of a peaceful and good government by and for blacks. Her father, a popular Baptist preacher, was mayor of the town several times and warned his daughter that the world outside would be vastly different. She bounced among various relatives until, at fourteen, she headed out to make her own way in the world, working as a maid for a group of Gilbert and Sullivan traveling players. Landing in New York City, Zora made some fateful connections with leaders of the Harlem Renaissance, including Langston Hughes, Alan Locke, and Montgomery Gregory.

With financial aid, Zora received an excellent education at Barnard College in New York City where she was mentored by Franz Boas, the leading anthropologist of the day, who also had mentored Margaret Mead. Boas saw Hurston's endless drive and curiosity and set her to the task of gathering the cultural history of her people. After graduation, Hurston returned to Florida to record black folklore. She married a man she met there, Herbert Sheen, but divorced not long after, one of three divorces. She got a fellowship in 1934 to collect more folklore and went on a quest for knowledge about her people that took her to New Orleans, Jamaica, Haiti, and the Bahamas where she studied voodoo in addition to her usual linguistics and tall stories. The data she accrued in this epic trip constituted the foundations for *Mules and Men* and *Tell My Horse*. *Jonah's Gourd Vine* is regarded as one of her finest works of fiction and *Their Eyes Were Watching God* is hailed as her masterpiece. One of Hurston's greatest proponents, novelist Alice Walker, offers a powerful endorsement of Hurston's opus, "There is no book more important to me than this one."

Unfortunately, her friendship with the great Langston Hughes broke down over a play they were collaborating on, *Mule Bone*. The forties saw further decline of Zora Neale Hurston's career. Her essay, "How it Feels to Be Colored Me" drew fire for its inflammatory frankness regarding what Hurston saw as the wholly unfair system of Jim Crow injustice. In 1940's America, Hurston's literary protests fell on unwilling ears.

In 1948, she was the victim of a trumped up charge of child molestation in New York City. The case was thrown out, but Hurston was devastated and headed back to Florida. Undaunted, she continued to act from her conscience, protesting 1954's *Brown vs. Topkea Board of Education*, taking the position that it smacked of a bias toward black students and southern schools as inferior. Huston, one of America's most original literary scholars, linguists, mythographers, and novelists, had to work as a librarian, a substitute teacher, and even as a maid to try to pay her bills. She was working on a book and still submitting articles to the *Saturday Evening Post* and *American Legion Magazine* even in her most desperate of circumstances.

When she died of heart failure in January of 1960, she was penniless and homeless, taking shelter at the Saint Lucie Welfare Home. Hurston's work languished, almost forgotten, until her masterful writing was "rediscovered" in the 1970s. Zora saw black culture as a treasure to be celebrated and shared, considering Caucasian culture as feeble when placed next to the vitality of black idiom and storytelling. Alice Walker searched out Hurston's unmarked pauper's grave in Fort Pierce, Florida, and wrote about her pilgrimage to find her sheroic foresister for *Ms.* Magazine in 1975. Her article "In Search of Zora Neale Hurston" created an avalanche of renewed interest in the writer who had been at the very epicenter of her Harlem Renaissance. The gravestone Walker had made read, "Zora Neal Hurston, A Genius of the South. Novelist, Folklorist, Anthropologist."

> *"I was not comfortable to be around. Strange things must have looked out of my eyes like Lazarus after his resurrection... I have been in sorrow's kitchen and licked out all the pots... I have stood on the peaky mountain with a harp and a sword in my hands."*
>
> —Zora Neale Hurston from *Dust Tracks on a Road*, Hurston's autobiography in which she predicts her whole life in twelve visions, including her ultimate destitution.

Martha Graham:
Grande Dame of Dance

Modern dance innovator, Martha Graham was born into a medical family in 1894. Her physician father was fascinated by how the body expresses the psychological, and the young girl was an eager student, adopting this physiognomic approach in her work. Martha's family settled in Santa Barbara, California in 1908 where she was further influenced by the crashing of the ocean's waves and Eastern art. In 1916, she began dancing professionally at Denishawn, the Los Angeles dance school and troupe founded by Ruth St. Denis and Ted Shawn. Martha eagerly enveloped herself in the global dance tradition at Denishawn—native American tribal, classical, folk, and ecstatic religious mysticism. Shawn worked with Martha on "Xochitl," a stunning Aztec ballet that showcased Martha's hidden power and passion. She stayed with Denishawn until 1923 when she decided their eclectics bordered on scattered, heading east for the Greenwich Follies. The next year found Martha teaching and experimenting with dance in Rochester's Eastman School.

Martha Graham appeared in New York as an independent dancer and choreographer for the first time in 1926. Critics were pleased with her grace and elegance in "Three Gopi Maidens" and "Danse Languide." The following year, Graham had dug deeper into her own creative source. Her new dances were stripped-down, purer, less to the taste of the New York's dance taste-makers who declared her work,"ugly, stark, and obscure." Her signature movements spiraled out from a contracting of the torso. She was compared to Nijinsky for being completely unafraid to appear unattractive in the passionate throes of expression.

In 1927, she performed "Revolt," perhaps the first protest dance staged in America. With Arthur Honegger's modern avant garde music, Graham's "Revolt" shocked audiences, causing a hue and cry of protest to her protest dance. The following period proved Martha's hard work and dedication to innovation with "Frontier," that featured sculptural set-pieces by Isamu Noguchi, "Primitive Mysteries," scored for Martha by a fine composer, Louis Horst, "Night Journey," a retelling of the Oedipus myth through the eyes of Jocasta, and "Letter to the World," interpretations of Emily Dickenson's poetry and life. In a career that spanned more than fifty years, Martha Graham went on to create nearly 200 original dances, choreograph over 160 ballets, form her own school and company, and attain recognition as one of the most influential dancers of all time. The first to present modern dance seasons in ballet houses, Graham danced "to objectify in physical form my beliefs..."

> *"[Graham created] a dance technique that has become the basis of the education of hundreds of thousands of dancers around the world and establishing a new form for dance and twentieth-century theater."*
> —from the Scripps American Dance Festival award
> honoring Martha Graham

Pearl Primus: Pearl of Great Price

Trinidad dancer shero Pearl Primus was born in 1919 and became the top interpreter of her African heritage via her choreography and performance. She received international attention and respect even though she had no formal training in dance and had intended on being a physician. Pearl was a Jill of all trades, working as a switchboard operator, photographer, health counselor, and as a welder in New York's shipyards, as well as many blue-collar factory jobs. Once Pearl committed to dance as her profession, she went at it with fierce dedication and concentration, viewing dance as a way to express her ideas about social conditions and the state of humanity. She was incredibly innovative, mixing dance and musical styles constantly. Fairly quickly, her pieces, such as "Strange Fruit" became classics. She also recited African, West Indian, and African American poetry and literature during freestyle dance performances such as Langston Hughes' "Our Spring Will Come" and "The Negro Speaks of Rivers." Pearl Primus really dug into the Afro-Indian culture, learning and in turn teaching, through her dance, about the cultures, tribes, and history of her people. She once said, "Dance is my medicine. It's the scream which eases for a while the terrible frustration common to all human beings who, because of race, creed, or color are `invisible.'"

Margaret Bourke-White:
The Mirror's Eye

] wonder what Margaret Bourke-White would think of her hauntingly beautiful photograph of Mohandas Gandhi at his spinning wheel being used in the Apple ad captioned "Think Different." As if the grammatical issue weren't irritating enough, it seems tragic for a work meant to preserve the memory and honor of a man dedicated to peace and simplicity (he's spinning his own cloth so as to not wear manufactured foreign goods) now being used to market computers. Really!

Born in the Bronx in 1904, Margaret Bourke-White "dared to become an industrial photographer and a photojournalist at a time when men thought they had exclusive rights to those titles, then rose with startling speed to the top of both professions," writes her biographer Vicki Goldberg. Indeed, her abilities did much to contribute to the rise of photojournalism and many of our memories of important twentieth-century history are thanks to her effort to document them for posterity. Although the Gandhi photograph may end up being the most famous thanks to some fairly insidious marketing, others are seared onto our memory: the Indian holocaust that took place during the partition when all Hindus were forced to leave the new northern state of Pakistan and all Muslims traveled north to the new state. The dead are still unnumbered in this trail of tears, estimates are as high as three million. She also photographed the Moslem massacre in Calcutta, horrendous and powerful pictures of dead Hindus being devoured by vultures.

As a *Life* staff photographer, she traveled the globe. In Moscow, she caught on film the Nazi air invasion of the Russian city. In South Africa, she photographed apartheid-beleaguered blacks slaving in diamond and gold mines for the gain of their oppressors. In Korea, she photographed guerilla warfare. She covered the war fronts in Africa, Italy, and Germany, and was with the Allied force that entered the death camp of Buchenwald, where she shot some of her most painful and important work. "I saw and photographed the piles of naked, lifeless bodies, the human skeletons in furnaces, the living skeletons."

In America, the 1934 drought and Dust Bowl migration were her subjects, as well as an unvarnished view of the abject poverty in Appalachia and other parts of the rural South. She and her husband, writer Erskine Caldwell, collaborated on several photo essay books, including *You Have Seen Their Faces,* reminding an insular America about her own forgotten people. During World War II, she was the first Army Air Force woman photographer in action in Italy and North Africa.

Margaret Bourke-White's sheroic dedication to telling the truth with pictures has left us with a fascinating chronicle of the twentieth century. In her pursuit of visual verity, she often put herself in danger, walking on steel beams to get the height for the best shot, going deep into dangerous mines, flying with a bomb squad in Tunisia, and even going down in a shipwreck in World War II. She died in 1971 of Parkinson's disease. In her lifetime, Margaret Bourke-White returned to us our own history and gave us the opportunity to learn from it.

"The impersonality of modern war has become stupendous, grotesque."
—Margaret Bourke-White, who put a face on the horrors

Dorothea Lange: Activist Photographer

"The discrepancy between what I was working on in the printing frames and what was going on in the street was more than I could assimilate," wrote Dorothea Lange of the reason she quit her job as a society photographer to record the misery of the Depression of the 1930s. Lange's sympathy for human suffering shines through in the luminous photographs, including her famous "Migrant Mother" and "White Angel Breadline." Her compassion came under attack later, however, when she was viewed as being overly empathetic with the Japanese American's internment in camps during World War II. Though she was hired to record this event for posterity, the photographs were impounded and not shown until 1972, seven years after her death. Nonetheless, Lange was not deterred from her personal mission to capture the essential and universal humanness shared around the world. Her genius was in documenting that which might be ignored if not for her artistic eye compelling us to look.

Frida Kahlo:
Cultural Patriot

Frida Kahlo's posthumous pop culture deification has eclipsed that of her husband, Mexican muralist Diego Rivera. A total iconoclast, Frida's visceral painting style has an intensity matched by few artists. Her fleshy fruits, torn arteries, tortured birthings, and imago-packed surrealist dreamscapes terrify and mesmerize. Her burning eyes in both self-portraiture and photographs maker her hard to forget. Her pain seems to emanate from many wounds—psychic, physical, and romantic.

Born Magdalena Carmen Frieda Kahlo y Calderón outside of Mexico City in 1907, her exotic looks, which have mesmerized millions, are a product of her heritage. Frida's father, one of Mexico's preeminent photographers, was a first generation Mexican born of Hungarian Jews, while her mother, Matilde Calderon, was a Mexican of mixed Spanish Indian ancestry. Frida contracted polio when she was seven, stunting her right leg. Her father took charge of her recovery from polio, encouraging her to play sports to build back the strength of her right foot and leg. At fifteen, Frida was in a horrendous trolley-car accident, crushing her spine, right foot, and pelvis, leaving her crippled forever. Later, she depicted the crash as the loss of her virginity when the trolley car's handbrake pierced her young body. In pain for the remainder of her life, she underwent thirty-five surgeries, the amputation of her gangrenous right foot, and what she deemed as imprisonment bedridden in body casts. Indeed, several of Kahlo's greatest works were done while flat on her back, using a special easel her mother had made for her.

Her tempestuous relationship with world renowned painter Diego Rivera was also a source of great suffering. Often described as "froglike" in aspect, the Mexican art star was quite a ladies' man. During a hiatus between marriage to each other, Frida hacked off her beautiful long hair and dressed in baggy men's suits. She bitterly rued her inability to bear Rivera a child, grieving over several miscarriages. They went about making art in very different ways—Rivera's huge paintings were political messages on the walls of public buildings; Frida's paintings were deeply personal, vibrant colored paintings often done on tiny pieces of tin.

Frida and Diego were a very public couple. Coming of age in the wake of the Mexican Revolution, they were both very political, becoming friends with Leon Trotsky, Pablo Picasso, Russian filmmaker Sergei Eisenstein, Andre Breton, and the Rockefellers. Both artists embraced "Mexicanismo," Frida going so far as to wear traditional Indian peasant costumes at all times, cutting a striking and memorable figure with the rustic formality. Frida's stalwart adherence to all things "of the people" made her a national shero, with papers commenting on her resemblance to an Indian princess or goddess. In his article "Portrait of Frida Kahlo as a Tehuana," art critic Hayden Herrera asserts that the Latina artist was "unrestrained by her native Mexico's male-dominant culture. Tehuantepec women are famous for being stately, beautiful, smart, brave, and strong; according to legend, theirs is a matriarchal society where women run the markets, handle fiscal maters and dominate the men."

More than forty years after her death, Frida and her work hold a fascination that shows no sign of fading. Her dramatic personal style and wild paintings have captured the public's imagination. She has been hailed as a role model for women artists, a stylistic pioneer and idealist who pursued her craft despite physical handicaps that would have stopped many others. Her body was broken but her spirit was indomitable, like the Tehuana women she identified with. As Herrera notes, "she became famous for her heroic *'allegria.'*"

Sheroic Influences

Dancer **Anna Pavlova** adopted the "Frida look" when she came to Mexico City. She danced a Mexican ballet in a native Indian costume, causing a sensation. Soon, bohemian intellectual types the world over were sporting the garb of Mexican peasant women.

Another Wild Woman

Frida Kahlo met Diego Rivera, twenty years her senior, through photographer **Tina Modotti**. Tina was really the catalyst for the direction Frida's life took toward art and leftist politics. Frida met Tina after her hospitalization from the trolley wreck where Modotti urged her to join the Communist party and gave her a hammer and sickle brooch to better show her affinities.

Tina Modotti left her home in Italy and moved to San Francisco in 1913. Theatrical in every way, she gained the respect of the Italian theater community for her acting, marrying Roubaix de l'Abrie Richey, a famously romantic painter and poet. Seven short years later, she moved to southern California and set her sights on a career in Hollywood films. Seeking out the bohemians of the day, she met photographer Edwin Weston, who soon became her lover. Weston taught Modotti photography and took many hauntingly beautiful shots of her.

Ultimately finding movie-making boring, Tina turned to the melting-pot of Mexico City where she had a quick fling with Diego Rivera and hooked up with other artists, writers, and revolutionaries. Tina Modotti straddled the line between popular and notorious; she was even accused of the murder of her Cuban lover, who was murdered in cold-blood as he and Modotti walked together in the streets of Mexico City. Maligned by the press, she was kicked out of Mexico in 1930. She went to Berlin and the Soviet Union where she devoted herself full-time to political activism with radicals Sergei Eisenstein, Alexandra Kollontorai, La Pasionaria, Ernest Hemingway, and Robert Capa. Tina Modotti lived in constant danger from her espionage on behalf of Stalinism. She went on to play a major role in the Spanish civil war before dying alone under mysterious circumstances in 1942. Pablo Neruda read a poem he had written especially for Tina Modotti at her funeral service.

Simone de Beauvoir:
Individuality and Intellectus

Existentialist writer Simone de Beauvoir was the leader of the feminist movement in France. Her book, *The Second Sex,* immediately took a place of importance in the feminist canon upon its publication in 1949 and established Beauvoir's reputation as a first-rate thinker. Although her brutally honest examination of the condition of women in the first half of the twentieth century shocked some delicate sensibilities, others were gratified to have someone tell it like it was. Beauvoir described the traditional female roles of wife and mother as that of "relative beings" dependent on context. She urged women to go after careers and endeavor to achieve fulfillment through meaningful work.

Beauvoir avoided the trap of "relative being" (and nothingness) by remaining partners and lovers with Jean-Paul Sartre, whom she met in her early twenties in a salon study group at Paris famed university, the Sorbonne. They recognized each other as soulmates immediately and stayed together for fifty-one years in a highly unorthodox partnership wherein they left openings for "contingent loves" so as not to limit their capacity for enriching experience. She eschewed motherhood and all forms of domesticity; the duo rarely dined at home, preferring cafes for all their meals. They lived together only very briefly during World War II and had difficulty protecting their privacy as word of the trendy new existentialist philosophy, ultimately espousing ambiguity, spread and their international prestige heightened. While Sartre is generally credited as the creator of existentialism, Simone was no philosophical slouch. Her treatise *Existentialism and the Wisdom of the Ages* postulates the human condition as neutral, neither inherently good nor evil, "[The individual] is nothing at first," she theorized, "it is up to him to make himself good or bad depending upon whether he assumes his freedom or denies it."

Beauvoir's first efforts toward her writing career were fictional including her aptly titled maiden voyage as a novelist in 1943's *She Came to Stay*, a fictionalization of Sartre's youthful protegee Olga Kosakiewicz who entered into a triangular living relationship with the two French intellectuals. Next, she tackled the male point of view in her epic novel treatment of death *All Men Are Mortal*, whose central character was an immortal she tracked for seven centuries. In 1954, after the success of her feminist classic *The Second Sex*, Beauvoir returned to fiction with *The Mandarins*, a novelization of the splintered and disenchanted French intelligentsia, which won the illustrious Goncourt Prize.

She continued to write and publish, creating a weighty body of work. She outlived Sartre and died on a Paris summer day in 1986 after a long and thoughtful life, living a legacy of significant contributions to gender and identity issues as well as philosophy and literature.

"One is not born a woman, one becomes a woman."
—the first line of *The Second Sex*

Clara Isaacman:
A Life in Hiding

Clara's family moved to the Belgian city of Antwerp in 1932 to escape the Romanian persecution of Jews after her father was beaten just because he tried to vote. They got a good start in Antwerp, where they ran a bottle-packing operation from their home. As the talk of anti-Jewish activities started to spread through Europe, the family kept on working hard, trying to go on as best they could, always keeping on the lookout for trouble. Clara's first experience with the cause of her parents' frightened whispers came when a troop of Nazis came and searched her school.

After that, the nightmare accelerated. Clara was shunned by her former playmates for being Jewish and lived in constant fear of being taken away. The family ended up going on the run, hiding wherever they could, oftentimes just one step ahead of Nazi soldiers looking for Jews to relocate to rumored camps. When the family ran out of money, Clara's father dared to leave their hiding place to get money to continue paying people to allow them to live in attics and rodent-filled, filthy basements.

Clara's survival is thanks to the many Belgian heroes and sheroes she encountered during her secret life in the shadows. Her mother's vigilance saved the family countless times. One of the constant threats was that their "landlords" would take their money to let them hide, only to turn them into the Gestapo for a reward. Clara's mother had a sixth sense and seemed to know exactly when betrayal was about to strike, and they would flee again.

A cherished memory of Clara's concerns her brother Heshie who was taken by the

Germans and put to work on a Jewish prison crew. When Heshie refused to act as a "kapo," a prisoner who got extra food and better treatment in return for doing anything the Nazis demanded, including helping kill other Jews, he was executed. Heshie's courage in the face of such cruelty and degradation made him a hero to the other prisoners, one of whom searched out Clara's family to make sure they knew of Heshie's heroism and honor in the face of death.

Like many survivors of the Holocaust, Clara suffered from enormous guilt about being one of the Jews who was spared while six million others, including her beloved brother, died. For many years after the war, she was silent about her experience out of shame for living. Clara decided to break her silence after hearing Nobel Prize winner Elie Weisel speak about being Jewish and practicing the faith in the post-pogrom era. Clara realized that she needed to share her story and help the healing process. Clara Isaacman now lectures around the world about the Holocaust, especially to young people. An Anne Frank who lived to tell her story, she has written a book for young adults entitled *Clara's Story* about her years of hiding. In dedicating her life to telling her story to help create peace, healing, and remembrance, Clara's sheroic survival is a testament to the human spirit.

Selma Lagerlöf & Nelly Sachs:
Nobel Nobility

]n 1909, Selma became the first woman and the first Swedish writer to receive the Nobel Prize in Literature. The Prize was awarded for her body of work, including the 1891 novel *To the Story of Gösta Berling* and the 1902 two-volume work of fiction *Jerusalem,* the chronicle of Swedish peasants who migrate to Jerusalem. Selma became the preeminent Swedish writer of her day and produced an impressive body of work—

33 novels and four biographical narratives. Shero Selma wasn't content to merely be the most brilliant novelist of her age, however, she also worked extremely hard at obtaining the release of Jewish writer Nelly Sachs from a Nazi concentration camp. Sachs, inspired by her savior, won the Nobel Prize for Literature herself in 1966!

Anne Frank:
Behind the Attic Wall

If Anne Frank had lived, what would she think of the fact that her diary of the two years her family spent in hiding from the Nazis would go on to become not only a classic of war literature, but one of the best-read and most loved books of all time? *The Diary of Anne Frank* is now handed down from one generation to the next, and reading the records of Anne's emotions has become a rite of passage for the teens of today. It has been translated into more than fifty languages, made into a play and a movie; a new English version, published in 1995, restored one-third more material that was cut out of the original by her father.

Why such popularity? Anne Frank's diary shows the human face to an inhuman war while it records Anne's emotional growth with great insight. When she passed through the walls behind the bookcases into the secret rooms of the attic in Amsterdam, she left her real life behind. At thirteen, Anne became a prisoner and fugitive at once. Torn from her friends at the onset of her teens, she poured her heart into the diary she called "Kitty," her imaginary friend and confessor. It's an intense experience for the reader who knows what Anne couldn't know—she wouldn't survive. Anne believed she would make it and shares her hopes and wishes for the children she will one day have. But at sixteen, she died at the concentration camp, Bergen Belson.

There is heartbreak also in the realization of what a gift for writing Anne had—it is almost unfathomable that some of the passages were written by an adolescent! Her honesty about her feelings, not all of them noble, is the quality that makes Anne's diary eternal. Caged in a hidden world, Anne showed us that a life of the mind could be full, no matter what the circumstances. For her courage and optimism, Anne Frank will always be a shero.

> *"The best remedy for those who are afraid, lonely, or unhappy is to go outside, somewhere where they can be quite alone with the heavens, nature, and God . . . I firmly believe that nature brings solace in all troubles."*—Anne Frank

More Inspiring Authors

The stories of Clara Isaacman and Anne Frank may inspire you to search for more of these precious documents of sheroic spirit from the Holocaust. I suggest Etty Hillesum's *An Interrupted Life*, the diary of a young Jewish girl hiding from Nazi's in the Netherlands, Eva Figes' *Little Eden: A Child at War*, about a shero who escaped to London, and Hanna Szenes: *A Song of Life*.

Audre Lorde:
A Burst of Light

Poet activist Audre Lorde is finally receiving the recognition she has so long deserved. A black lesbian poet who never hid her truth, Audre started writing poetry seriously in grade school. Born in the winter of 1934, her parents were West Indian immigrants who escaped to New York City from Grenada in 1924, just in time for The Great Depression. Audre grew up feeling different from her two older sisters, feeling like she was really an only child or "an only planet, or some isolated world in a hostile, or at best, unfriendly firmament."

Dazzlingly bright, Audre read voraciously. After a stint at the University of Mexico where the atmosphere of racial tolerance really opened her eyes to the racism in the United States, she began attending Hunter College and earned a degree in library science from Columbia. Married and with two small children, she worked for several New York libraries for eight years. Divorcing, she again moved toward her true passion—creative writing, both prose and poetry. In 1968, she started teaching creative writing at City University of New York. She also spent a year as poet in residence at Tougaloo College in Jackson, Mississippi, and went on to teach at many prestigious schools throughout America, where her reputation as an extraordinarily gifted poet grew.

The rare combination of gifted writer *and* teacher, Audre Lorde challenged her students. According to biographer Joanne S. Richmond in *Handbook of American Women's History,* Lorde urged her writing students to "Claim every aspect of themselves and encourage(d) them to discover the power of a spirited wholeness, knowing that in silence there is no growth, in suppression there is no personal satisfaction."

Her prose includes *The Cancer Journals* disclosing her battle with breast cancer, from which she ultimately died. Audre encountered a feminist's nightmare in her treatment, refusing to wear the prosthetic breast her doctor tried to force upon her. In 1982, *Ami: a New Spelling of My Name* was Lorde's foray into creating a new genre, what she called "biomythology" and her literary outing of her own lesbianism. In *Ami,* she digs deep into archetype, myth, and women's mysteries through the story of her mother's birthplace, the West Indian island of Carriacou. Lorde reveled in the lore of African goddesses and matriarchal tales, her lusty lovemaking with other black women, the intrinsic egalitarianism of nature. A staunch feminist and political activist, in her work she also pointed to the patriarchal "I" centeredness of Judeo-Christian traditions and confronted the hypocrisy of her times, angrily decrying sexism and bigotry in such poems as "Cables to Rage" and "The Black Unicorn."

On many occasions, Lorde read her poetry with fellow black poets Amiri Baraka, Nikki Giovanni, and Jayne Cortez. She began, as many poets do, in coffeehouses and humble church basements. But soon she was filling theaters and winning awards, including the American Book Award for *A Burst of Light,* a nomination in poetry for the 1974 National Book Award, and the Walt Whitman Citation of Merit, for which she became New York's Poet Laureate shortly before losing her life to cancer in 1992.

Audre Lorde is a poet's poet. Scratch the surface of many of today's best writers' influences and her name will come up repeatedly. Jewelle Gomez cites Audre Lorde as a major influence on her writing life and on the lives of many others in the African American creative community. In an article for *Essence* magazine, Gomez recognizes Lorde's work as a "a mandate to move through . . . victimization and create independent standards that will help us live full and righteous lives . . . She was a figure all women could use as a grounding when they fought for recognition of their worth."

> *"Poetry is the conflict in the lives we lead. It is most subversive because it is in the business of encouraging change."* —Audre Lorde

Maya Angelou:
How the Caged Bird Sings

Marguerite Johnson's childhood was marked by the hardship of the Depression years in which she grew up. Her parents divorced and packed her off to live with her granny, "Momma" Henderson, who eked out a living in Stamps, Arkansas, running a little general store. Marguerite, known as Maya, attended church devotedly with Momma who gave her stability and taught her the importance of values and a strong work ethic. The young girl found love and roots from her grandmother and the congregation at their church.

But tragedy struck when she visited her mother in St. Louis for eight months. Her mother had a boyfriend who spent a lot of time at her mother's house and often touched and hugged the seven-year-old much, but, in her innocence, she mistook it for a father's love. Later, he raped her and Maya felt guilty and responsible for his jailing and subsequent death at the hands of other inmates who exacted their own brand of justice on the child molester. She became catatonic as result of this onslaught of catastrophic violence. With the support of her family and an adult friend, Bertha Flowers, who introduced her to literature, Maya gradually reentered the world, speaking after five years and graduating first in her eighth grade class.

Maya and her mother then moved to San Francisco where her mother ran a boardinghouse and worked as a professional gambler. Maya met many colorful characters among the boarders and threw herself into school where she flourished. She got pregnant at sixteen and took on the full responsibilities of motherhood with the birth of her son, Guy. For a few years, Maya walked on the wild side: working a Creole restaurant, waitressing in a bar in San Diego, even an accidental and brief stint as a madam for two lesbian prostitutes. After a two-year marriage to a white man, Maya started dancing at the Purple Onion and got into show biz in the road show for "Porgy and Bess," which toured Africa and Europe. After cowriting "Cabaret for Freedom" with Godfrey Cambridge for the Southern Christian Leadership Conference, Maya drew Martin Luther King's attention for her talent and contribution to the civil rights movement, and he invited her to serve as an SCLC coordinator.

Maya's career was absolutely astonishing after this point, living in Egypt with Guy and her lover, a South African freedom fighter, and working in Ghana writing for *The*

African Review. She has remained involved with the theater, writing and performing in plays, acting in *Roots,* and writing several volumes of poetry as well as the script and music for the movie of her autobiography. But it is for the six best-selling volumes of her autobiography, starting with *I Know Why the Caged Bird Sings,* that she will go down in literary history. (The *New York Times* called her "one of the geniuses of Afro-American serial autobiography.") Written with captivating honesty, color, and verve, they are read by youth and adults alike for their inspirational message. Listen to this powerful passage from *I Know Why the Caged Bird Sings*: "If growing up is painful for the Southern Black girl, being aware of her displacement is the rest on the razor that threatens the throat. It is an unnecessary insult." When she was criticized for not being completely factual as a writer, Maya responded, "There's a world of difference between truth and facts. Facts can obscure truth."

Maya Angelou, a name combined from a nickname her brother called her and a variation on her first husband's name, truly reinvented herself. No moment in her wonderfully colorful life illustrates this as much as her reading of her beautiful poem, "On the Pulse of Morning" at President Bill Clinton's first inauguration. She had come a long way from the scared and silent little seven-year-old to a woman come fully into her power, unafraid to share that with the world.

> *"The ability to control one's own destiny . . . comes from constant*
> *hard work and courage."* —Maya Angelou

Maxine Hong Kingston:
Warrior Woman

Maxine Hong Kingston's appropriately titled magic realism autobiography, *The Woman Warrior: Memoirs of a Girlhood Among Ghosts,* came out in the bicentennial year, 1976. It was perfect timing because Kingston's story is an American story and a rebellion as well. Her tale of a Chinese American girl coming of age in California won the National Book Critic's Circle Award and set off a wave of writing by women of color; suddenly Maxine was a literary shero at thirty-six years old. Her subsequent book *China Men* won the same award in 1980, while her 1989 debut novel *Tripmaster Monkey: His Fake Book* thrilled both readers and critics.

Born in 1940 to Chinese immigrants who ran a Stockton, California, gambling house, Maxine got her name from a very successful blonde patron of their establishment. When some shady fair-weather friends swindled the Hongs out of the gambling business, they operated a laundry that employed the whole family, including Maxine and her five sisters and brothers. It was a life with a lot of drudgery, but Maxine was able to attend the University of California on eleven scholarships. Intending to study engineering, she quickly switched to English literature. Upon graduation, she married a white man, Earl Kingston.

Throughout her childhood, Maxine Hong Kingston struggled with being left out of the books she read. There were no stories of Chinese Americans in the Stockton library, and very few that featured girls. "In a way it's not so terrible to be left out," she said years later in the *Los Angeles Times,* "because then you could see at a very early age that there's an entire mother lode of stories that belong to you and nobody else."

The girl in *Woman's Warrior* had her tongue snipped by her mother in accordance with the superstition that it would allow her to speak many languages. (In *Ami,* Audre Lorde relates having undergone the same frenum cutting!) Juxtaposed with the mundane school and laundry work of Maxine's childhood in *The Woman Warrior* are fantastic imaginings of a girl unfettered by chores and mere reality. Kingston cycles through her mother's women ancestors and speaks frankly of Chinese folk antifemale expressions such as "When fishing for treasures in the flood, be careful not to pull in girls" and "There's no profit in raising girls. Better to raise geese than girls."

Perhaps then, it is little wonder that Kingston has come under the strongest attacks from those within her own culture. Several Chinese men have gone after Maxine, criticizing her for everything from her creative license with Chinese legends to her marriage to a white man. Playwright and activist Frank Chin, on behalf of Chinese American male pride, has issued the most vicious and vitriolic assault on Kingston's *Woman Warrior,* derogating it as "kowtow" and "persona writing." Chin also lays siege to her person as an example of "Ornamental Orientalia," calling her "a false goddess" created by "the worship of liars."

Clearly, Kingston struck a nerve with the power of her writing, touching on the critical issues of race and gender in a way that has caused it to become "the book by a living author most widely taught in American universities and colleges," notes former Poet Laureate Robert Hass. In *Warrior Woman,* Kingston's protagonist's inner battle rages silently within the confines of her mind— race, gender, spirit, identity, straddling the duality of a culture that devalues girls at the same time the legends say "that we failed if we grew up to be but wives or slaves. We could be heroines, swordswomen."

A Warrior Woman's Literary Shero

Kingston credits Virginia Woolf as being a major influence on her work. "Virginia Woolf broke through constraints of time, of gender, of culture. Orlando can be a man. Orlando can be a woman." Inspired by Woolf to experiment with point of view along gender and race lines, Kingston has crossed over, she says, to where she "can now write as a man, I can write as a black person, as a white person; I don't have to be restricted by time and physicality."

Judy Chicago:
Guess Who Came to Dinner?

Judy Chicago set the art world on its ear with The Dinner Party, her mixed media installation made from traditional women's crafts—needlework, weaving, ceramics, china-painting, and plastics. Born Judy Cohen in Chicago in 1939, she soon left for the burgeoning art scene in Los Angeles in the early 1960s. After her husband Jerry Gerowitz died in an automobile accident, Judy changed her name to Judy Chicago at the prompting of gallery owner Rolf Nelson. Nelson called her that partially because of her heavy Midwest accent and partially because of her strong sense of purpose. At a show at Cal State Fullerton in 1969 a sign with the following hung at the font door: Judy Gerowitz hereby divests herself of all names imposed upon her through male social dominance and freely chooses her own name, Judy Chicago.

Starting in 1973, Chicago began work on The Dinner Party, but soon realized her ambitious art project was going to require some help and ended up with an army of researchers, assistants, artists, and professional embroiderers. The Dinner Party has six huge banners spelling out the names featured on the forty-eight foot triangular table set with uniquely designed vulvic plates and sumptuously handmade and embroidered placemats. Every plate is in honor of a woman who made a significant contribution to herstory. The incredibly detailed work of The Dinner Party Table shows the research, thoughtfulness, and thoroughness of the project. The Amazons' placemat is replete with a labyris, the sacred double-axe, and breastplates, a crest moon, and many other minutiae. A total of 999 women are named in Chicago's opus, with engravings on triangular (Triple Goddess Power!) ceramic tiles on the Heritage Floor.

The Dinner Party was probably the climax of artistic expression of the feminism of the 1970's. Despite this splendid achievement, most museums were unwilling to show The Dinner Party. However, San Francisco feted Chicago and her masterwork with the largest crowd ever gathered to see the opening of a show—more than 100,000 people! Although the uptight suits that run the art world keep spinning out excuses, The Dinner Party has had a life of its own. It has been celebrated in photographs, books, performance art, and is indelibly imprinted in art herstory. Judy Chicago, whose latest undertaking is The Birth Project, certainly achieved what she set out to do in "symbolizing the long history of female achievement," underscoring the realization that "the history of Western Civilization, as we have understood it, has failed to represent the experience of half the human race."

Guest List at Judy Chicago's Dinner Party:

Primordial Goddess	Amazon	Boadaceia
Fertile Goddess	Hetshepsut	Hypatia
Kali	Judith	Marcella
Snake Goddess	Sappho	Saint Brigid
Sophia	Apasia	Theodora

Hrosvitha	Artemisia Gentileschi	Elizabeth Blackwell
Trotula	Anna Van Schurman	Emily Dickinson
Eleanor of Aquitaine	Anne Hutchinson	Ethel Smyth
Hildegarde of Bingen	Sacajawea	Margaret Sanger
Petronilla de Meath	Caroline Herschel	Natalie Barney
Christine de Pisan	Mary Wollstonecraft	Virginia Woolf
Isabella d'Este	Sojourner Truth	Georgia O'Keeffe
Elizabeth R	Susan B. Anthony	

bell hooks:
an Untamed Tongue

Born Gloria Jean Watkins in the small town of Hopkinville, Kentucky, in 1952, poet, feminist theorist, and professor bell hooks grew up as one of six kids watching her father work as a janitor and her mother clean houses for white people. Gloria was in the first round of desegregated classes and grieved for the loss of community and safety desegregation caused: "It hurt to leave behind memories, schools that were 'ours,' places that honored us." She was raised to be polite and mind her manners, but she "had a mouth." By talking back and saying what she really thought, she was chided by a neighbor as being "kin to bell hooks [her maternal grandmother]—a sharp-tongued woman.... Gloria was to have been a sweet southern girl, quiet, obedient, pleasing. She was not to have that wild streak that characterized women on her mother's side. With that, Gloria changed her name and continued finding her own voice and speaking out.

She found her calling at a young age—by the time she was ten, she was composing poems. Then, while working as a telephone operator to pay for classes at Stanford, nineteen-year-old bell shared her writing with her coworkers, working class black women who nurtured her talent and encouraged her to tell the world about the truth of being black and a woman. Since then, while she has continued to write poetry, her fame as a writer has come from critical essays on race, gender, and class.

Obtaining a Ph.D. in English literature, she has taught English and African American studies at various institutions around the country, including Yale, Oberlin, San Francisco State, and City College of New York. She first published her work in 1981 in the book *Ain't I a Woman*, a title quoting and honoring the great shero Sojourner Truth. bell's book had an immediate impact, named as one of the top twenty most important women's books. More importantly to bell, she received hundreds of letters from black women, including many poor and working class readers all over America who told them *Ain't I a Woman* changed their lives. For bell, the goal of a fully inclusive feminism rather than an "old girl's school" of Ivy League white women was on the way to being realized, a pursuit she continues to this day. "Moving from silence into speech is for the oppressed, the colonized, the exploited, and those who stand and struggle side by side a gesture of defiance that makes new life and new growth possible. It is that act of speech, of 'talking back,' that is no mere gesture of empty words, that is the expression of our movement from object to subject—the liberated voice." She continues to write, including a book with Cornel West, *Breaking Bread: Insurgent Black Intellectual Life,* and to ask us to wake up to the various isms that are socially created and personally painful.

"I was always saying the wrong thing, asking the wrong questions.
I could not confine my speech to the necessary corners
and concerns of my life."—bell hooks

Guerrilla Girls: Graffitti Goddesses

The Guerrilla Girls are a group of women artists and arts professionals who make posters about sexism and racism in the art world and the culture at large. These self-styled feminist do-gooders see themselves as counterparts to Robin Hood, Batman, and the Lone Ranger, using humor to provoke discussion and wearing gorilla masks to focus on the issues, not their personalities. In ten years, they have produced seventy posters that have been passed around the globe by kindred spirits. Their slogan? "We could be anyone; we are everywhere." To join the cause, contact hhtp://www.voyagerco.com/gg/

Celluloid Sheroes:
Conquering the Cathode Ray and Dominating the Silver Screen

Fictional sheroes are no less important than real-life ones; after all, in many ways they are more role models than flesh and blood women, particularly for young girls. In the movies, on TV, in books and comic books, in computer games, and on the Internet, fantasy sheroes are lighting up the screens of our minds, becoming more tough and more outrageous as time goes on. Celluloid sheroes are also doing some very important recognizance work on the collective male unconscious, as well, showing women to be powerful, fearless, smart, and independent. It's mind-boggling to consider the impact of a show like Xena broadcast in parts of the world where women are still oppressed. Thanks to Rupert Murdoch's SkyTV in India, Xena is fantastically popular among the one billion people of the subcontinent. Who knows? Maybe India's "Bollywood" might spring forth with a Xenaesque Phoolan Devi Warrior Shero series! Best of all, Xena has blown the ridiculous T & A fest, *Baywatch*, out of its polluted water, out-rating the sunbleached, surgically altered Barbies and providing a positive and strong image of women on a global level.

Strong women have always been on TV screens. Starting with *I Love Lucy* in 1951, the beloved character Lucy Ricardo mugged her way through three decades of early television, and the actress/creator built an entertainment empire and raised a doting family. While silver screen goddesses like Marilyn Monroe, Jean Harlowe, Jane Mansfield, and Joan Crawford played everything from vamps to victims, the actress shero Lucille Ball exacted the undying loyalty of millions of fans by letting us know in no uncertain terms she was packing an enormous brain beneath the carrot-colored curls. She reigned as queen in the formative years of television, which has gone on to become the most influential medium in the world, for better or worse.

Some fantastical silver screen sheroes were conjured from pages of favorite books and became instant archetypes: P. L. Travers' "Mary Poppins" was brought to life by Disney in their charming and quirky production of *Mary Poppins*. Golden-voiced Julie Andrews played the suffragist time-traveling nanny who believed in magic and could make it happen. The animation classic based on the timeless book *Alice in Wonderland* showed that intellectual curiosity in little girls is not only OK, it can make for some fascinating adventures and occupy scholars and children alike until the end of time. Similarly, the live action fantasy *The Wizard of Oz* featured Dorothy, a Kansas farm girl played by Judy Garland, who took us over the rainbow and back. On her shero's journey down the Yellow Brick Road, she helps the weak, battles evil, and learns from Good Witch Glinda that she has the power to return home!

On the fairy-dusted heels of the magic-making femmes in *Bewitched* and *I Dream of Jeannie* of sixties' television, Lieutenant Uhura, Mary Richards, Rhoda Morgenstern, and Marlo Thomas' *That Girl* were indicators of changes on the psychosocial horizon, portraying career women with sass and spunk who probably read *Cosmopolitan* and *The Feminine Mystique* and invariably acted rings around their dullard male counterparts. While women characters drowned in the bitchy, glitzy suds of bloated eighties' super-soaps *Dynasty, Falcon Crest,* and *Dallas,* the big screen emerged as a proving ground for the material decade's fictional feminists with Clarice Starling, Thelma and Louise, and *Alien's* ravishingly superior space shero, Ripley. In the fin de siècle days of the late nineties, women have completely taken over, from single mom Murphy Brown who singlehandedly destroyed the political career of that mentally challenged chauvinist Veep to *Melrose Place's* blunt and brilliant corporate shero Amanda and Ally McBeal attorney and everywoman who is sheroic by being smart, funny, bitingly honest, and very, *very* human. And while I'm passing out kudos, a big round of applause for Ellen DeGeneres, who became the first major TV star (and character) to come out of the closet. Thanks to them all, a powerful woman doesn't need to be a genetic witch, a skimpily clad genie in a bottle, or a gushingly nice (heterosexual) doormat to make it! The new sheroes don't need to worry about the glass ceiling anymore. Now the sky's the limit (watch out for unidentified flying objects, though!) and it's OK to be flawed. The celluloid sheroes of the new millennium are looking an awful lot like you and me.

Hey, who can take a nothing day and suddenly make it seem worthwhile? Well, it's you grrrrrl and you should know it!

Samantha Stephens:
The Good Witch

The most empowered woman in America in 1964 who still got invited into people's living rooms was probably Samantha Stephens of *Bewitched*! Able to exact her will with a mere twitch of her upturned nose, Samantha was witch royalty who gives it all up (not really) to stand by her man, a mere mortal by the name of Darrin. Polar opposites in every regard, he was as plain and hum drum as she was glamorous. Played by actress Elizabeth Montgomery, who later stunned audiences in her role as the axwielding murderess, Lizzie Borden, Samantha Stephens had the best of both worlds—normal suburban life and the ability to enact her fantasies in a twinkling. Darrin, an ad exec employed by the oily Larry Tate was talented but bumbling and always needed Sam to twitch him out of a jam.

▲ *Elizabeth Montgomery as TV witch Samantha Stephens.*

Sam's parents were cream-of-the-crop sorcerers; her mother Endora was an extremely powerful witch who suffered no fool gladly, thought Darrin (Durwood, Dum Dum, she never ever said his proper name) was a total loser, and virulently objected to her daughter's decision to forgo magic. Sam's father, the dramatically dressed warlock Maurice, appeared less frequently than Endora and often took his daughter's side in disputes. He had trouble remembering Darrin's name, too, and called him Dobbin, Duspin, and Duncan in a never-ending series of failed but creative attempts to address his son-in-law.

A very happy couple when not embroiled in

one jam or other, Darrin and Samantha had two children, Tabitha and Adam, whose genetic heritage endowed them with magical powers, much to the delight of Sam's entire family. With the birth of baby Tabitha, another character made her debut, Sam's raven-haired cousin Serena, a swinging "mod" witch who looked a lot like Samantha and was, in fact, played by Elizabeth Montgomery under the stage name Pandora Spocks. Serena was quite a gadabout flirt, a card-carrying member of the Cosmos Club who played at being a singer-songwriter. Other relatives constituted a veritable coven of eccentrics including Hagatha, Enchantra, Hepzibah, and Clara. Samantha remained the calm center of the chaos she created.

Bewitched was a top-rated show for its entire run, including two different Darrins. In Christine Lunardini's wonderful book *What Every American Should Know About Women's History,* she points out that *Bewitched* was "the perfect show for a nation on the cusp of 'women's liberation.... What made the show such an interesting commentary about the early sixties, and a portent of the women's movement that came shortly thereafter, was the fact that the husband Darrin was so threatened by his wife's powers that he insisted they be bottled up entirely."

Descendants of the Nose Twitcher

Sabrina the teenage witch and Buffy the vampire slayer would seem to be the descendants of Samantha Stephens. Buffy, a stylishly clad TV shero, has the bad luck to attend a high school built over of a nest of the undead and, on a daily basis, fights evil and slays vampires to keep her schoolmates, teachers, and family safe. Sabrina is also a high-schooler with special powers. She is trying to fit in at her new school and make new friends. On her sixteenth birthday, her genetic witchiness kicks in.

To Sabrina's utter amazement, she discovers she is from a whole clan of witches and warlocks from way back. Try blending in when you have magical powers you just found out about!

Agent 99:
The Spy Who Loved Us

The "better half" of 1968's Spy Couple of the Year, Agent 99 captivated America in *Get Smart,* the popular television show. Sleekly played by Barbara Feldon, Agent 99 was the "straight woman" to a cast of comedic klutzes, exhibiting a powerful combination of beauty and brains.

Agent 99 was a meat and potatoes Emma Peel, just as professional but more approachable. Her sympathy for her partner Agent 86, the woebegone Maxwell Smart, was tangible. For the television viewer, if 99 could put up with him, so could we, despite his often irritating klutziness and ineffectuality.

Agent 99 and her partner were kept busy saving the world from evil in the form of a corrupt group, KAOS. The good guys, Agents 99 and 86, and company work for the U.S. government's secret organization CONTROL, formed specifically to stop KAOS in its diabolical tracks. As agents of CONTROL, 99 and 86 get to enjoy the latest technological wonders such as shoe phones, a highly intelligent canine agent, Fang, a robot assistant named Hymie, and an antibugging device referred to as The Cone of Silence. The other agents of CONTROL, all men such as the completely clueless Agent 13 and the "Chief" Thaddeus, were either utterly inept or simply uninvolved, leaving Agent 99 to save the day over and over again with her winning combination of optimism, competence, and concern. Because of her warmth and eagerness to do her job well and be a vital member of her team, 99's superiority to the men in the organization works on the level of a subtle undercurrent, and therefore, was not at all disturbing to the television audience of sixties America.

Agent 86, as played by Don Adams, posed as a salesman for the fictional Pontiac Greeting Card Company while Agent 99, kept up an everchanging series of aliases to protect her identity. Interestingly for 60s TV, the other top agent in CONTROL was Charlie Watkins, whose alias as a woman (really a man in perpetual drag) was played by the stunning actress Angelique Pettyjohn. The usually dim-witted Agent 86 was quite right to believe that Charlie was really a woman. Sexy Pettyjohn went on to a wide ranging career as a beautiful alien in *Star Trek* and leads in several successful porn films including *Body Talk* and *Titillation.*

Perhaps the most fascinating aspect of Agent 99 is that we never see behind her facade, for her true identity is never revealed! The real genius of it is that we believe she is simply Agent 99, open, perky, and pretty; never mind that she is a crack-shot and the best agent of the lot by a long shot. Even when Agent 99 and Agent 86 marry, she remains 99 and her mother is always referred to as Mrs. 99 or 99's mother. Wonderfully played by Barbara Feldon, Agent 99 remains a complete mystery, winning over new generations of fans in a perpetuity of reruns.

Julia Barnes: Beyond Cool

If Agent 99 and company from *Get Smart* were the rather unhip *Odd Squad*, they were counterpointed brilliantly in the sixties by The Mod Squad. *The Mod Squad* was a trio of hipsters—two men, one woman—with lefty leanings and a political consciousness who refocussed their rebelliousness into doing good and upholding the law. The Mod Squad wore beads but eschewed guns and had a killer boogie nights soundtrack with cheesy Hammond organ riffs keeping a nonstop acid groove.

At the center of the trio was Peggy Lipton's Julia Barnes. With Nico-like bangs and long blond hair, Peggy Lipton was definitely the coolest chick on the small screen, a veritable oasis of sophisticated modernity in a sea of dorky TV characters. The daughter of a San Francisco prostitute, Julia was a runaway booked for vagrancy in Los Angeles when she was spotted by Captain Adam Greer who handpicked the trio to constitute a special "youth squad" with enough street cred and cool points to pass as "counterculture." Julia posed as trailer trash, a Hollywood starlet, and a high-school girl in her mission to save the youth of America from drug lords, crooks, and the "underground." Julia Barnes would definitely be the only TV character Andy Warhol would ever have wanted to party with!

Emma Peel:
Avenger Angel

The sixties were a hot bed of sexy spies. One of those who left behind lasting memories was Diana Rigg's Emma Peel from the British ensemble show, *The Avengers*. Emma Peel, *neé* Knight, was an extremely independent woman whose husband, test pilot Peter Peel, died in a crash. The head of Knight Industries since the age of twenty-one when she inherited the family business upon her father's untimely death, Emma maintained a dazzling lifestyle. She drove a 1966 Lotus Elan and was a student of anthropology and an extraordinary bridge player who authored the article "Better Bridge with Applied Mathematics."

A yen for adventure, speed, and risk convinced Emma that she should join John

Steed in his spy adventures after they met in a minor fender-bender. Steed was a handsome and urbane ministry agent who worked for the British government in a mission to "avenge crimes perpetrated against the people and the state." Emma joined forces with the other Avengers and became, for many viewers, the one to watch. Exuding intelligence and not at all hard on the eyes, Emma was a clever chameleon who invariably saved the day. Famous for wearing all black, Emma's trademark was her "Emmapeeler" catsuit, still much imitated to this day. When her husband Peter was found alive in the Amazonian jungle, several years after his plane crash, Emma left The Avengers to join her husband, who looked eerily like Patrick McNee's John Steed! Her parting advice was "Always keep your bowler on in times of stress and watch out for diabolical masterminds."

▶ *Diana Rigg as The Avengers sexy spy Emma Peel wearing her trademark "emmapeeler" cat suit.*

Modesty Blaise:
Night of the Morningstar

Comic strip character (and later movie star) Modesty Blaise is a survivor. Surviving a war in Europe (you pick, it could be World War II or the Balkans), Modesty came to consciousness at the age of six, wandering barefoot, hungry, homeless, and alone. She awoke with the distinct feeling that something really terrible had happened and that her mind had locked it away to protect her. She scurried around like a wild thing, stealing food, running, running, always running. While working as a goatherd in Malaurak, Modesty was captured by a "flesh gang" who sold her for a slave. Modesty's childhood ended here when she learned that men can do terrible things to a girl. Fortunately, Modesty encountered a kindly man named Lob who taught her book learning and gave her the name of Modesty. Lob had been a professor, but was now displaced, like his student. Her eager mind grasped onto everything, and she was soon speaking many languages and gave herself a last name—Blaise, a name she took from the Arthurian wizard Merlin's mentor.

Upon Lob's death, Modesty was again left entirely to her own devices and the game she knew best, survival in a rough world. In Tangier, Modesty found herself in the midst of a terrible gang war and seized control of the powerful Louche gang, reforging the ragtag ruffians into a sophisticated group called The Network. Modesty's Network became a megacorporation, successfully operating in the gray areas between criminality and big business. She made a best friend when Willie Garvin joined her crew, a man who dedicated his life to protecting and adoring Modesty as a platonic soulmate. When money and possessions lost their luster, Modesty and Willie retired, Modesty to travel the world and Willie to run his pub, The Treadmill. Their reputation remained behind and soon enough, the British Secret Service sought them out. Modesty Blaise took up the challenge and worked with Sir Gerald Tarrant and his agents, unraveling many puzzles and opening the door to a new life of adventure.

Modesty Lives!

Modesty Blaise is the creation of Peter O'Donnell, first appearing in the form of a comic strip in 1963 in the *London Evening Standard* and last seen in the *Detroit Free Press*. Modesty quickly developed a cult following for her survivalist pluck and ability to go on no matter how much pain she witnessed and experienced. In 1966, Monica Vitti starred in a

Modesty Blaise movie and Miramax is reportedly working up a redo feature film starring the orphan shero. The volumes of strips have been collected into books that all have wonderfully romantic and tantalizingly colorful names like "The Impossible Virgin," "The Silver Mistress," "The Xanadu Talisman," "Dead Man's Handle," and "The Night of the Morningstar." Like all supersheroes, Modesty has a plethora of webpages dedicated to her, but this one is the best bet to date: http://www.cs.umu.se/~kenth/modesty.html where the riddle of Modesty Blaise is explored intelligently and imaginatively!

Barbarella:
Forty–first Century Femme Fatale

]n 1968, Roger Vadim and his wife Jane Fonda offered the movie-watching world a delectable bombshell bon bon—*Barbarella*. French artist Jean-Claude Forest originated the erotic science fiction comic strip in the early sixties for the sheer entertainment of his friends who convinced him that it had potential for mass popularity. They were quite right; the strip soon took Europe by storm. Director Roger Vadim and Italian movie mogul Dino De Laurentis took notice and felt that a live-action *Barbarella* would find an audience with the new generation whose interests included sexual freedom and space exploration. Amazingly, both Vadim and De Laurentis had Jane Fonda in mind for the role. When they got together to work out the conversion from comic strip to feature film, *Barbarella* emerged as fun, fluffy, and titillating entertainment.

Barbarella is a forty-first century shero, so evolved that she bests her enemies fairly effortlessly even when the odds seem insurmountable. Jane Fonda was the epitome of fresh American femaledom, playing Barbarella as an innocent abroad who triumphs over violence and debauchery with her gullible Gulliverlike guilelessness and perfection. (An unexpected result of the film is that Jane Fonda's Barbarella contrasts the American sensibility to the European—naive versus decadent. Fortunately, the film pokes fun at itself, allowing us to have a laugh and some thrills at the expense of the extremely earnest cast.)

Barbarella begins with the eponymous sheroine leisurely suspended in the weightless comfy confines of her fur-lined spaceship while she removes her spacesuit. In a very-advanced-for-the-time cinematic sleight-of-hand, letters form from each item of clothing Barbarella takes off to spell out the credits. Nude and ready, her video phone announces she has an incoming message from the president of Earth who assigns her the task of finding Durand-Durand, the inventor of the positronic ray—the ultimate weapon. Unable to entirely understand the concept of violence ("a primitive state of neurotic irresponsibility"), the president beams aboard the last remaining weapons on Earth from the Museum of Conflict for Barbarella to use in her dangerous assignment. Donning the first of several sexy costumes, the space-babe bids her companion computer/alarm clock, Alfie, goodnight and begins her misadventures.

Crash landing on Pythin, a nasty planet with an earthlike atmosphere, she is bound and tortured by children with remote control-attack dolls. Before Barbarella's beauty is blemished, however, Mark Hand, who lives in a lustrous skimcraft that zips over the icy surface of the planet, rescues her. The grateful Barbarella, lamenting her inability to properly thank hero Hand, is shocked when he suggests a proper thank-you would involve lovemaking. "You don't even know my psychocardiagram!" she exclaims, forty-first century culture having substituted exaltation transference pills for physical coupling. Though dubious, Barbarella agrees to the antiquated ways of sex and is soon humming delightedly and remarking upon the superiority of "old-fashioned ways." Hand offers his new honey her pick of the skimcraft's closets and she steps out sporting a fabulous fur outfit with a six-foot tail!

She sets out again in search of Durand-Durand. This time, she encountered a chronically depressed blind angel Pygar, whom she deems as her only chance to help her get to the evil empire of Sogo. She also meets a professor Ping, played by French mime Marcel Marceau in one of his only speaking roles, who gives invaluable information about the evil rules and citizens of Sogo. Barbarella and her blind angel run into many obstacles, including imprisonment in the deadly Chamber of Ultimate Solutions by the antishero known as The Great Tyrant, played by Anita Pallenberg. Oddly, they are rescued by the Tyrant's Concierge before their certain deaths. One of Pallenberg's more ingenious punishments for Barbarella is

▲ *Jane Fonda as the highly evolved space shero Barbarella.*

to lock her in a cage to be pecked to death by brightly plumed parrots.

The mercurial Concierge, turns on Barbarella and recaptures her. This time, he installs a machine that kills through excess sexual pleasure. His plans fail, though, when Barbarella's capacity for sexual enjoyment blows the machine's circuits without fazing her. In fact, reaching new sexual heights empowers her anew and she figures out that the Concierge is actually Durand-Durand, who is ultimately destroyed by his own positronic ray. Barbarella, the sex kitten of space, prevailed through her own ingenuousness. If the film contained any message, it is that a woman in command of her own sexuality is the most powerful being in the universe.

Jane Fonda: Cause Celebre

It's impossible to address the sheroism of *Barbarella* without a look at Jane Fonda. Even in the lightweight *Barbarella*, Jane stirred controversy. The movie's celebratory sexuality and nudity was greeted with shock and rebuke upon its release, except among more sophisticated audiences.

Though her lengthy career has included an immense array of powerful women characters, Jane sparks debate even now with her outspoken approach toward the concerns she deems important. To some, she will always be "Hanoi Jane" who protested the Vietnam War. While married to California Congressman Tom Hayden, Jane pumped millions of dollars into his campaigns and her liberal causes, and threw everyone for a loop when she emerged as a diet guru whose mantra "feel the burn" made America sit up, literally. Her marriage to CNN magnate Ted Turner amazed her fans and detractors equally as she threw herself into the role of glamour wife. Observant Fondaphiles knew, however, it was just a matter of time before a new passion drew her back to center stage. Jane is now using her considerable celebrity and money to draw the nation's attention to teen pregnancy. When the Republican majority in Congress moved to withhold funding for sex education to any school providing condoms to high-schoolers, Fonda teamed up with Durex, the condom manufacturer famous for their logo, "Only the Feeling Gets Through," to support the Georgia Campaign for Adolescent Pregnancy Prevention. She's also helping to raise consciousness on another taboo subject—depression. This one hits close to home; Fonda's mother committed suicide when she was twelve. She has recently narrated a film on the subject in hopes that it will be seen as a treatable medical condition.

Jane Fonda's life, though colorful, is exemplary of risk-taking sheroism for never backing down from a fight and pursuing her passions with zeal and self-sacrifice. *Time* magazine journalist Margaret Carlson describes Jane as "always more interested in making a difference than in making a movie."

Lieutenant Uhura:
Living Long and Prospering

S *tar Trek*'s Lieutenant Uhura was the coolest chick in space before Captain Janeway womaned the helm of *Star Trek's Voyager*. Uhura has several firsts under her miniskirted belt; she was one of the first black women to star as a regular on a television series, and she participated in the first interracial TV kiss. Named Swahili for "freedom," Uhura was a crack communications technician, a wonderful musician who crooned to her crew, and a crack-shot with a phaser, who "stunned" all manner of bizarre, low-budget aliens with compassion and efficiency.

Nichelle Nichols, the actress who immortalized Uhura, has had a life nearly as colorful as her TV character. While pregnant with Nichelle, her mother was nearly shot by Al Capone's gangster brother. And her baby brother, Thomas, was killed with other members of the suicidal Heaven's Gate cult in 1997's San Diego suburb catastrophe. Believing the Hale Bopp comet to be the harbinger of the arrival of the spaceship that would transport him to a wonderful new world, the connection to his Star Trekking sister's career is tragically ironic.

In her autobiographical book, *Beyond Uhura,* Nichols reveals her family herstory as the granddaughter of a Welsh slave owner and the daughter of a slave. As a girl, she danced with Katherine Dunham and sang with Duke Ellington. Nichols also sheds light on the dishy goings-on behind the sci-fi scenes—her affair with producer Gene Roddenberry, the discriminatory treatment at the hands of NBC execs, and the difficulties of working with that egocentric pill, William Shatner.

Nichelle seems to have embraced space as the central theme of her life, recording an album "Dark Side of the Moon" and speaking on behalf of NASA's campaign to employ women and people of color for the space shuttle program. Nichols stays busy, appearing in the highly successful Star Trek films, singing with orchestras across the country, and producing films for the Smithsonian Air and Space Museum. She now cruises cyberspace, connecting with fans who will always remember her graceful portrayal of Lieutenant Uhura on board the USS Enterprise. Her favorite episodes of the original series *Star Trek*? "Anything where Uhura got to get off the bridge; for example, "Gamesters or Triskelian,' 'Mirror Mirror,' 'Plato's Step Children,' and our beloved 'The Trouble with Tribbles.'

> *"Black super-star actress Whoopi Goldberg . . . told me her heroine was Uhura. Because of Uhura, she decided she could be anything she wanted to be, so she decided to be a super star! Keep reaching for your star! And, never look back."* —Nichelle Nichols

Captain Kathryn Janeway: Now Voyager

Space Shero Captain Kathryn Janeway outclasses Kirk and is every ounce the peer of Picard as she heads the helm of the starfleet ship USS Voyager through the twenty-fourth century on *Star Trek: Voyager*. Her mission is, if anything, more difficult than her predecessors in that her ship is lost in space at the utter ends of the universe with a crew made up of enemies. Janeway is a wonderful admixture of confidence and competence with plenty of spunk to see the crew through their dangerous encounters with the unknown. Janeway can navigate the Voyager thorough plasma storms and wormholes in time, and she can control the chaos of warp-core microfractures with elan. Thanks to speed-of-light advances in computer animation, Janeway faces horrors the other Trekkie commanders could never have imagined.

The search for Captain Janeway was akin to the search for the perfect Scarlett O'Hara. Other actresses considered for the role were *Bionic Woman's* Lindsay Wagner, *Bladerunner's* android stripper, Joanna Cassidy, and *Terminator's* Linda Hamilton. After a bumpy beginning with the miscast Genevieve Bujold who beamed almost immediately back to earth, Kate Mulgrew took the captain's chair and has delighted audiences ever since. Died in the wool Trekkie purists are ecstatic about her hands-on, down-to-earth (yes, it's possible even in deep space!) impulsiveness so reminiscent of the original Captain James T. Kirk. Kate Mulgrew says, "Captain Janeway is the quintessential woman of the future . . . both commanding and discerning in her warmth, she's authoritative while remaining accessible."

Batgirl:
Not Just Another Caped Crusader

The third partner of Batman and Robin, Batgirl is a shero created by DC Comics, who debuted on the printed page in 1967, but has gone on to see life on TV in an aminated TV series, a live-action series, and a movie. This girl knows how to cross-promote!

Batgirl is, by day, librarian Barbara Gordon, the daughter of Gotham's police commissioner. When dear old dad was falsely accused of and framed for a crime, Barbara suited up, tossed back her cape, and assumed the guise of shero, Batgirl. She had learned a thing or two from Batman and, after clearing her father of the false charges, joined the Dynamic Duo for some estrogen-powered crime-solving.

Batgirl really didn't need superpowers, as she had developed her inherent abilities so well. Equipped with only a batarang and wind-proof hair, Batgirl brought an arsenal of natural talent to her role. She is a superb athlete, researcher, and computer hacker extraordinaire, and held brown belts in Karate and Judo. She excells in the stick-fighting martial art, Escrima, and is a great gymnast and dancer. Oh, yes, she also rides a mean motorcycle! Played by Yvonne Craig in the live action TV series, Batgirl entered the show by rescuing Batman and Robin from the Killer Moth. After her debut, the powers-that-be decided to make her ultrastreamlined costume more feminine and added ruffles and bows!

Batgirl and Catwoman were pitted against each other in the episode *Batgirl Returns* where Batgirl bested the feline antishero, and then unexpectedly teamed up with her to became the more dynamic of duos. Even Batman couldn't handle the two fighting femmes! Turning to the movies, Batgirl, played by Alicia Silverstone, nearly stole the movie *Batman Forever* from the boys with her English schoolgirl-turned-biker chick act.

Bionic Woman Batgirl finally got her very own comic in 1997, and actress Yvonne Craig's life story is being told in the biography *"From Ballet to the Batcave and Beyond."* Yvonne enjoys a rabid cult following for her role in the perennial rerun fave. She makes public appearances and participates in net chats with her fans, both original sixties TV watchers and kids who discovered Batgirl anew in syndication. A typical message to Yvonne comes from an anonymous Alaskan: "Thank you, Yvonne, for being a female role model for me and letting me know I did not have to be like June Cleaver and stay home in the kitchen." Our sentiments exactly!

Check out Batgirl online for fans of the "Dark Night Damsel of Gotham City" :http://www.netvista.net/~mpg/batgirl/batgirl.html. And don't forget another web site devoted to Batgirl; it was created by a fourteen-year-old boy, Jonathan Sanders: http.//www.geocities.com/EnchantedForest/2635/why.htm

▶ *Yvonne Craig as batgirl, librarian by day, crime solver by night.*

Caped Crusaders Wage the War for Women Everywhere!

In 1974, the U. S. Department of Labor created a wonderfully tongue-in-cheek and right-on public service announcement featuring Batman and Robin hogtied in an abandoned warehouse with a ticking bomb set to explode any minute. Upon Batgirl's arrival, the not-so-dynamic duo command our girl to untie them "before it's too late!"

Batgirl: "It's already too late. I've worked for you for a long time and I'm paid less than Robin."

Robin: "Holy discontent!"

Batgirl: "Same job, same employer means equal pay for men and women."

Batman: "No time for jokes, Batgirl."

Batgirl: "It's no joke, it's the federal equal pay law."

Batman: "Can we talk about this later?"

Voiceover: Will Batgirl save the dynamic duo? Will she get equal pay? Tune in tomorrow or contact the Wage and Hour division listed in your phone book under the Department of Labor.

Mary Richards:
She Turned the World on With Her Smile

Mary Richards seized America's heart with her first toothy grin. Having played second banana to Dick Van Dyke on the 1960s show of the same name, Mary Tyler Moore already had fans, but she also brought several concerns to producers who feared American TV viewers would be confused by the absence of Dick Van Dyke and might get upset by her character's status as a single woman. But, beginning in 1970, Mary Richards made TV history, becoming the first single, white female over the age of thirty to star in a weekly TV show. As such she helped open the minds of a stodgy America, uneasy about the idea of independent, childless women.

Mary's pre-pilot history was that she left New York after breaking up with her boyfriend and took off for Minneapolis to start a new life and new career. Renting an apartment from her old friend Phyllis Lindstrom, she got a job as assistant producer of WJM-TV's "Six O'Clock News" show. Curmudgeonly booze-hound boss Lou Grant saw "spunk" and spark in Mary, who had applied for a job as a secretary and hired her in at a higher position, soon promoting her to associate producer. Aside from Mary, Lou was surrounded by has-beens, losers, and sadsacks, resigning himself to the fact that the "Six O'Clock News" would never be great—or even very good. Anchorman Ted Baxter is dumb as a rock and egomaniacal, but is endowed with an impressive head of silver hair and a deep, booming voice—essential tricks of the trade. Murray, the news writer, has low self-esteem and a wicked wit that occasionally erupts into fits of anger. Fellow WJMer Sue Ann Nivens has a cooking show, a nonstop libido, and a yen to generally cause trouble. Mary's neighbors, the nosy and irritating Phyllis Lindstrom, and sassy New Yorker Rhoda Morgenstern rounded out the cast of one of the most beloved shows in television's history.

▼ *Mary Tyler Moore in her role as seventies' icon Mary Richards.*

Mary was the bedrock of her namesake show. Throughout the ups and downs of her own life, she was the one everyone depended on when the chips were down. *The Mary Tyler Moore Show* dealt with issues that were very cutting edge for the seventies—aging for single women, sex out of wedlock, the struggle for equality for women on the job, and the pressure from friends and relatives to be married. Mary Richards was hugely appealing and very human; her weaknesses and self-doubts were never hidden. She became a role model for the millions of American women who were going through the same struggles in their daily lives and looked at Mary as a friend and sister.

The show was canceled after seven stellar years. The ending was sad and hilarious, fitting for the end of a legend. Chuckles the Clown, the star of WJM's most popular show died a tragic death when he was "shelled" to death by a rogue elephant in his Peter Peanut costume as grand marshall of a parade. After the demise of Chuckles, the station manager fired the entire staff, including Mary and Lou, keeping the hapless Ted on as his only employee. *The Mary Tyler Moore Show* spawned new series for Lou Grant, Rhoda, Phyllis, and Betty White, whose Sue Anne Nivens chewed up scenery with such regularity. Murray didn't get his own show, but actor Gavin Macleod had quite a success with the unexpected role as the suave captain of *The Love Boat*.

The Mary Tyler Moore theme song was written and performed by Sonny Curtis. Careful listeners probably noticed several telltale changes after the first season:

First Season
How will you make it on your own?
This world is awfully big, girl, this time you're all alone.
But it's time you started living.
It's time you let someone else do some giving.

Love is all around, no need to waste it.
You can have the town, why don't you take it?
You might just make it after all.
You might just make it after all.

Second Through Seventh Seasons
Who can turn the world on with her smile?
Who can take a nothing day, and suddenly make it all seem worthwhile?
Well, it's you girl and you should know it.

With each glance and every little movement you show it.

Love is all around, no need to waste it.
You can have the town, why don't you take it?
You're gonna make it after all.
You're gonna make it after all.

Rhoda Morgenstern: Prime Time's First Feminist

Mary Richard's upstairs neighbor in Minneapolis was New Yorker Rhoda Morgenstern, a single Jewish artist who came to the upper Midwest when she couldn't find either a job or an apartment in Manhattan. Working as a window dresser in the Twin Cites, Rhoda was a breath of fresh air, contrasting sharply with the waspy cast of the show. At first, she and Mary rubbed each other the wrong way in a tiff over Mary's apartment, which Rhoda desperately wanted. After settling in the attic of the Weatherly Street Victorian, however, Rhoda decorated her cramped apartment with her singular dramatic style and set about becoming Mary's best friend. Frank, open, and funny, Rhoda exhibited yet another set of issues for single women of America through her battle with weight, never getting dates, and problems with money.

Rhoda stood out like a sore thumb in Minneapolis, but never stopped being herself. She got a $40 dollar fine at the city zoo for feeding a buffalo yogurt, and she constantly shocked Phyllis with her brutal honesty and catty barbs. Rhoda was definitely a strong woman and, upon moving back to New York and heading up her own TV show, took on even stronger issues than "The Mary Tyler Moore Show." She married and divorced on prime time, dieted down with her sister Brenda, and took on the issue of unmarried sex and infidelity much more openly. Rhoda was very much a modern career woman, feminized, and ready to fight for her rights.

Foxy Brown, Sheba and Coffy:
Three Sheroes in One

In the seventies, Pam Grier was one of only three "bankable" Hollywood actresses, along with divas Liza Minelli and Barbara Streisand. Her success was in the very different milieu than the singer-actresses who rivaled her in ticket sales. Rather, Pam Grier was the queen of "blaxploitation" films with her action-shero characters Foxy Brown, Sheba, and Coffy. It's easy to see why Grier has prevailed in this medium—the camera loves her. When she is on the screen, no one else matters—her charisma draws the eye and keeps it. Strikingly beautiful, Grier always manages to rise above the material and imbue her characters with charm and intelligence. Called the "Mocha Mogul of Hollywood" by author Jamaica Kincaid, Pam is the lucky result of Black, Caucasian, Asian, and Native American gene pools colliding. An Air Force brat, she spent her formative years in Europe until her family relocated to Denver, Colorado, where she experienced the culture shock of a dangerous high school.

Entering a beauty contest in the hopes of winning a year's tuition for her second year of college as a premed student, Grier was spotted by a Hollywood agent who took her to Hollywood and groomed her to be an actress. Working as a switchboard operator while taking classes and auditioning, Grier made a fateful move one day when she approached Roger Corman, the king of B movies. After some bit parts, she starred in his version of *The Defiant Ones* called *White Mama, Black Mama,* a women-in-prison chick-flick. The move was quickly forgotten but Black Mama was not.

Grier became the premiere black star of the day, a sort of female Shaft. In *Coffy,*

▲ *Pam Grier rose above blaxploitation to powergirl Foxy Brown.*

Grier slays a pusher who got her sister hooked on dope and in *Foxy Brown,* she pulled out all the stops in her revenge for the murders of both her brother and her boyfriend. In a startling turn, Foxy castrates the killer and pickles his member in a jar she presents as a gift to his girlfriend! *Sheba, Baby* has Grier going up against the mob to save her father's loan company, offing the Godfather with a spear gun.

Grier herself points out that, aside from Coffy, Foxy, and Sheba, there were virtually no powerful black women characters in film. Journalist Darius James, a blaxploitation scholar, puts it eloquently: "Grier reigned over the altars of adolescent onanism in a dangerous double-D cup like a black-skinned goddess Kali." Roger Ebert, a huge Pam Grier fan beginning with her pre-Black Mama bit parts (she was featured in Russ Meyer's *Beyond the Valley of the Dolls,* a script Ebert wrote) draws parallels between Grier and Sean Connery, "She knew how to keep her action in character, make it believable. She remained likable in the serial while doing some truly horrible things to her enemies. She should have done them to her directors."

Eventually Pam grew tired of the redundancy of the roles she was playing and drew back from acting. As she lay dying from cancer, a close friend, the singer Minnie Ripperton urged Grier to start "giving" again. Grier gives a great deal to her personal charities—fighting drugs and helping improve educational opportunities for mentally retarded children.

She returned to acting in the eighties with a vengeance, surprising everyone with her comeback role as an anything but glamourous doper-prostitute in the critically acclaimed *Fort Apache: The Bronx*. Grier gave the performance of a lifetime; Pauline Kael in the *New York Times* expressed the effectiveness of Grier's performance in her review of the film: "each time Pam Grier's angel-dusted hooker appears, she give us a feeling of obscene terror." Having escaped being typecast, she went on to myriad roles in TV's *Miami Vice*, plays like Sam Shepherd's *Fool For Love*, Disney films, and as action king Steven Seagal's partner in the smash hit *Above the Law*.

Idolized by a new generation of filmmakers and fans who discovered her in the video store, Pam Grier remains an object of fascination. One of her biggest fans is Quentin Tarantino, whose debut *Pulp Fiction* is a modern classic. A purveyor of "bad taste at its best" he wrote the lead role in *Jackie Brown* specifically for Pam Grier and paired her with Samuel L. Jackson, one of the finest black actors of this generation.

The queen of the genre she helped create, Pam Grier is more than a pin-up girl. She became a role model for women of all colors, emblematic of women's lib and a positive image of black women in cinema. In *Notable Black Women*, Jessie Cszrney Smith declares Grier a "pioneer." "With her independent and forceful persona, she set a precedent for all black women in film and her work is important in black film history."

"When I grew up I knew a certain kind of Black woman who
was the sole support of her family and who would, if you disrespected her,
beat you into the cement. She was the glue that held her family together, got

them through. I admired her greatly. I still do. And she still exists. I brought that lady to the screen—played her to the bone!"—Pam Grier

Charlie's Angels:
Triple Goddesses

Too often put down for simply being drop-dead gorgeous, *Charlie's Angels'* sheroic authenticity is made clear through a careful attention to the show's intro. After graduation from the police academy with flying colors, all three angels were given dead-end jobs with the tacit understanding that as highly attractive women, they were either too threatening to the L. A. police patriarchy or not taken seriously at all, dismissed into no brainer clock-punching activities such as meter maids and crosswalk guards.

So, when the mysterious Charles Townsend, aka "Charlie," pursued them to be private detectives for his classy agency, who can blame them for jumping at the chance? Jill Munroe, Kelly Garrett, and Sabrina Duncan prove Charlie's instincts right when they unfailingly catch the crooks every time. It is also clear that the L. A. police force lost three crack agents by not treating the gorgeous girl cops respectfully. What a career move! They made a ton more money, had more fun, and were treated like the stars they were by the Wizard of Oz-like agency owner, Charlie, who saw their talent, deemed them "pretty, bright, and gutsy," and loosed the sassiest squad of "dicks" the seventies had ever seen!

Charlie's Angels was hugely popular with both men and women and was almost equally controversial with bralessness, plenty of bikinis, and lots of "jiggle quotient": courtesy of plots that required the tightly clad angels to run, jog, or trot in nearly every episode. Despite the tinge of prurience, though, the bottom line was that the angels were good-looking women who were also super-competent. Every week had them outsmarting some feckless man, spurning unwanted advances with a roll of the eye and a click of the handcuff.

Starting with the unforgettable cast of Farrah Fawcett, Jaclyn Smith, and Kate Jackson, *Charlie's Angels* was an out-and-out phenomenon. Though the cast changed to substitute Cheryl Ladd, Shelly Hack, and Tanya Roberts as the women left, the initial crew has achieved cult status, wearing quite well through the years in constant rerun rotation. Farrah, whose character Jill quit the show with aspirations to become the first woman racecar driver to win Europe's Le Mans race, became an international celebrity in her own right with her famous poster, the best-selling one of all time, showing her at her toothy and toothsome best with a tumble of hair imitated by millions of seventies women. Smith, a relative unknown, was beloved for her elegance and cool beauty, while Kate Jackson was the Xena of her day, beloved by lesbian fans for being smart, no-nonsense, and "butch."

Pepper: Salt of the Earth Police Woman

Angie Dickinson of *Police Woman* dealt with the issue of pretty women as law officers more directly than *Charlie's Angels*. Lee Ann Anderson, aka Pepper, was a high-fashion model who quit while at the top of her game when she found it boring and meaningless. After completing her training, Pepper worked vice before getting her promotion to sergeant and transfer to the L. A. Police Department's Criminal Conspiracy Division. Independent, caring, and hardworking, Pepper sends her sister Cheryl to the Austin School for Learning Disabilities, doubtless the first such character for television circa 1974. Pepper's fellow officers are all men, experienced, good cops who seem to accept Pepper completely. *Police Woman* enjoyed solid popularity for four years.

Angie has gone on to portray several other police women and crime solvers in subsequent series and movies. Her most important work as Pepper was probably the ground she broke as a woman playing the lead in a crime drama. Pepper's predecessor in the policewoman business was non other than Beverly Garland, the stepmother in *My Three Sons*. Garland had a brief stint as Patricia "Casey" Jones who worked for the 16th Precinct of New York City's finest. We know she made $75 dollars a year, was treated as a novelty by her coworkers and only lasted for one year, fall 1957 through spring 1958. The name of the show was *Decoy*. Need we say more?

Nancy Drew:
Sweet Sixteen Forever

While Pepper Anderson busted criminals as an LAPD detective sergeant, a very different kind of female detective hit the airwaves in 1978. Pamela Sue Martin, who went on to became a fabulously histrionic and troubled member of the cast of *Dynasty*, played the plucky girl detective, "a girl with a very inquisitive mind who loves to unravel a mystery." The daughter of a successful criminal attorney, Carson Drew, Nancy did part-time investigative work for her father's firm. Set when Nancy was a young adult five years out of school, *The Nancy Drew Mysteries* began with her doing the dregs of drudgery for her father, sifting through files and checking car tags.

Longing to become a real detective, Nancy waited for her chance to sink her teeth into a genuine mystery—and she got her chance on every show!

Based on the cherished book series by Carolyn Keene begun in the thirties, the nome de plume of author Harriet Adams who worked with writing partner Andrew Svenson and four ghostwriters who authored the Tom Swift, Jr. the Hardy Boys, and the Bobbsey Twins series. Astonishingly popular, Nancy Drew outsold all other books put together. Classics about the adventures of the crime-solving girl including *The Hidden Staircase, The Secret of the Old Clock, Mystery of the Whale Tattoo, The Clue in the Crossword Cipher, The Spider Sapphire Mystery, The Sign of the Twisted Candle,* and dozens of others have been translated into dozens of languages around the world and have sold-out countless printings.

Beloved by each new generation of grade schoolers and adolescents to come along, Nancy Drew seems to live in a pleasant time-warp where everyone's parents belong to the country club, all the kids have new cars, and the concerns of the outside world don't touch their Midwestern town. Nancy is quite a shero; she's a star swimmer, ace mechanic, prize-winning gardener, crack-shot, a talented artist and ballet dancer, knows classics throughout history though she never seems to have to attend school, and has a beau, Ned Nickerson, who helps her solve mysteries when not on the football field. Despite constant kidnapping and threats to her life, Nancy and her gal pals George and Bess do good and have a grand old time, which they share with every girl who picks up a Nancy Drew mystery. For generations of women now in adulthood, she represented virtually the only fictional model of a girl who was extremely competent, physically active, and didn't need any males to rescue her. What a role model!

Harriet: Spy Girl

Louise Fitzhugh's 1964 *Harriet the Spy* created quite a reaction upon publication. Very different from any other children's book, it is the hilarious story of a young girl who wants to be a writer when she grows up and starts observing people to hone her craft, making notes of their conversations. The would-be writer, Harriet M. Welsch, manages to record some fascinating tidbits in her secret notebook, revealing an eye and ear for human foibles. Accompanied by Harriet's delightful drawings, her notebook is a highly entertaining look at the private lives of various New Yorkers, a very absorbing project for our spy until the notebook falls into the hands of the people she spied upon. Harriet's hijinks continued in *The Long Secret* and were made into a very popular movie. Harriet's popularity, based on her dead-on observations about life, seems to have grown with every passing year. Harriet's ultimate realization from her observations? "That is that some people are one way and some people are another and that's that."

The Bionic Woman:
A Sommer's Day

The seventies featured a potpourri of live-action super-heroes including Wonder Woman, the Six-Million Dollar Man, and The Bionic Woman. While Farrah Fawcett burned up the screen on *Charlie's Angels,* her husband was enjoying celebrity as American astronaut Steve Austin on *The Six-Million Dollar Man.* Critically injured in a jet crash testing an experimental plane for the Air Force, character Austin became the six-million-dollar-man after an operation to replace his legs, right arm, and left eye with atomic powered prosthetic parts. After the operation, Steve Austin was a cyborg, complete with super-human speed and x-ray vision, purchased at the expense of his humanness. Naturally, he used these powers to combat the forces of evil in the world.

In a wonderfully SoCal plot twist, Steve lives in Ojai, California, the New Age capital of the Western world. Ostensibly, a hyper-evolved human would belong there. His girlfriend, Jaime Sommers, is lissome, tan, and athletic. The high-school sweetheart of the astronaut hero, Jaime is actually one of the top five tennis players in the world and is honing her skills to go up against the legendary Billie Jean King in a match set in Barcelona. A few day before heading to Spain, Steve and Jaime go skydiving. When Jaime's parachute malfunctions, she suffers near-fatal injuries in a body-crushing fall, "Her legs have so many breaks that we can't count them; her right ear is hemorrhaging, and her right arm and shoulder are crushed beyond repair."

Steve convinces his doctor to repeat the bionic surgical procedures that saved his life. Oddly, while the cost of Steve's operation is well-known, Jaime's operation is "cost-classified." Jaime Sommers is distraught when she recovers consciousness and learns that she is now bionic— until her beau reveals his secret cyborg status. Like Steve before her, she learns to walk again and is soon running a mile in fifty-eight seconds, two seconds faster than super-Steve! Jaime's body begins to reject the artificial limbs and she actually died briefly on the operating table until a physician specializing in cryogenics employs an experimental procedure to save her life. Unfortunately, Jaime's memory is compromised after a massive cerebral hemorrhage and she's a bit foggy about life before bionics.

Eager to begin anew life and show her gratitude for being alive at all, Jaime joins the team of special agents assigned to extremely dangerous secret missions and works with Steve Austin until she gets her own show, *The Bionic Woman!* In her new life, she foregoes her professional tennis career to teach junior high. This is a good thing, because a tennis ball hit by Jaime is as deadly as a cannonball. Jaime ran like the wind, listened with inhumanly acute hearing, and tossed bad guys around like rag dolls for a memorable two years. She had a bionic German Shepherd named Max and returned to the screen with Steve twice to battle evil, most recently with a bionic girl, played by *Speed's* sheroic bus driver Sandra Bullock.

Jaime Sommers, played by Lindsay Wagner, was a rather unusual tv supershero for the seventies. She was beautiful, but in a more real, earthy way with a visible facial scar and long, uneven and unstyled hair. She rarely smiled and didn't seem particularly overjoyed by her bionic superpowers. Lindsay Wagner also played the role of Lisa Galloway, Jaime's evil twin doppelganger, who underwent plastic surgery to pass as Jaime in order to learn the secret of her superpowers. Years later, in a reunion movie, a possible reason for Jaime's reticence and Mona Lisa smile was revealed. It turns out that Jaime was ultimately unsatisfied by working for the government; she wanted to make a contribution in a completely different way, by giving back to her community. Upon retiring from the "team," Jaime seems to find her right livelihood working at a rehabilitation center, proving herself indeed to be a total shero!

Wonder Woman: Natural Wonder

Lynda Carter burst onto the seventies scene in her tight red, white, and blue costume with a lasso, a pair of sapphire eyes, and a bodacious body that made her truly seem like she was supernatural in some way. She fought evil, worked an incognito day job in frumpish spectacles that in no way detracted from her dazzling beauty, and made everyone forget about Superman. Wonder Woman was timed so perfectly with the women's movement that it seemed like she was the physical incarnation of the new feminized, empowered, modern woman. It is no accident that the first issue of *MS.* magazine featured Wonder Woman on the cover. Actress Lynda Carter has since married well, works D.C.'s Capitol Hill circuit quite handily, and has never had a role that eclipsed her embodiment of Wonder Woman. But her magnificent figure and powerful presence are indelibly engraved in pop culture herstory.

Pippi Longstocking: Swedish Supergrrrl

Jaime Sommers wasn't the first female to boast of super-human strength. Pippi Longstocking of the revered children's book and television cartoon, was the first pop-star to have such awesome powers. Created by Astrid Lindgren in 1945, she could lift a horse effortlessly and picked up two policemen by their belts when they tried to haul her off to the Children's Home.

Pippi is as renowned for her red pigtails and her dishevelment as she is for her strength, pictured wearing one black sock and one brown sock. Enormously wealthy, Pippi is also a little strange and rather rude, though smart as a whip. On her only day at school, Pippi mocked the formal Swedish school system with great sarcasm and some quite excellent points. Pippi's only family are her pals, Tommy and Annika, well-behaved children who are often shocked by Pippi's outlandish behavior, but loyal to the end. Like the Bionic Woman to come thirty years later, Pippi was orphaned. Nine-year-old Pippi, "Lamgstrump" as she is called in her native Swedish, lives alone down a lane in Villekula Cottage with her horse and an ape where she dreams of her mother, whom she believes to be an angel. Curiously, her ideas about her father are not so positive. Pippi believes her father, believed to be lost at sea, survived and made passage to a distant land where he rules as Cannibal King. Pippi will always be a favorite with kids worldwide, providing a positive example for kids who are different!

Ripley:
Take No Prisoners

Fighting a monster more terrible than all the earthly monsters put together, Ripley is one shero who survived against all the odds. Played by the stalwart Sigourney Weaver, who increasingly buffed up for the *Alien* series as time went on, Ripley virtually created singlehandedly a new image for women—smart beauty with muscles.

It began in 1979, when director Ridley Scott sealed his reputation with the excellent sci-fi thriller *Alien* and vaulted Ripley into sherodom. A visual masterpiece of futurist gothic with sets by artist H. R. Giger, *Alien* pitted a space salvage crew against a hostile atmosphere and an unknown evil on the sinister planet LV426, with unrelenting suspense until Ripley escapes with her beloved cat, Jonesy, for whom she risks her own life. The scariest moments of the entire movie might be when Ripley prepares for her cryogenic sleep in the escape pod during the long trip back through space, after having blown up the Alien-infested ship. Vulnerable and very female in her underwear, she discoveries that an alien has made it aboard the pod, and she has to battle once more to save herself and her cat. Using her ample intelligence, she opens the hatch to jettison the hideous creature out into space, for a last, long, and disturbing look at the vaguely humanoid figure of the alien as it is catapulted into the void.

Ripley appears in three more *Alien* films, most recently *Alien: Resurrection*. The Ripley at her most sheroic is the Ripley of *Aliens*, the 1986 sequel. This time, Ripley is rescued from her fifty-seven-year-long drift through space by a robotic probe. During her stay in a hospital to heal from her over-long cryogenic sleep, Ripley is haunted by dreams of aliens. When she discovers that the planet she escaped from has been colonized by seventy families, she protests loudly, to the scorn of those around her. Though reassured that there have been no sightings of any alien creatures in the twenty-year colonization effort, Ripley doesn't believe for a minute that danger no longer exists for the colony. When earth loses contact with the people on LV426, Ripley is encouraged to accompany the space marines, a motley, coed crew of pumped-up toughs who compensate for their lack of discipline with plenty of swaggering macho to investigate the situation. The marines disregard all warnings and shoot off their heavy artillery at the first excuse, setting off a meltdown of the colony's nuclear reactor core. So, now the crew is up against aliens and a nuclear chain reaction. One of the marines, a Latina by the name of Vasquez, emerges as a kamikaze shero in this, the most gynocentric of the *Alien* quartet, when she sets off a live grenade and holds it triumphantly while an alien approaches, knowing that killing the creature means her own death, as well.

Ripley, when she sees that none of the marines have the necessary leadership qualities, takes charge. She rescues several of the marines from the plant as well as a little girl, Newt, the only survivor of the Aliens. Surrogate motherhood seems to really bring out the ferocity in Ripley; she struts through the alien queen's egg chamber, destroying as many of the queen's unborn progeny as she can with a flame-thrower. Escaping with the surviving crew in tatters, Ripley is exhausted and tearfully thankful for living through her second encounter with the terrible extraterrestrials. To her horror, she then realizes that the queen has smuggled herself aboard the ship. Ripley kicks out the jams in this action sequence. Clad in a Power Ranger-like space suit, she battles it out with the huge alien queen set on taking Newt, shouting, "Get away from her, you bitch!" Through sheer determination alone, Ripley prevails, protecting her foundling "daughter" in an adrenaline charged cinematic roller-coaster that gave new meaning to the popular concept of an eighties Super Mom.

Tank Girl: The Anti-Shero Down Under

Comic turned live-action movie shero, Tank Girl is a post-apocalyptic punk who is pretty much all that stands between total evil and mayhem in her world. One of a tough new breed of comic-book sheroes, Tank Girl is the brainchild of Jamie Hewlitt and Alan Martin, who in 1988, decided to create a female character every bit as kick-ass as any man. She first appeared in *Deadline* magazine where, with her pet 'roo Booga and her gal pals, Jet Girl and Sub Girl, the Aussie goes about her business in a nightmare battle zone after a comet crashes and turns planet Earth into a decimated desert that bears a strong resemblance to White Sands, Arizona. In 1995, Lori Petty did a credible job of fleshing out the comic-book shero in the movie role Emily Lloyd dropped when she found out she had to shave her head! The release of "Tank Girl" was accompanied with a bloated merchandising campaign that featured Tank Girl fashions available at finer department stores like Macy's. Tank Girl, the strip series, has continued to thrive underground. Tank Girl's personal philosophy of survivalist pragmatism is summed up nicely in the early episodes of the comic: "People worldwide are living a lie and run their lives around a system that is complete bollocks."

Roseanne:
Power Barr

Roseanne knew at three years old she was destined for fame as a comic. She put on little shows for her family on Friday's at her grandmother's house for Sabbath in her hometown of Salt Lake City, Utah, garnering rave reviews from the critics which confirmed for the toddler that she was on the right track. She says that her family's reaction told her she was the "Center of the Universe," a belief she holds to this day.

Roseanne took her act to the far reaches of her neighborhood, writing, producing and starring in school productions. At sixteen, she suddenly felt stymied in Salt Lake City, and at eighteen she headed for a more progressive part of the Rockies—Colorado. Roseanne hooked up with fellow thespians and moved into an artists' colony. She met a man, one of the few "with a bathtub in the county," and married him, and in 1973, they moved to Denver, where they had three children in rapid succession. The family of five lived in a tiny house of 600 square feet. Roseanne started working part-time jobs to help bankroll the expanding family, pulling stints as a cocktail waitress and window-dresser.

At the bars where she slung drinks, her customers told her she should be a professional comedian because she was downright hilarious. Roseanne listened, remembered her dream, and by 1983 was "Queen of Denver Comedy." Though it took ten hard years of working every club in Denver and thereabouts, Roseanne's success after that seemed rapid-fire. She, again, took some good advice and tried out for Mitzi Shore's Comedy Store and immediately was hired to do stand-up in Los Angeles at the star-making club. That same day—a banner day—she was also asked to appear in a George Schlatter (of Laugh-In fame) produced show for ABC called *Funny*. At the rehearsals for *Funny, The Tonight Show*'s talent scout, Jim McCawley, thunderstruck by her comedic brilliance, approached her exclaiming, "Roseanne, I love you!" Jim put her on *The Tonight Show* the very next Friday where she was a huge hit.

By 1988, Roseanne had a hit show *Roseanne,* on ABC, based on the character she had created for her comedy routines, which held a top spot in the ratings for its duration. Roseanne's accolades and awards for the show are countless—Emmy Awards, Golden Glove Awards, American Comedy Awards, as well as the Peabody Awards and the Eleanor Roosevelt Award for being an outstanding American woman. Her two books, *Roseanne: My Life as a Woman* and *My Lives* were runaway bestsellers, as well as quite controversial for her unvarnished honesty.

Roseanne the TV character was a sensation, a self-proclaimed "domestic goddess" with a smart mouth, a messy, but loving family, and the most realistic scenario since Archie Bunker's Queens digs. The Connor family were a loud crew, whose blue-collar concerns resonated

▲ *Roseanne: outspoken "domestic goddess" and queen of comedy.*

with a part of America usually ignored or patronized. Their tract home was always in disarray with some meal in process and kids and neighbors running in and out. They dealt with tough issues like teenage sex, lay-offs, marital discord, and money woes.

In her autobiography, Roseanne talked about the strongly feminist roots of her work. She also revealed the sexual abuse she suffered at her home growing up and the escapist lengths it drove her to later. In the seventies, Roseanne read everything she could get her hands on having to do with women's issues. Her "domestic goddess" comic personality, developed long before she hit the national airwaves, was her response to a feminism that seemed to speak mainly to educated, upper-class white women. The show gave her a fantastic opportunity to reach out to what she felt were her people, the working-class women of America—check-out clerks, waitresses, housewives, the underpaid, and almost invisible or, as Roseanne says, "in other words, the coolest people."

While the show found a niche and kept it, Roseanne herself, determined to live life on her own terms, seemed to attract controversy and relish it, referring to herself as "an accident that keeps on happening" and "one happy, smart, fat, happy woman" and generally acting fairly outrageously. Her one-time husband and evil-twin, Tom Arnold, said it very succinctly, "We're America's worst nightmare—white trash with money!" Greg Brennan, who produced a documentary about the superstar comic, explained her reputation as contentious after working closely with the brilliantly gifted, but edgy actress. "The trouble is she doesn't play by Hollywood rules . . . no hair-dos . . . but instead (is) always trying to engage in reality. It's something Hollywood finds very hard to reward."

When she announced the end of *Roseanne* after its record-setting nine-year run, Roseanne also gave notice that she was putting together a daily talk-show for King World syndication, for whom *Oprah!* is also a property, to debut in the fall of 1998. A huge fan of Rosie O'Donnell and Winfrey, Roseanne says a talk show is "a dream come true" and can only guarantee "I'm not going to try to be like everyone else, but I'm not sure exactly what it is I'm going to try to do."

Roseanne conceived of the domestic goddess shtick in tribute to housewives and pink- and blue-collar women of America. Insofar as being completely, unrepentantly herself and still creating huge success, Roseanne is the working-class shero of the nineties, for sure!

"Women should try to increase their size rather than decrease it, because
I believe the bigger we are, the more space we'll take up, and the more we'll have to
be reckoned with. I think every woman should be fat like me." —Roseanne

Thelma and Louise:
Girlfriends

Director Ridley Scott has a way of taking unlikely characters and revealing their unsung sheroism. Like the alienated loner Ripley before them, Thelma and Louise were a pair of rather forlorn femmes before life presented them with a challenge that awakened something within them. Thelma was a ditzy housewife who rarely left the confines of her cluttered house; was ignored by her creepy husband; her chief excitement before hooking up with Louise was melting Velveeta in the microwave. Louise was a worn and world-weary waitress whose rockabilly boyfriend wasn't around all that much either before the duo hit the road and changed their lives forever.

A buddy film for women, 1991's *Thelma and Louise* starts off with the innocently fun idea of two girlfriends taking a roadtrip to get away from their stagnant lives. Louise's husband's objections and insistence upon them taking his pistol set the stage for the unexpected turn of events. A few hours later, the two women stop at a honkytonk for drinks and the whole vacation goes up in flames.

Thelma and Louise struck a chord in America as they exacted their own brand of vigilante justice when a boozed-up barfly got innocent housewife Thelma drunk and tried to rape her. Street-smart Louise got worried when Thelma seems to be spending too much time in the parking lot with her dance partner and interrupted a violent sexual assault upon her friend. When the would-be rapist hit Thelma as hard as he could in his anger at her protests and showed no sign of remorse at his actions, Louise flipped out and shot him with Thelma's husband's pistol. Louise admits she had been raped once and could never stand by and watch it happen to another woman. As they contemplated how to deal with the situation, they realized that Thelma will be accused of asking for it (shades of *The Accused*) and wrestle with the notion that they are outlaw fugitives.

The rest of the film depicts their irrevocable bonding, adventures, and mishaps in escaping the law, and their complete and total rebellion against sexually repressive patriarchy, culminating in blowing up a trucker's rig when he makes sexually obscene gestures to them. Mild-mannered and repressed Thelma, played by Geena Davis, becomes a wild woman and discovers her latent talent as a stick-up artist. Susan Sarandon's portrayal of Louise is simply transcendent in the depth of emotion she is able to express through her character. For Louise, all the waiting around has ended once and for all and she is able to turn the ultimate dead-end into ultimate freedom.

When *Thelma and Louise* debuted, edgy and not entirely feminist, it sparked a lot of debate. Screenwriter Callie Khouri certainly achieved her aim to "put two women on the screen you haven't seen before. I'd had it with going to the movies and seeing women I do not relate to." We could relate all right, finally a road movie for women, starring two sheroes out to end the scourge of sexism!

> *"Just for the future, when a woman's crying like that, she's*
> *not having any fun."* —Louise

Agent Scully:
Something Xtra

Special FBI Agent Dana Scully has something her male counterpart doesn't—the respect of her peers and superiors in the Agency. Perhaps that's one of the reasons *The X-Files* is so universally popular—the creators cleverly reversed the roles of the leading woman and leading man. Dana Scully, a highly trained officer and physician/scientist, is super-rational, logical, skeptical. Fox Mulder, the other half of the team is all emotion and intuition, traits traditionally associated with women.

Scully, poker-faced, in plain suits and pumps and seemingly the most serious person on the small screen, is assigned to the X-Files to work with trouble-making Mulder to debunk his alien abduction conspiracy theories. She always looks for and, often provides, the logical and reasonable answer to the puzzles they're unraveling as they face an endless stream of bogeymen, human hybrids, and other inexplicable phenomena. In the character's own words, "No one does anything without a reason." However, Scully's involvement with the dangerous X-Files missions has cost her enormously on a personal level—the loss of her father, her sister, good friends and fellow FBI agents. Sheroically, she doesn't wallow in misery, insisting on working and remaining active to keep balance and perspective.

Scully is a pre-Raphaelite beauty with more brains than anyone else on the show. The rabid Internet fans of the actress Gillian Anderson and her alter ego, Agent Scully, call it IDDG—Intellectual Drop Dead Gorgeous. Amazingly, producer/writer Chris Carter had to fight tooth and nail to have Gillian Anderson cast as the cerebral Scully; the network bigwigs would have preferred a leggy, bosomy blonde for ratings. Duh!

Special Agent Dana Scully holds the world in her thrall. In more than 60 countries, people watch transfixed as she goes about her work. Scully is always thinking; when things get too weird, she is the one with the scientific experience and understanding to help string the pieces back together. Scully can heal the sick and, just as expertly, saw apart the dead bodies for autopsies, providing the needed evidence.

Scully fascinates with her ability to remain calm, sane, and clearheaded in the face of the truly bizarre she and Fox face on a weekly basis. She is the rock in the pool of turbulence that is *The X-Files*. In situations where anyone else would throw in the towel, she's the consumate professional, never giving up. Little wonder Gillian Anderson as Scully went from obscure starlet to sheroic superstar nearly overnight. In a fractured, technocratic world that sometimes makes very little sense, Dana Scully shines a light of strength, intelligence, and hope that, like her, we might be able to make sense of it all. This shero looks the heart of darkness right in the eye, solving crime and confronting ultimate evil (in the form of our own government), daring to makes this a better world!

> *"I'm back and I'm not going anywhere."*
> —Dana Scully, upon returning from an alien-induced disappearance

Not to be out-Foxed!

Actress Gillian Anderson echoed shero foremother Betty Friedan when she demanded "Equal Work for Equal Pay" in a public appearance after discovering she was being paid half of what fellow actor David Duchovny made.

Clarice Starling:
Silent No Longer

It should not have been such a surprise that *The X-Files'* Agent Dana Scully would be so appealing. Her character was carefully modeled on that of Jodie Foster's Clarice Starling from Jonathan Demme's hugely popular film, *The Silence of the Lambs*.

Hannibal Lector, brilliantly played by chameleon Anthony Hopkins, is a daunting opponent for Clarice. An extremely intelligent and shrewd psychiatrist before his imprisonment, he is unrepentantly evil and can't be touched by the usual police tactics of intimidation and interrogation. He is unmatched—until a rookie FBI agent by the name of Clarice Starling, who is at the top of her class and the apple of her supervisor's eye, is sent to interview the cannibalistic killer Dr. Lector to suss out whether he has any information about a new serial killer known only as "Buffalo Bill." Bill's modus operandi involves kidnapping plump young women, starving them, murdering them, and stripping off their skin. Lector, ostensibly, might shed light on such a diabolical method.

The film centers on the unusual bond that develops between Starling and Lector. As her supervisor Jack Crawford suspected rightly, Clarice connects with Lector where all others before failed. The moment Crawford asks Clarice if she "spooks easily" and offers dolorous warnings not to let "Hannibal Lector inside your head," we know we are in for a dark, scary, and thrilling ride. Beginning with a walk through the gauntlet of prison cells to his cell in what must be the prison's dungeon,

▲ *Jodie Foster: her portrayal of FBI cadet Clarice Starling is the basis for X-Files agent Scully.*

Clarice is balancing on a tightrope, with the eerily accurate Lector dissecting her like a lab animal. He suggests a tit-for-tat exchange of information she needs about Bill for information about Clarice personally. "You're one step removed from poor West Virginia white trash," he pronounces, drawing Clarice out slowly and surely until she tells him of her painful childhood memories of trying and failing to save a lamb from slaughter, to still the screaming of the lambs who somehow knew they were doomed.

Lector probed Clarice to the very core of her sheroism, analyzing her need to be a rescuing hero and her comparing the latest victim of Buffalo Bill, Catherine, to the lamb—"thought if I could save just one, but—he was so heavy . . ."—Clarice tried to carry away. Chillingly, Lector delves into Clarice's very being, "You still wake up some-times, don't you, wake up in the dark. And hear the screaming of the lambs . . .You think if you save poor Catherine you could make them stop, don't you? You think if Catherine lives you won't wake up in the dark ever again to that awful screaming of the lambs."

Fans and reviewers pronounced Demme's movie to be as compelling as a Greek tragedy, and perhaps without exactly knowing why, they are exactly right. Clarice Starling is on a shero's journey and she goes underground and encounters all the demons of Hades—Lector is a perfect devil and he brings out her own demons as well. Shaken, but unswerved, she learns what she needs to know and then slays the monster and rescues the damsel in distress.

Beautiful and with visible pain in her eyes, Clarice's primary weapon is her courage. Like her aggrieved lambs, she nearly walks into slaughter, but triumphs against an enemy she can't even see. Sensitively, the movie deals with Clarice Starling's sheroic struggle on several levels. She is an orphan, had a hard life, and, as a woman, had to go up against many odds in her FBI training. We admire, even as Lector does, Clarice for trying to raise herself above her humble roots. We know that it is not cold ambition, but the desire to be a good person, to be closer to her deceased policeman father, and to have success on her own terms that drive Clarice. *Salon* magazine's Joyce Millman puts it beautifully in her column "Personal Best": "What does Jane Austen have in common with a gory serial-killer thriller . . . a super-heroine, of course. . . most of all I prefer—OK, I'll say it, I want to be—Clarice Starling, the gutsy FBI Academy student who singlehandedly takes down a nasty woman-flaying serial killer in *The Silence of the Lambs.*

We've not heard the last of Clarice Starling. Her creator, novelist recluse Thomas Harris, has finally set to work on the long-awaited sequel to his supremely successful book upon which the beloved scary movie is based. While we know, indeed are told by

Harris, that Clarice now sleeps well, basking in the abated bleatings, we also know that, as a shero, she will again have to battle monsters in human skin. And we sleep the better for it.

Jodie Foster:
Miss Authoritiva

While directing Jodie Foster in her portrayal of Clarice Starling, Jonathan Demme was amazed when she "nailed" Clarice's very important transitional scene on the second take. This striking and memorable scene was the autopsy of one of Buffalo Bill's victims, palpably grisly. The scene begins with the seasoned and chauvinistic male cops and agents urging Clarice Starling to leave because it would be too upsetting for a woman to view. Demme positioned this as the scene when Starling goes from student to agent, a very important moment when we are to see through facial expression only Starling's movement from a young woman relating and identifying with the corpse on the slab to a cool professional going about her job with the efficiency and detachment necessary to get the job done. A lot to express in a few silent seconds! Demme was prepared to do the scene again and again, but Jodie only needed one warm-up. "Watching Jodie's face during take two was one of the most thrilling moments I've ever experienced on the set of any movie," he enthused, "more than anything she's every done, [Clarice is] the first character I can think of where Jodie didn't have to hide the intelligence she possessed as a person; I think she's always had to mask that one way or another."

Demme originally had Michelle Pfeiffer in mind for the role until, after a reading, "It became apparent that she was unable to come to terms with the overpowering darkness of the piece." Foster loved the novel and the character of Clarice and lobbied hard to get the part. Her instincts were right on target; her Clarice Starling is one of the most unforgettable performances ever, for which she won her second best-actress Oscar.

Foster rarely accepts parts offered to her and prefers to go after the ones she feels an affinity for. "You fight for the ones you have a serious personal connection with," she claims. Her filmography shows a predilection for carnies, hookers, and assorted other damaged people. She doesn't see them as losers, though, and prefers to depict such marginal types in order to "portray their stories in fiction and have them resolved and be heroes in the end." Sarah Tobias, the rape victim Foster played in *The Accused,* was no victim, says Foster, but a "very imperfect heroine," a hardworking waitress who toughed her way through a gang rape and fought back for justice with the help of a sheroic attorney. Her characterization of Sarah Tobias as a white trash survivor was a hard sell; she fought hard for her interpretation of the raped woman, bucking the suits at Paramount in order to play Tobias authentically with overpermed hair, clothes right off the KMart rack, and a hard-bitten look and attitude. One wonders if the suits remembered their reluctance when Jodie won the Academy Award for her performance that year.

Jodie's stock-in-trade determination to portray the truth about the downtrodden and her stringent privacy about her personal life has accorded her a rarity—the absolute respect of the entire industry. From her Coppertone modeling days as a toddler to her preteen prostitute in *Taxi Driver* and on to her own critically acclaimed directorial debuts, Jodie Foster is a shining example of uncompromising artistry: "You have to take those risks or all you're ever going to be is mediocre," says this shero.

"A real hero to me is a woman who has five kids and no money and takes care of them and survives. That's a heroic feat." —Jodie Foster

Xena:
A Law(less) Unto Herself

P erhaps the ultimate embodiment of sherodom as she kicks butt in the ancient world, sporting a chakram, breastplate, and the most blazing blue eyes this side of the New World, Xena Warrior Princess is a phenomenon unto herself. She started out as a character on the live-action myth series, *Hercules,* starring Kevin Sorbo and Anthony Quinn, no less, but soon was busting out into her own series. In no time at all, Xena overtook strongman Hercules in the ratings and has even set new records for popularity.

In her incarnation as Hercules' enemy, the Warrior Princess so impressed Hercules and the producers, they realized they couldn't let her be killed off and, voila!, she undertook a transformation from icy killer queen to warrior princess with a heart of gold. With the second episode in the trilogy of Xena on *Hercules,* vibrant New Zealand actress Lucy Lawless, totally unknown before taking on Xena, was approached by the producers to do her own series and accepted immediately, ready to rock! Lawless recalls, "Rob and Sam had always wanted to do a female hero and just didn't know where, when, or who. . . And it was me. Here and now!"

The rest is cathode ray herstory! *Xena: Warrior Princess* began production in May 1995 with twenty-two filmed episodes to air in September 1995. While creators and the newly-minted star hoped for a success at least equal to *Hercules: The Legendary Journeys,* no one could have every predicted the huge hit *Xena* was to become with hundreds of sites on the Internet, Xena dress-up fan clubs and conventions, lesbian cults, and immense popularity among children and adults, particularly women, all over to the world.

"I'm thrilled the show has struck such a chord with women," says Lawless, "because it's been brought to my attention that an awful lot of women need that." Lawless reports that, as Xena's living counterpart, she received mail that touches her deeply. "A lot of women write to me after they've been through a rape or something," to tell Lawless that, thanks to Xena, "they're not going to let themselves be victims."

Xena's superpowers bring new meaning to the word "awesome." She brings enemies to their knees with the "Xena touch," a pinch on the neck that either kills or forces the pinchee to tell the truth. Lawless demonstrated this skill on a clueless David Letterman; when he didn't seem to know who Xena was, she proclaimed, "Xena is a bad-ass, kick-ass, pre-Mycenaen girl who traverses time lines." Xena's forte is her special combination of acrobat and martial arts. She wields many weapons, but her signature piece is the chakram, a razor-edged discus, which she throws with deadly speed and accuracy. Xena differs from the perennial do-gooder Greek Hercules in that her character has much more depth and shading, thanks to her transformation from bad-ass to evil-fighter.

To some, Xena is reminiscent of the beautiful brunette SuperShero of the seventies, Lynda Carter's Wonder Woman, who would lasso her villains. To still others, she is a postfeminist answer to the world's problems, showing that women can be bold and bodacious, self-sufficient survivors (after Lucy Lawless' fall off the stage on Jay Leno's *Tonight Show,* her pelvis was broken in four places, but she was back on the horse next season and kicking just as hard!) who can outfight any man.

Xena's mission is to rid the ancient world of evildoers: "I'm Xena. I'm a problem solver." In real life, she has shattered many taboos and ideas about women's limitations, women's sexuality, and most importantly woman power. An inspiration to women and girls the world over, Xena makes us know we *can* do anything we want, overcome any obstacle, and make the world a better place. Xena: Warrior Princess, you rule!

"Xena's power doesn't come from her sexuality . . . It is not that she can seduce men, but that she can out-strategy them; that she is a great leader, a great sword person, and is inspirational to others." —Lucy Lawless

314

News from the "Xenaverse"

- This connection between Agent Scully and Xena is straight out of the *X-Files*. The evil Cigarette Smoking Man behind Scully's abduction by aliens is played by William B. Davids, who taught acting to Lucy Lawless!

- Xenaware! The global popularity of *Xena: Warrior Princess* has spawned merchandising empires including silver-plated, jewel-studded charkrams, videos, comic books, tee-shirts, coffee mugs, action figure dolls, warrior princess costumes, *Xena: The Official Magazine* on newsstands everywhere, and in cyberspace@ www.topps.com!

- Hard to believe, but Lucy Lawless wasn't the first choice to play Xena. The producers had actually chosen a much more delicately feminine actress, Vanessa Angel, who fell ill at the last minute. Angel recovered to go into her own syndication immortality with the *Weird Science* series.

Lara Croft:
CyberCipher

Lara Croft is no boy toy. She holds her own in skimpy outfits that would make even a Spice Girl blush; she fights evil with elan and keeps herself to herself. Star of *Tomb Raider* and *Tomb Raider II,* she is the first female action star to really make it big in the boy-dominated world of video games. Lara has, in fact, become a full-on international phenom, selling more than three million games around the world, with sales accelerating fast. As of this writing she's developing a line of merchandise including dolls, watches, a comic book, and "LaraWear" so we can all look like Lara—well, except for the 16-inch waist.

Lara toured with superband U2 in their 1997 PopMart world tour and a Lara look-alike, actress Rhona Mitra, tours as Croft at gamer trade shows. Scuttlebutt has it that Sandra Bullock and Demi Moore are contenders for the under-discussion Lara movie.

A British girl and daughter of nobleman Lord Hensingly Croft, Lara is twenty-nine years old. She was on her way to be married when her plane crashed in the icy Himalayas forcing her to survive alone against a hostile environment, marauding wolves, and mysterious enemies. Lara's interests are reminiscent of Indiana Jones; she loves to travel the world in search of the lore and treasure of ancient civilizations. In Lara's upcoming comic book, she'll go up against Top Cow's star, Witchblade, for a sheroic showdown.

The creators of Lara Croft are carefully considering any moves to expand Lara's empire. Due to the intensity of the action and dearth of dialogue in the *Tomb Raider* games, Lara has remained an enigma up to this point and creators want to deliberate on her future. "We're sitting on it," claims Jeremy Smith, founder of Core design, "because we're trying to decide what to do with Lara Croft, and who she is exactly . . . She's the perfect fantasy woman. That's what has made her such a phenomenon." What Smith will say about Lara is that she is "single and still looking."

Sheena: Queen of the Jungle

A foxy Amazon from the comic book series that started in 1938 came to the big screen fleshed out, very impressively, by Celtic pin-up girl Irish McCalla. Like Tarzan, for whom she is the female counterpart, Sheena is white, even though her adventures take place in the African wilds of Kenya. Sheroic Sheena was taught to command the animals of the jungle by the Logi tribal chief who adopted her when she was orphaned in a plane crash in 1928. Befriended by a white trader, she battles all manner of sinister foes in her adopted homeland with her sidekick, Chim, a chimpanzee. Sheena was very successful and remains a favorite midnight movie series. The popularity of the Sheena comic books spawned quite a few jungle Amazon comics swinging their way through the jungles and rainforests in the skins of zebras, tigers, leopards, lions, and panthers, including Zegra, Judy of the Jungle, Rulah, Tiger Girls, Princess Pantha, and Camilla, Queen of the Jungle. Often these strapping viragos were environmentalists, saving the wildlife from poachers and hunters.

Saturday Morning Sheroes and Other Assorted Animated Amazons

The decade of bra burnings, *Ms.* magazine and women's lib ushered in a whole new breed of TV sheroes. No longer relegated to sidekick, set decoration, or stereotypical "smart chick," the new animated and live-action sheroes inspired a generation of neo-feminist pre-teens. By the 1980's superwomen of every stripe and off-beat cartoon anti-sheroes had a firm hold on the hearts, minds and remote controls of America's youth. Who could ever forget:

Electra Woman and Dyna Girl

Played by Deidra Hall and Judy Strangis, this dynamic duo were the feminist flagship of the Sid and Marty Krofft entertainment empire. By day, they maintained their cover as mild-mannered girl reporters, but one bleep of the "Electracom" (cleverly disguised as fashionable wrist jewelry) and they discarded career-wear for spandex and notebooks for phaser guns. Keeping house at home base was the unflappable Frank, a middle-aged curmudgeon who, we can only speculate, relished his duty as dispatcher and den father. Electra Woman and Dyna Girl, unlike, say Wonder Woman or Catwoman, were unencumbered by romantic longings and unrequited crushes. In each other, the mature blonde and the pony-tailed brunette, appeared to have found not only a partner in crime-fighting, but a soul sister.

Isis

"With this amulet, you shall have powers over the forces of nature and the animals. You will soar as the falcon soars, run with the speed of gazelles, and command the elements of the earth. To summon the powers you must say aloud the words, 'OH MIGHTY ISIS." So began each episode of *The Secrets of Isis*. Though forced to share a time slot with the Winnebago road warrior Shazam!, Isis nonetheless made the most of her airtime. Andrea Thomas, as played by Joanna Cameron, was a school teacher not above transforming herself into the living incarnation of an ancient Egyptian Goddess to get a point across to her students. She drew upon the eco-power of the ancient deity to fight crimes, manipulating nature to do her benign bidding through twenty-five action-packed live-action episodes (including three co-starring Shazam!), and five Freedom Force cartoons. There were not many sheroes of color in this era, and ISIS was no exception, but *Secrets of Isis* did feature African American and Asian teenage girls in the cast.

Pinky Tuscadero

While not technically a Saturday morning shero (in fact, a Tuesday evening at 8:00 P.M. EDT/PDT shero), Pinky Tuscadero, as portrayed by Roz Kelly, held the nation in her thrall and left an indelible mark on TV history while appearing in only three episodes of the immensely popular *Happy Days*. The only female ever to match Fonzie cool-for-cool, Pinky strutted into the 50's family sitcom wearing pink hot pants, a pink leather jacket and a saucy red scarf tied at her neck. As Arthur Fonzerelli would say, "Whoa!"

She-Ra, Princess of Power

The animated foremother of Xena, She-ra was born Princess Adora of Etheria. Princessing a people waging a war of rebellion might have been enough of a challenge for a mere mortal, but Adora was destined for more. Summoned from a dreamy sleep by a sorceress to claim the "Sword of Protection," she declared "For the Honor of Grayskull! I am She-Ra!" A supernatural costume change marked the complete transformation of the royal miss into the Princess of Power. Her first acts at She-ra was to free her brother He-Man—so-called "Master of the Universe" from the MagnaBeam. She-ra was created by the "Masters of Marketing" at Mattel, who observed that girls playing with Barbie dolls began to, "act out action, adventure . . . fantasies" and that the number of girls buying action toys had risen 6 percent from 1983-1985. Mattel also discovered that girls expect a little something extra from their sheroes. Boys view power as possessing "physical stamina, strength and muscles," but girls believe it "means a lot of things that are not physical . . . it means being beautiful, and having a strong body, but also having a power that's within to guide your own destiny." Qualities She-ra has in spades!

Daria

"I'm Daria Morgendorffer, I love to see the first bloom of a wild rose, to smell the salt spray of an ocean breeze, to hear the laughter of little children at play. Oh no, wait, that's somebody else." Daria began her animated life as the intellectual foil to MTV's *Bevis and Butthead*. It soon became apparent that the cynical teen with the Mona Lisa smile needed a more stimulating environment, so she and her family moved from Highland County to Lawndale, and from B & B guest appearances to her own show. Daria's dry wit and acerbic retorts fly above the head of her dim-witted sister, Quinn, and well-meaning but clueless parents. Daria's one weakness is Trent, the wanna-be rock star brother of her best friend, the equally sardonic Jane. Like many sheroes of superior intelligence, Daria seems to like 'em cute and stupid. *TV Guide* called her "a hero for the alienated teen in us all." Hmm, shouldn't that be *shero?*

Holly Marshall

Land of the Lost's Holly, played by Kathy Coleman, was cast as a typical helpless girl on this live-action adventure series about a family who falls through a door in time (while on a "routine expedition") and finds themselves battling dinosaurs and other odd prehistoric creatures in a vain attempt to get home. She did however use her budding woman's intuition to form the all-important bond with Chaka, the helpful Neanderthal. Chaka was integral to their survival, and Holly—as the only surviving female in the Marshall clan—sheroically took on the role as mother to Chaka in addition to her many around-the-cave duties.

Lisa Simpson

Follow the soulful sounds of an expertly played saxophone through the streets of Springfield, and you'll find yourself at the bedroom door of Lisa Simpson. A eight-year-old spikey-haired shero in a strapless mu-mu, Lisa is the heart, soul, and brain of TV's wackiest animated family, the Simpsons. Lisa is clearly wise beyond her years—she's explored vegetarianism with Paul McCartney, created a realistic "Lisa Lionheart" fashion doll, and prowled the jazz clubs with her mentor, the late, great axe-blower, Bleeding Gums Murphy. But although Lisa possesses an obviously advanced intellect, she's also very much a little girl. She pines away for a series of teen-idol Coreys, develops an impetuous school-girl crush on neighborhood bad boy Nelson, and delights in the random acts of violence perpetrated on her brother Bart's favorite cartoon, "Itchy & Scratchy." Lisa's true sheroism is her ability to rock the boat when it needs it, but to also accept the love and respect that lie beneath the obvious shortcomings of her family. The Simpsons know Lisa is destined for a life of accomplishment beyond Springfield, and she knows she will soon soar above their bright yellow heads.

▲ *Lisa Simpson: girl wonder and Springfield's smartest citizen.*

Joy, "The Girl Bugaloo"

The Bugaloos were some of the most bizarre characters ever to grace the TV screen. A quartet of cockney insects, the Bugaloos composed and performed weird little pop songs and foiled the attempts of Benita Bizarre (played by Martha Rae) to eradicate them from existence. Joy held her own among her male bandmates, and flitted about the forest in a fetching green mini.

Velma

The undisputed brains of *Scooby Doo,* Velma Dinkley was a symbol of substance over style on Saturday morning. While pretty Daphne and beefcake Fred went off God Knows Where to do Who Knows What, Velma valiantly saddled herself with schleppy Shaggy and the loveable yet-useless Scooby Doo (who after all was a *dog*!) and proceeded to get to the bottom of every case. Just before the gang piled back into the Mystery Machine to head off for another adventure, the villain would inevitably claim he could have gotten away with his crime if is wasn't for "you meddling kids." Always the lady, Velma graciously shared the credit with her cohorts.

Josie

Voiced by Janet Waldo, Josie of *Josie and the Pussycats* proved a woman need not give up a thriving musical career in order to take up crime fighting, or later, on *The Pussycats in Outer Space,* intergalactic space travel.

Zan and Jayna

Zan and Jayna were the second set of teenage twins on the evolving superhero series, *The Superfriends.* The first, Wendy and Marvin, were human, had no powers, and therefore not technically "super." In 1977 the "All-New Superfriends" introduced Zan & Jayna, and the immortal battle cry "Wondertwin Powers—Activate!" Upon utterance of such, the twins could turn themselves into any animal or form of water they wished. Though Jayna was reliant on her brother to fulfill her sheroic potential, together they often stole the show from the more macho and established superfriends, including Batman and Superman. Jayna's voice was provided by the sheroically named Liberty Williams.

Dot, the Warner Sister

"The name is Dot ... call me Dotty and ya die." *Animaniacs* cartoons revived the Warner Brothers tradition of animated adventures silly enough to entertain kids, but written with plenty of puns, in-jokes, cultural references, and sarcastic remarks so the 'rents stay glued to the tube as well. What sets Dot apart from previous animated kid characters is that she's not content to merely be cute. Dot hostesses her own "Poetry Corner," leers at animated male guest stars such as Male Gibson, and gleefully reeks havoc on the Warner Brothers Studio lot with her brothers, Yakko and Wacko. Her famous line, "I can't help it if I'm cute" speaks volumes about her own place in the world of cartoons and for sheroes everywhere who strive to be taken seriously beyond their physical attributes, however adorable they may be.

Interplanet Janet

Years before Sally Ride made herstory as the first American woman in space, Interplanet Janet ("She's a galaxy girl, a solar system Ms. from a future world,") showed young viewers of ABC's *Schoolhouse Rock* that they too could reach for the stars. The classic series of animated lessons in math, science, history, and grammar set to catchy tunes was the educational foundation for a generation of kids. Other sheroic episodes include "Suffering Until Suffrage" a soul-funk tribute to the first women's movement, and "Mother Necessity" which honored the true mothers of invention—the mothers of inventors.

Trixie

Trixie is the seventeen-year-old right-hand girl to Japan's most famous teen racecar driver in *Speedracer*. She also happens to be a helicopter pilot, navigation whiz (she once quickly calculated that Speed's car, the powerful Mach Five, had to average 160 mph to win the big race). Trixie, like Speed, is also a well-trained, fearless martial artist. Like any warrior goddess, she's protective of her man and can shoot a withering glance at any animated chippie who dares set her wide eyes on Speed. But Trixie need not fear. The helpless waifs flit in and out of episodes, but she rides a permanent shotgun in Speed's car *and* his heart!

Æon Flux

Æon Flux was the scantily leather-clad, gun-toting, full-time assassin/part-time dominatrix of the MTV showcase of experimental animation, *Liquid Television,* and the eponymously named, short-lived series. A super-sexy, super-violent, super spy, Æon is an agent of the Monikans, trapped in a perpetual love/hate relationship with her Breen competitor, Trevor Goodchild. Spurned by a dark sense of justice and a thirst for revenge, Æon Flux leads her loyal fans on otherworldly animated adventures that defy linear logic (she dies in every other episode) and titillates them with sexual ambiguity. Creator Peter Chung described her prowess in his original proposal to MTV: "She dances unscathed through storms of gunfire while massacring her grotesque, anonymous enemies without mussing her hair."

Sailor Moon

Sailor Moon, the character, is by day a typical teen named Serena. By night, she and her Sailor Scouts—Sailor Mercury/Amy, Sailor Mars/Raye, Sailor Jupiter/ Lita, Sailor Venus/ Mina, and token male, Tuxedo Mask/Darien—fight the evil forces of the Negaverse. *Sailor Moon,* the show, is an internationally popular example of Anime, Japanese animation. Sailor Moon began in Manga, Japanese comics, but her spunk and spirit could not be contained within its pages. She was first animated for a one-time special, but a captivated public demanded more of the swabby shero with the split personality. Because of Aime's more sophisticated style and stories, *Sailor Moon* is popular not only with its target audience of six-to-twelve-year-old girls, but among twenty-something college students as well.

Acknowledgments

I have many to thank for this book, many sheroes and heroes are behind this effort:

Jay Kahn, for his magical touch. He is a truly gifted researcher and an original thinker whom I hope to assist on his book of obscure musical minutiae one day.

Ann Foley, whose wonderful combination of intuition and perspicacity made her invaluable to the project and who suggested and then excavated many, many of these incredible women.

Lara Morris, a cybershero every bit the equal of Lara Croft who could Net up anything I requested and whose grace balanced me in some scary, underground passages of this shero's journey.

Mary Jane Ryan, my indefatigable editor, who was able to structure the unstructurable in tackling the daunting task of trying to contain the lives of 300 sheroic women in one book and for reeling me in when I kept wanting to add dozens of women at the last minute!

Will Glennon, for always being able to see the big picture and support the frisky females he publishes with vision and good sense and great humor.

Nina Lesowitz, whose enthusiasm and good friendship have meant a lot to me in the gestation of this book and who is gromming two sheroes of the future—Mara and Jaime!

Laura Marceau, who seems to be able to bend time to her advantage and produce books with utter excellence in less time than anyone I know.

Jennifer Brontsema, warrior woman, and Pohahaesque bookmaker and muse.

Suzanne Albertson, who not only encouraged the book into being, but made Sheroes extraordinarily beautiful.

Ame Beanland, whose cover designs rock!

Claudia Schaab, whose herstoric library preferred many jewels.

Tom King, Everton Lopez, and Annette Madden who keep all the balls in the air without dropping any.

Phil Cousineau, who patiently listened to my ramblings and supplied unfailing insight into the mythic realm.

Vicki Leon, for wisdom, excellence, and inspiration. One day, I aspire to be a her storian such as you!

Mary Norbert Korte, for her contribution of ecoshero Judy Bari, which is beautifully moving and essential to this book; Mary's activism and poetry are a goddess send.

Patricia Kelly and Elise Cannon, sales sheroes, who immediately grokked the essence of the book and are the source of some wonderful inclusions.

Leslie Rossman, who made several invaluable suggestions of sheroic women and, as always, offered good counsel at exactly the right time.

Lastly, I would like to thank Nancy Fish who, in conversation one day about a mutual friend exclaimed "She's my total shero!" and lit the lightbulb over my head to do this book of sheroes.

Thanks to you one and all from the bottom of my heart and soul!

Bibliography

A & E Television Networks. "Biography." 1997. http://www.biography.com.

Willis J. Abbot. *Notable Women in History.* London, England: Greening & Co., 1913.

African Americans: Voices of Triumph-Creative Fire. Alexandria, VA: Time-Life Books, 1994.

African Americans: Voices of Triumph-Leadership. Alexandria, VA: Time-Life Books, 1993.

African Americans: Voices of Triumph-Perseverance. Alexandria, VA: Time-Life Books, 1993.

Helen Ashton and Katharine Davies. *I Had a Sister.* London: Lovart Dickson Limited, 1937.

Seale Ballenger. *Hell's Belles.* Berkeley, CA: Conari Press, 1997.

Daniel B. Baker, ed. *Explorers and Discoverers of the World.* Detroit, MI: Gale Research, 1993.

Olive Banks. *The Biographical Dictionary of British Feminists,* Vol. 1. NY: New York University Press, 1985.

Jane DuPree Begos, ed. *A Women's Diaries Miscellany.* Weston, CT: MagiCircle Press, 1989.

Robert E. Bell. *Women of Classical Mythology.* Santa Barbara, CA: ABC-CLIO, Inc., 1991.

Ginia Bellafante. "Kudos for a Crusader." *Time,* October 20, 1997, p. 65.

K.A. Berney, ed. *Contemporary Women Dramatists.* Detroit, MI: St. James Press, 1994.

Iris Biblowitz et al. *Women and Literature.* Cambridge, MA: Women and Literature Collective, 1976.

Hans Biedermann. *Dictionary of Symbolism: Cultural Icons and the Meanings Behind Them.* New York, NY: Facts on File, Inc., 1992.

Barbara Carlisle Bigelow, ed. *Contemporary Black Biography,* Vol. 5. Detroit, MI: Gale Research Inc., 1994.

_____. *Contemporary Black Biography,* Vol. 6 Detroit, MI: Gale Research Inc., 1994.

_____. *Contemporary Black Biography,* Vol. 7 Detroit, MI: Gale Research Inc., 1995.

Jean F. Blashfield. *Hellraisers, Heroines, and Holy Women.* New York, NY: St. Martin's Press, 1994.

Danuta Bois. "Distinguished Women of Past and Present." 1997. http://www.netsrq.com/~dbois.

Martha Bremser, ed. *International Dictionary of Ballet,* 2 vols. Detroit, MI: St. James Press, 1993.

Ward W. Briggs, ed. *Ancient Greek Authors.* Detroit, MI: A Bruccoli Clark Layman Book, 1997.

Ivor Brown. *Dark Ladies.* London, England: Collins Press, 1957.

Karlyn Kohrs Campbell, ed. *Women Public Speakers in the United States, 1800–1925.* Westport, CT: Greenwood Press, 1993.

_____. *Women Public Speakers in the United States, 1925–1993.* Westport, CT: Greenwood Press, 1994.

Margaret Carlson. "Back in the Saddle." *Time,* October 27, 1997, p. 27.

Humphrey Carpenter and Mari Prichard. *The Oxford Companion to Children's Literature.* New York, NY: Oxford University Press, 1984.

John Cech, ed. *American Writers for Children, 1900–1960.* Detroit, MI: Gale Research Inc., 1983

Hsiao-hung Chang. "Gender Crossing in Maxine Hong Kingston's *Tripmaster Monkey@* Society for the Study of the Multi-Ethnic Literature of the U.S., 1997.

Neva Chonin. "The Women of Rock Interviews: Joan Baez." *Rolling Stone,* n773, November 13, 1997, p.155.

Anatole Chujoy and P. W. Manchester, eds. *The Dance Encyclopedia.* NY: Simon and Schuster, 1967.

Ella Clark and Margot Edmonds. *Sacagawea of the Lewis and Clark Expedition.* Berkeley and Los Angeles, CA: University of California Press, 1979.

Barbara Naomi Cohen-Stratyner. *Biographical Dictionary of Dance.* NY: A Dance Horizons Book, 1982.

John Coulson, ed. *The Saints.* NY: Hawthorn Books, 1958.

Nadine Crenshaw. *Scully X-posed.* Rocklin, CA: Prima Publishing, 1997.

_____. *Xena X-posed.* Rocklin, CA: Prima Publishing, 1997.

Kathryn Cullen-DuPont. *The Encyclopedia of Women's History in America.* NY: Facts on File, Inc., 1996.

David DeLeon, ed. *Leaders from the 1960's.* Westport, CT: Greenwood Press, 1994.

Katherine Dunn. "The Women of Rock Interviews: Courtney Love." *Rolling Stone,* n773, November 13, 1997, pp. 164–66.

Electronic Nobel Museum. "The Nobel Prizes." [Online] Available
http://www.nobel.se/prize, 1997.

Wolfgang D. Elfe and James Hardin, eds. *Dictionary of Literary Biography, Vol. 75.
Contemporary German Fiction Writers.* Detroit, MI: A Bruccoli Clark Layman
Book, 1988.

Elizabeth Ellet. *The Women of the American Revolution.* Vol. II. NY: Haskell House
Publishers Ltd., 1969.

Encyclopedia Britannica. [Online] Available http://www.eb.com:180.

Glenn E. Estes, ed. *American Writers for Children Since 1960: Fiction.* Detroit, MI:
Gale Research Inc., 1986.

John Mark Faragher, ed. *The Encyclopedia Colonial and Revolutionary America.* NY:
Facts on File, 1990.

Deborah G. Felder. *The 100 Most Influential Women of All Time.* NY: A Citadel Press
Book, 1996.

Malcolm Forbes. *Women Who Made a Difference.* NY: Simon and Schuster, 1990.

FOX News Network. "India's Bandit Queen Threatens Suicide." [Online] Available
http://www.pennyarcade.com/phoolan.html, November 21, 1997.

John Hope Franklin and August Meier, eds.. *Black Leaders of the Twentieth Century.*
Urbana, IL: University of Illinois Press, 1982.

Antonia Fraser. *The Warrior Queens.* NY: Alfred A. Knopf, Inc., 1989.

Frontline. "The Karen Silkwood Story." [Online] Available
http://www.pbs.org/wgbh/pages/frontline/shows/reaction/interact/silkwood.html,
November 13, 1997.

Gillian Gaar. *She's a Rebel.* Seattle, WA: Seal Press, 1992.

Ute Gacs. *Women anthropologists : Selected Biographies.* Illini Books ed. Urbana : University of Illinois Press, 1989, c1988.

Gale Research, Inc. "Celebrating Women's History Month Biographies." [Online] Available http://www.thomson.com/gale/whmbios.html, 1997.

Elysa Gardner. "The Women of Rock Interviews: Bonnie Raitt." *Rolling Stone,* n773, November 13, 1997, p. 157.

Janeane Garofalo. "The Women of Rock Interviews: Jewel." *Rolling Stone,* n773, November 13, 1997, p. 162.

GeoCities. [Online] Available http://www.geocities.com, 1997.

Carol Gerten-Jackson. "Georgia O'Keeffe (1887-1986)." [Online] Available http://www.yawp.com/cjackson/okeefe/okeefe_bio.htm, October 31, 1997.

Ronnie Gilbert. *Ronnie Gilbert on Mother Jones.* Berkeley, CA: Conari Press, 1993.

Jim Gillogly. "Modesty Blaise Chronology." [Online] Available http://www.cs.umu.se/~kenth/modesty.html, November 20, 1997.

Beverly E. Golemba. *Lesser-Known Women.* Boulder, CO: Lynne Rienner Publishers, 1992.

Mike Gonos. Batgirl On-line. [Online] Available http://www.netvista.net/~mpg/batgirl/batgirl.html, December 18, 1997.

Jill Hamilton. "The Women of Rock Interviews: Ani DiFranco." *Rolling Stone,* n773, November 13, 1997, p. 150.

James Hardin and Donald Daviau, eds. *Dictionary of Literary Biography, Vol. 85. Austrian Fiction Writers After 1914.* Detroit, MI: A Bruccoli Clark Layman Book, 1989.

Walter L. Hawkins. *African American Biographies.* Jefferson, NC: McFarland and Company, 1992.

James D. Henderson and Linda Roddy Henderson. *Ten Notable Women of Latin America.* Chicago: Nelson-Hall, 1978.

Hayden Herrera. "Portrait of Frida Kahlo as a Tehuana." *Heresies #4*, Winter 1978, p. 245.

Mark Hertsgaard. "Who killed Petra Kelly?" *Mother Jones,* 18(1), Jan–Feb, 1993, p. 13.

Ralph Hickok. *The Encyclopedia of North American Sports History.* NY: Facts On File, Inc., 1992.

Darlene Clark Hine, ed. *Black Women in America: An Historical Encyclopedia,* 2 Vols. Brooklyn, NY: Carlson Publishing, 1993.

Gerri Hirshey. "The Women of Rock Interviews: Madonna." *Rolling Stone,* n773, November 13, 1997, pp. 98–100.

Gerri Hirshey. "Jodie Foster." *Rolling Stone,* n600, March 21, 1991; pp. 34–41, 88–89.

Fred Ho, ed. *Sheroes Womyn Warrior Calendar.* Brooklyn, NY: Autonomedia, 1998.

Margaret Hooks. *Tina Modotti: Photographer and Revolutionary.* San Francisco, CA: Pandora, 1993.

The International Who's Who of Women. London: Europa Publications Limited, 1992.

Edward T. James and Janet Wilson James, eds. *Notable American Women 1607–1950.* 3 Vols. Cambridge, MA: The Belknap Press of Harvard University Press, 1971.

Anne Janette Johnson. *Great Women in Sports.* Detroit, MI: Visible Ink, 1996.

Pauline Kael. *5001 Nights at the Movies.* NY: Henry Holt and Company, 1991.

Christina Kelly. "The Women of Rock Interviews: Melissa Etheridge." *Rolling Stone*, n773, November 13, 1997, p. 159.

Ethel M. Kersey. *Women Philosophers*. Westport, CT: Greenwood Press, 1989.

Jamaica Kincaid. "Pam Grier: The Mocha Mogul of Hollywood." *Ms*. August 1975, pp. 49-53.

Nancy Kline. *Elizabeth Blackwell: A Doctor's Triumph*. Berkeley, CA: Conari Press, 1997.

Gretchen Kopmanis. "Modesty Blaise." [Online] Available http://www.cs.umu.se/~kenth/modesty.html, November 20, 1997.

Howard Kohn. "Malignant Giant." *Rolling Stone*, June 11, 1992, pp. 92–97.

Mary Norbert Korte. "Judi Bari: Hero of the Forest Movement." Original unpublished article, 1997.

Cheris Kramarae and Paula A. Treichler. *Amazons, Bluestockings, and Crones*. London, England: Pandora Press, 1992.

Annette Kuhn and Susannah Radstone, eds. *Women in Film. An International Guide*. NY: Ballantine Books, 1990.

_____. *The Women's Companion to International Film*. Berkeley, CA: University of California Press, 1994.

Michael L. LaBlanc, ed. *Contemporary Black Biography* Vol. 1. Detroit, MI: Gale Research, 1992.

Vicki Leon. *Uppity Women of Ancient Times*. Berkeley, CA: Conari Press, 1995.

Rayford Logan and Michael Winston, eds. *Dictionary of American Negro Biography*. NY: W. W. Norton & Company, 1982.

Christine Lunardini, Ph.D. *What Every American Should Know About Women's History*. Holbrook, MA: Bob Adams, Inc., 1994.

L. Mpho Mabunda, ed. *Contemporary Black Biography,* Vol. 8. Detroit, MI: Gale Research Inc., 1995.

L. Mpho Mabunda and Shirelle Phelps, eds. *Contemporary Black Biography,* Vol. 11. Detroit, MI: Gale Research Inc., 1996.

Frank N. Magill. *Magill's Cinema Annual 1987*. Pasadena, CA: Salem Press, 1987.

_____. *Magill's Cinema Annual 1990*. Pasadena, CA: Salem Press, 1990.

_____. *Magill's Cinema Annual 1992*. Pasadena, CA: Salem Press, 1992.

_____. *Magill's Cinema Annual 1993*. Pasadena, CA: Salem Press, 1993.

_____. *Magill's Cinema Annual 1994*. Pasadena, CA: Salem Press, 1994.

_____. *Great Lives From History: American Series,* Vols. 1 & 4. Pasadena, CA: Salem Press, 1987.

_____. *Magill's Survey of Cinema: English Language Films,* First Series, Vol. 4. Englewood Cliffs, NJ: Salem Press, 1980.

_____. *Magill's Survey of Cinema: English Language Films,* Second Series, Vol. 1. Englewood Cliffs, NJ: Salem Press, 1981.

Sharon Malinowski, ed. *Notable Native Americans*. Detroit, MI: Gale Research, Inc., 1995.

Rick Marin and Veronica Chambers. "High Heels, Low Esteem." *Newsweek*, October 13, 1997, p. 71.

Evelyn McDonnell. "The Women of Rock Interviews: Queen Latifah." *Rolling Stone,* n773, November 13, 1997, p. 122.

Susan McElrath. "Mary McLeod Bethune Council House." [Online] Available http://www.nps.gov/mamc, 1997.

Robert McHenry, ed. *Famous American Women*. New York, NY: Dover Publications Inc., 1981.

Joyce Millman. Personal Best: Silence of the Lambs. *Salon*. [Online] Available http://www.salonmagazine.com/weekly/lambs960930.html, 1997.

Kay Mills. "Literature by Lode and By Lore." *Los Angeles Times*, August 25, 1985.

Isaac Mizrahi. *The Adventures of Sandee the Supermodel*. 3 Vols. NY: Simon & Schuster Editions, 1997.

Chantal Mompoullan. *Interviews with Eight American Women of Achievement*. Voice of America, 1985.

Burleigh Muten, ed. *Return of the Great Goddess*. Boston, MA: Shambhala Publications, 1994.

Peter O'Donnell. "How It Could Have Been . . ." [Online] Available http://www.cs.umu.se/~kenth/modesty.html, November 20, 1997.

Olga S. Opfell. *Women Prime Ministers and Presidents*. Jefferson, NC: McFarland & Company, Inc., 1993.

Diane K. Osbon, ed. *Reflections on the Art of Living: A Joseph Campbell Companion*. NY: HarperCollins Publishers, 1991.

Mary Rosetta Parkman. *Heroines of Service*. Freeport, NY: Books for Libraries Press, 1969.

Shirelle Phelps. *Contemporary Black Biography*, Vol. 12. Detroit, MI: Gale Research Inc., 1996.

_____. *Contemporary Black Biography,* Vol. 15. Detroit, MI: Gale Research Inc., 1997.

Steve Pond. "Wild Things Run Fast: Joni Mitchell." *Rolling Stone,* November 25, 1982, pp. 27–29, 87.

Arthur Prager. "The Secret of Nancy Drew: Pushing Forty and Going Strong." *Saturday Review,* January 25, 1969, pp. 18–19, 34–35.

Bruce A. Ragsdale and Joel D. Treese. *Black Americans in Congress, 1870-1989*: U.S. Government Printing Office, 1990.

Susan Raven and Allison Weir. *Women of Achievement.* New York, NY: Harmony Books, 1994.

Phyllis J. Read and Bernard L. Witlieb. *The Book of Women's Firsts.* NY: Random House, 1992.

Don Reisman, ed. *Portraits of American Women,* Vol II. NY: St. Martin's Press, 1991.

Phyllis Rose, ed. *The Norton Book of Women's Lives.* NY: W.W. Norton & Company, 1993.

Bob Rosenberg. "Frequently Asked Questions About Tank Girl." [Online] Available http:// www.cs.ucl.ac.uk/staff/b.rosenberg/tg/FAQ.html, December 15, 1997.

Dorothy C. Salem, ed. *African American Women: A Biographical Dictionary.* NY: Garland Publishing, 1993.

Jessica Amanda Salmonson. *The Encyclopedia of Amazons.* NY: Paragon House, 1991.

Jonathan Sanders. Why Batgirl? [Online] Available http://www.geocities.com/EnchantedForest/2635/why.htm, December 18, 1997

Virgilia Sapieha (Peterson), Ruth Neely, and Mary Collins. *Eminent Women: Recipients of the National Achievement Award.* Menasha, WI: George Banta Publishing Company, 1948.

Kathleen Scalise. "The Humanities Medal for Kingston." *Berkeleyan,* October 1–7, 1997.

Paul Schlueter and June Schlueter, eds. *An Encyclopedia of British Women Writers.* NY: Garland Publishing, Inc., 1988.

Bent Schonberg, ed. *World Ballet and Dance 1992–93. An International Yearbook.* London: Dance Books Ltd., 1993.

Arvind Sharma and Katherine K. Young, eds. *The Annual Review of Women in World Religions.* Vol. II, *Heroic Women.* Albany, NY: State University of New York Press, 1992.

Joanne Shattock. *The Oxford Guide to British Women Writers.* NY: Oxford University Press, 1993.

Jessie Carney Smith. *Epic Lives: One Hundred Black Women Who Made a Difference.* Detroit, MI: Visible Ink, 1993.

_____. *Notable Black American Women.* Detroit, MI: Gale Research Inc., 1992.

Jessie Carney Smith, ed. *Notable Black American Women,* Book II. Detroit, MI: Gale Research Inc., 1994.

Autumn Stephens. *Wild Women.* Berkeley, CA: Conari Press, 1992.

Esther Stineman. *American Political Women.* Littleton, CO: Libraries Unlimited, Inc., 1980.

Willow Ann Sirch. *EcoWomen: Protectors of the Earth.* Golden, CO: Fulcrum Publishing, 1996.

Joseph C. Tardiff and L. Mpho Mabunda, eds. *Dictionary of Hispanic Biography.* Detroit, MI: Gale Research Inc., 1996.

Vincent Terrace. *Television Character and Story Facts.* Jefferson, NC: McFarland and Company Inc. 1993.

Herbert Thurston, S.J. and Donald Attwater, eds. *Butler's Lives of the Saints.* London, England: Burns and Oates, 1956.

Marion Tinling. *Women Remembered.* Westport, CT: Greenwood Press, 1986.

_____. *Women into the Unknown.* Westport, CT: Greenwood Press, 1989.

Peter Travers. A Women on the Verge: Thelma & Louise.@ *Rolling Stone,* April 18, 1991, pp. 97–98.

Jennifer S. Uglow. *The Continuum Dictionary of Women's Biography.* NY: Continuum, 1984.

Jennifer Uglow and Frances Hinton, eds. *The International Dictionary of Women's Biography.* NY: Continuum; Macmillan, 1982.

_____. *The Continuum Dictionary of Women's Biography.* NY: Continuum, 1989.

Vietnam Veterans of America Foundation. "The Nobel Peace Prize for 1997: International Campaign to Ban Landmines (ICBL) and Jody Williams." [Online] Available http://www.vvaf.org/landmine.html, December 30, 1997.

Marina Warner. *From the Beast to the Blonde: On Fairy Tales and Their Tellers.* NY: Farrar, Straus and Giroux, 1994.

Marjorie Weiser and Jean Arbeiter. *Womanlist.* Canada: McClelland and Stewart Ltd., 1981.

Alden Whitman, ed. *American Reformers.* NY: The H.W. Wilson Company, 1985.

Ora Williams. *American Black Women in the Arts and Social Sciences.* Metuchen, NJ: The Scarecrow Press, 1994.

Justin Wintle, ed. *Makers of Modern Culture.* NY: Facts on File, Inc., 1981.

_____. *Makers of 19th Century Culture 1800-1914.* Boston, MA: Routledge & Kegan Paul, Ltd., 1982.

Women's International Center Biographies. [Online] Available http://www.wic.org/bio, 1997.

Marion Woodman. *Leaving My Father's House: A Journey to Conscious Femininity.* Boston, MA: Shambhala Publications, 1992.

Elizabeth Wright, ed. *Feminism and Psychoanalysis.* Cambridge, MA: Blackwell Reference, 1992.

Yahoo's Web CelebSite Biographies. [Online] Available http://la.yahoo.com/external/webceleb.

Zbigniew Zwolinski. "Maria Sklodowska-Curie, 1867-1934." [Online] Available http://hum.amu.edu.pl/~zbzw/ph/sci/msc.htm, November 21, 1997.

Helen Zia and Susan B. Gall, eds,. *Notable Asian Americans.* Detroit, MI: Gale Research, 1995.

Angela Howard Zophy and Frances M. Kavenik, eds. *Handbook of American Women's History.* Garland Reference Library, 1990.

Editorial Department
Merriam-Webster, Inc.
47 Federal Street
Springfield, MA 01102

Dear Editors/Lexicographers:

I am writing to express my interest in including the word "shero" in Merriam-Webster's Collegiate Dictionary, Eleventh Edition. The word "shero" communicates the idea of female courage, wisdom, and no-holds-barred individuality.

Based on the definition of "hero" in Webster's 10th Edition, the definition should be as follows: **she-ro** \ *n, pl* **sheroes** [fr. *she*] **1 a :** a mythological or legendary female figure often of divine descent endowed with great strength or ability. **b :** an illustrious warrior woman. **c :** a woman admired for her achievements, wisdom, and noble qualities. **d :** a woman role model. **2 :** the principal female character in a literary or dramatic work. **3 :** an object of extreme admiration and devotion.

Your dictionary states that ". . . the inescapable fact that emerges from considering language historically . . . is change" (p. 24). I would add another inescapable fact: the all-important relationship between language and power. As gender roles and relationships continue to evolve, it is important to continue to enrich the English language with words that define what power means to women today.

Currently there is no word in the lexicon to uniquely express the strength and power of women. "Hero" has distinctly masculine connotations, while "heroine" is a homonym of an addictive narcotic. The phrase "woman hero" is a diminishment, because it is merely a modification of "hero." So women and girls of power have coined the word "shero" to describe their own role models and legendary figures. Dr. Maya Angelou and others have used the word frequently in their speeches about women's achievements.

As a dictionary editor with an ear to the evolution of the English language, you may already be aware that the word "shero" is increasingly coming into the common parlance. Your decision to welcome this word into the lexicon would be a strong endorsement of a crucial concept for girls and women today. Please send your response to: Brenda Knight, Conari Press, 2550 Ninth Street, Suite 101, Berkeley, CA, 94710.

Thank you for your consideration of my request.

Sincerely,

_____

(sign your name)

Who's Your Shero?

I hope you've enjoyed this preliminary excursion into the ranks of the bold, brash, and unabashed! We know there are so many more sheroes who must be honored and included in the annals of herstory. In light of this important mission, we're asking *you* to nominate your personal shero(es). Please help us rewrite *his*tory by filling out this form and including the reasons for your choice. Any background information you can supply would be a goddess-send! We welcome all submissions—from fictional to actual, celestial to supernatural, ancient to modern. Feel free to copy this form and nominate as many as you wish. Thank you!

— And while you're remembering the shero sisterhood, don't forget to honor yourself!

Name of Shero Nominee:

Think globally! Country of Origin:

Significant Dates and Why:

Biography/Reason for Nomination:

Quotes:

Send to:

Conari Press
2550 Ninth Street, Suite 101
Berkeley, CA 94710

fax: (510) 649-7190
email: conaripub@aol.com

Index

A

Aba, 5

Abra, Queen of Babylon, 5

Abzug, Bella, 157-159

Ada, 5

Adams, Abigail, 157

Addams, Jane, 179, 220

Adelita, 17

Admete, "The Untamed", 5

Adora of Etheria (see She-ra)

Acthelburg, 8

Aëllopus, 5

Aelfwyn, 8

Aethelflaed, 8

Afra'Bint Ghifar al-Humayriah, 12

Agave, 4

Agent Dana Scully (*see* Scully)

Agent 99: 270-271

Akers, Michelle, 67

Alcott, Louisa May, 162

Aleksandrovna, Tamara, 10

Alice in Wonderland, 266

All-Girls Baseball League, 53-54

Ally McBeal, 267

Amanda (*Melrose Place*), 267

Anderson, Gillian, 307-308

Anderson, Marian, 102

Andrea Thomas (*see* Isis)

Andrews, Julie, 266

Angel, Vanessa, 315

Angelou, Maya, xix, 101, 254-256

Anthony, Susan B., 107, 123, 129, 135-137, 156, 261

Apple, Fiona, 210

Aquino, Corazon, 174-175

Arbus, Diane, 213

Arendt, Hannah, 95-97

Asantewa, Nana Yaa, 147

Ashford, Evelyn, 57-58

Atalanta of Boetia, 45

Austen, Jane, 213

Æon Flux, 324

B

Baez, Joan, 189, 199, 206

Balch, Emily Greene, 179

Ball, Lucille, 266

Barbarella, 275-278

Baraka, Amiri, 254

Barbudo, Maria de la Mercedes, 147

Bari, Judy, 19, 42-44

Barland, Beverly, 293

Barnes, Julia, 271-272

Wild Women Association

In 1992, with the publication of *Wild Women* by Autumn Stephens, Conari Press founded the Wild Women Association. Today there are over 3,000 card-carrying Wild Women in cities throughout the world—and some even meet regularly with their untamed and uproarious sisters in an effort to encourage wildness. The Association's primary purpose is to rediscover and rewrite our wild foresisters back into history.... and if there is a wild woman in your family we hope you might help by sending us information for possible inclusion in subsequent volumes of the "Wild and Ever-So-Uppity Women" series.

To become a member and to receive the Wild Women Association Newsletter, please mail this page to:

The Wild Women Association
2550 Ninth Street, Suite 101
Berkeley, CA 94710-2551

Let's rewrite history with women in it!

Other books in the
Uppity and ever so Wild Women series:

Hell's Belles
A Tribute to the Spitfires, Bad Seeds & Steel Magnolias
of the New and Old South

Seale Ballenger

Uppity Women of Ancient Times
by Vicki León

Wild Women
Crusaders, Curmudgeons and Completely Corsetless Ladies
in the Otherwise Virtuous Victorian Era

by Autumn Stephens

Wild Women in the White House
The formidable Females Behind the Throne,
On the phone, and (Sometimes) Under the Bed

by Autumn Stephens

Wild Women in the Kitchen
101 Rambunctious Recipes & 99 Tasty Tales

by The Wild Women Association

Wild Words from Wild Women
An Unbridled Collection of Candid Observations
& Extremely Opinionated Bon Mots

by Autumn Stephens